Faint Praise and Civil Leer

The "Decline" of Eighteenth-Century Panegyric

Jon Thomas Rowland

Newark: University of Delaware Press
London and Toronto: Associated University Presses

© 1994 by Associated University Presses

All rights reserved. Authorization to photocopy items for internal or personal use, or the internal or personal use of specific clients, is granted by the copyright owner, provided that a base fee of $10.00, plus eight cents per page per copy is paid directly to the Copyright Clearance Center, 222 Rosewood Drive, Danvers, Mass. 01923. [0-87413-543-5/94 $10.00 + 8¢ pp, pc.]

Associated University Presses
440 Forsgate Drive
Cranbury, NJ 08512

Associated University Presses
25 Sicilian Avenue
London WC1A 2QH, England

Associated University Presses
P.O. Box 338, Port Credit
Mississauga, Ontario
Canada L5G 4L8

The paper used in this publication meets the requirements of the American National Standard for Permanence of Paper for Printed Library Materials Z39.48–1984.

A portion of this book appeared as "Another Turn of the Screw: Prefaces in Swift, Marvell, and Gérard Genette" in volume 21 of *Studies in Eighteenth-Century Culture*. Used with permission.

Library of Congress Cataloging-in-Publication Data

Rowland, Jon Thomas, 1956–
    Faint praise and civil leer : the "decline" of eighteenth-century panegyric / Jon Thomas Rowland.
       p. cm.
    Includes bibliographical references and index.
    ISBN 0-87413-543-5 (alk. paper)
    1. English literature—18th century—History and criticism.
2. Praise in literature. 3. Laudatory poetry, English—History and criticism. 4. Satire, English—History and criticism.
5. Rhetoric—1500–1800. I. Title.
PR448.P68R68 1994
821'.509—dc20   94-17432
                                                            CIP

PRINTED IN THE UNITED STATES OF AMERICA

Upon Nothing

Great Negative, how vainly would the wise
Inquire, define, distinguish, teach, devise,
Didst thou not stand to point their blind
    philosophies!

—John Wilmot, earl of Rochester

Contents

1. "Panegyrike Congratulatorie" / 11
2. Andrew Marvell's Political Poetry and the Panegyric Tradition / 36
3. "Competing Versions:" The "Painter-Poems" and *Annus Mirabilis* / 52
4. *The Rehearsal Transpros'd:* The Panegyrical Paratext (1) / 85
5. From Cheated Sight to False Light: Analogy from Swift's "Odes" to *A Tale of a Tub* / 107
6. The Preface as Vehicle in *A Tale of a Tub:* The Panegyrical Paratext (2) / 124
7. Swift and Churchill: Postmodern Panegyrics / 145

Afterword / 166

Notes / 170

Bibliography / 177

Index / 187

Faint Praise
and Civil Leer

1
"Panegyrike Congratulatorie"

Panegyric and Satire as Rhetoric

THERE are two aspects to this study. The first is to indicate how certain works, including Marvell's *Rehearsal Transpros'd* and Swift's *Tale of a Tub*, participate in the panegyric tradition. The second is to describe developments within the tradition itself. These have principally to do with analogy, as is appropriate, since analogy has long been essential to discourse on transcendentals like the Good, which are properly the subject of panegyric.

Panegyric is a kind of writing that conforms very neatly to one branch of epideictic rhetoric, the other branch being satire. In discussing panegyric we end up saying something not just about satire, but about epideictic, about rhetoric, and finally about meaning. One cannot describe the branch unless one describes the whole tree, but fortunately from the standpoint of economy, to describe the branch accurately *is* to describe the tree.

Aristotle does not actually use the term "panegyric," but he accurately describes epideictic (the kind of rhetoric to which it belongs), identifies some of panegyric's most important devices, and remarks on its curiously overlapping relationship with other kinds of rhetoric, in particular deliberative rhetoric.

He first defines rhetoric by its function, which is "to find out in each case the existing means of persuasion."[1] He then defines the kinds of rhetoric—deliberative, forensic, and epideictic—according to "the three kinds of hearers" or judges: assemblymen, jurors, and spectators. Each kind has its proper subject and time. Deliberative rhetoric's subject is persuasion or dissuasion, and its time the future; forensic's is accusation or defense, and its time the past; and epideictic's is praise or blame, and its time the present. Each kind has also its "different special end": for deliberative it is "the expedient or harmful," for forensic it is "the just and unjust," and for epideictic it is "the honourable and disgraceful" (35).

Epideictic, then, is that kind of rhetoric whose judge is a "critic," whose subject matter is "praise and blame," whose time is "the present," and whose end is "the honourable or disgraceful." Panegyric and satire can easily be seen as its two branches. Their judges are (initially, at least) "critics," their time "the present" (we will consider the extremely topical character of some examples later), and their end "the honourable or disgraceful." Though epideictic is our primary concern, it is important to keep in mind what the other kinds are, because, as we shall soon see, none of them is entirely distinct from the others. In Aristotle's examples a mere change of phrase from the prohibitive to the nonprohibitive (as from "one ought not to pride oneself on goods that are due to fortune" to "he was proud, not of goods that were due to fortune") is all the difference between suggestion, advice, and encomium. Each branch of rhetoric only has meaning insofar as it is part of the whole: rhetoric is a synchrony.

When Aristotle proceeds to a more detailed discussion of "praise [ἔπαινος] and blame [ψόγος]," he exerts himself mainly to define it by defining what he calls its end above: "virtue [ἀρετή] and vice [κακία]" or "the noble [καλόν] and the disgraceful [αἰσχρόν]" (91). The reason for this emphasis, I think, is that he is dealing with terms that are extremely "value-laden" in a context that is extremely abstract and "valueless," not just because it is one of presentation only, but because it is one in which the presentation, ostensibly, is not intended to provoke any immediate action—the "judge" is just a "spectator," like our modern critics perhaps, whose judgment is on the order of a merely aesthetic decision.

Consequently, there is something unstable about the "end" of epideictic, and the effort Aristotle devotes to discussing this "end" seems intended to convey this. Such instability enables panegyric and satire to evoke one another, and requires the writer to be competent at both lest the satire unintentionally and unexpectedly become panegyric (or vice versa). When Aristotle defines "the noble" as "that which, being desirable in itself, is at the same time worthy of praise," he means something, to the orator, entirely different—his presentation not of something that *is* noble but of something *as* noble.

Similar problems arise with Aristotle's definition of virtue. It is quite easy to see Aristotle's virtue as wish-fulfillment, because it always seems to be defined from the standpoint of the nonvirtuous. Virtue being defined as "what is most useful [χρησιμώτατα] to others" (91), the effect of endeavoring to be virtuous would be the eradication of all virtue. Virtuous acts would soon become useless, and so no longer virtuous. Hence "virtue" seems to be a merely relative term or, at best, one that only has meaning synchronically. The length it takes him to convey its essential indeterminacy foreshadows the difficulty with transcendentals, especially the Good, which contributes as much as more topical factors to the (d)evolution of panegyric.

Perhaps it is because of the indeterminacy of "virtue" and "the noble" that so much persuasion depends on what Aristotle calls "ethical proof," the impression of "the moral character of the speaker" that renders his speech "worthy of confidence" (17). Equally important is "amplification," which from Aristotle's own examples could be defined as the presentation of something or someone in the most flattering terms.[2] Both these devices are used almost equally in satire and panegyric, and often together, *amplificatio* being used ironically in satire, or in its negative form, *minuendo*. Waller's "Instructions" is a splendid example of the unsuccessful use of amplification in panegyric. It fails partly because Waller does not accompany this device with "ethos," which might have made his exaggerations more credible, and partly because he did not observe Aristotle's recommendation that amplification be used for "actions which are not disputed" (105). Like the whole Second Dutch War, the Battle of Lowestoft, the action of the poem, was as hotly disputed as badly waged.

Amplification without ethos is like a gun in the hands of someone who cannot aim. In the "painter-poems," Andrew Marvell, or some other assailant, attacks Waller with his own weapon. Charles Allen Beaumont, in *Swift's Classical Rhetoric*, describes how the satirist uses these devices to support one another (24). In *A Modest Proposal* diminution is effective because it is accompanied by "ethical proof," "the moral character of the pleader himself" (Beaumont's definition). For the skilled writer, the very instability of this kind of writing is as much a plus, a means of manipulation, as for the unskilled it is a negative, a way to be manipulated and laughed at.

Vice and virtue begin to appear almost as labels for the same thing observed from different perspectives:

> We must assume, for the purpose of praise or of blame, that qualities which closely resemble the real qualities are identical with them; for instance that the cautious man is cold and designing, the simpleton good-natured, and the emotionless gentle. (Aristotle, *"Art" of Rhetoric*, 97)

Whether we praise or we blame will depend on which term we adopt. It will depend also on "what is esteemed among the particular audience," though not necessarily what is "actually existing there"; the same thing or person may be praised or blamed, flattered or denigrated, praised here and blamed there for the same thing, and praised or blamed for a thing that may be done or undone by "a change in the phrase [μετατιθέντα τῆς λέξεως]" (101). That praise and blame may themselves begin to appear as alternating vehicles for the same increasingly inscrutable tenor is important to later developments in epideictic writing, especially satire.

Quintilian stresses the utility of epideictic ("the class of *causes* which are concerned with praise and blame")[3] in court and at funerals. If anything, his emphasis on treatment over material is even stronger; very neatly, he shows how opposites can be made to appear equally praiseworthy or blameworthy. In discussing praise of the gods, for example, he says, "some again may be praised because they were born immortal, others because they won immortality by their valour"; similarly, in discussing praise of men, he says, "either it will be creditable to the objects of our praise not to have fallen short of the fair fame of their country and of their sires or to have ennobled a humble origin by the glory of their achievements" (469).

Quintilian suggests that since the things he praises are opposites, both cannot be true; but such an "either/or" does not make sense if both alternatives are equally so. One becomes aware that he is not dealing with virtue so much as the *appearance* of it. The passages toward the end of the chapter suggest a kind of moral arithmetic, as Quintilian neatly turns a list of "positives" into a list of "negatives," reinforcing his statement that "vice may be denounced, as virtue may be praised, in two ways." Opposites may be not only equally good, but equally bad: "some great men like Menander have received ampler justice from the verdict of posterity" but "some have been branded with infamy after death"; "children reflect glory on their parents" but "the vices of children bring hatred on their parents"; "cities [bring glory on] their founders" but "founders of cities are detested for concentrating a race which is a curse to others, as for example the founder of the Jewish superstition."

Finally, Quintilian restates Aristotle's point, unnecessarily I think, that "since the boundary between vice and virtue is often ill-defined, it is desirable to use words that swerve a little from the actual truth, calling a rash man brave," which seems implicit in the above examples. He adds, almost as a coda, that "*panegyric* is akin to deliberative oratory inasmuch as the same things are usually praised in the former as are advised in the latter" (479)— one of the three times he actually uses the term.

1 / "Panegyrike Congratulatorie" 15

While Aristotle and Quintilian, in discussing praise and blame, touch on some of the fundamental characteristics of panegyric, they do not deal with it in much detail. For that we must turn to more obscure rhetoricians, whose works are still accessible through modern studies. Their definitions of panegyric are provided by Garrison in his *Dryden and the Tradition of Panegyric*, the best study of panegyric in modern times.[4] He quotes seventeenth-century dictionaries that distinguish it from encomium, or mere praise; these definitions, "charged with emotion" (4), as he says, indicate how much more than mere praise it was. Blount's definition of 1656 is typical:

> *Panegyrick*. A licentious kind of speaking or oration, in the praise and commendation of Kings, or other great persons, wherein some falsities are joyned with many flatteries. (5)

That it "touches a political nerve" is confirmed by Garrison's example of Thomas Blount's *Glossographia*, in which the negative definition—"wherein some falsities are mixed with praise"—is deleted from the post-Restoration edition of 1661 (6). The definition that Blount appended in place of the deleted one—"Also any Feast, Game or Solemnity exhibited, before the General Assembly of a whole Nation"—indicates a Greek source: Philemon Holland's translation of Plutarch's *Morals* (1603). Blount's primary definition, on the other hand, indicates a Roman source: Thomas Thomas's *Dictionarium Lingua Latinae* (1587).

> A licentious and lascivious way of speaking or oration in the praise and commendation of Kings, wherein some do ioyne many lyes with flatterie. (6–7)

In the Greek tradition, panegyric ("a general assembly") "was a speech delivered before a mass audience on a festival occasion" (7). Oddly enough, the most famous of these "was never actually delivered as a speech" (7), an irony that suggests that not all of the tension in this kind of writing between "heard thing" and "read thing" or between "rhetorical occasion" and "private reading" is print-related. As remarked above, the word is rare in Latin (occurring in Quintilian only three times); the most important Roman panegyrist, Claudian, comes relatively late. The two strains are reflected in an early-eighteenth-century definition in John Kersey's *Dictionarium Anglo-Britannicum* (1708):

a Speech deliver'd before a solemn and general Assembly of People, especially in Praise of a great Prince. (9)

This definition is nearly complete for our purposes, since it indicates the tripartite relationship (between prince, poet, and people) that is a fundamental characteristic of panegyric distinguished from encomium or praise; it is also the definition that, historically, proves most durable and that, according to Garrison, "survives even the interregnum" (13).

Perhaps Garrison's most important contribution to our appreciation of panegyric is a reawakening of our sense of it as a respectable *genre*, not just because of its "overlapping" relationship to more respectable kinds of rhetoric like the deliberative, which Aristotle and Quintilian both remarked, but to paramount forms like the epic. Garrison recounts that his inspiration for a study of panegyric in the seventeen century came from a passage in Dryden's *Annus Mirabilis*: "[T]he same images serve equally for the epic poesy, and for the historic and panegyric, which are branches of it" (ix). Elsewhere, he remarks that "Dryden, by coupling [in the critical dedication to 'Eleonora'] Pliny and Pindar in his list of models for panegyric, suggests a broader notion of the genre, one that unites the Greek ode with Roman oratory" (28).

This linking of panegyric and heroism, panegyric and epic, should probably be less surprising than it is. Brian Vickers states in his introduction to *Rhetoric Revalued* that "For the early Renaissance, as O. B. Hardison has shown, Aristotle's *Poetics* was influential through Averroes's redaction of it, with its reduction of all literature to the functions of praise and blame, which helps account for the dominance of epideictic rhetoric."[5] Epic and panegyric would have been linked, from the Renaissance on, as forms of praise. Averroes's translation of the *Poetics* begins, "Every poem and all poetic discourse is blame or praise." Vickers suggests that "it is fully comprehensible that, even after the re-discovery of the authentic text, this conception of poetry should continue to be influential" (20). If Garrison is right that Dryden "offers no explanation that would justify such a lofty comparison [of panegyric to epic]" (29), it is possible that Dryden did not feel the need to because of the existence of this Renaissance tradition.

The "commonplaces" of panegyric, the commonplace observations that a panegyrist is apt to use (as opposed to Aristotle's more technical *topoi*, the forms of arguments), were articulated in some of the obscurer rhetorics mentioned above. Garrison cites in particular the *Rhetorica ad Herennium*, where they appear (as "demonstrative topics") in the *divisio*, organized under "external circumstances" (ancestry, education, wealth, titles, sources of power), "physical attributes" (agility, strength, beauty, health), and character (wisdom or prudence, fortitude, temperance, justice). The three divisions correspond conventionally to Augustus, Trajan, and Nerva, themselves "commonplaces" of panegyric. The organization of the panegyric into a six-part festival oration concluding with the *laus regis* is discussed in the rhetoric of Dionysius of Halicarnassus. It is, according to Garrison, Thomas Farnaby who, in his discussion of what he calls *panegyrica nova* in his *Index Rhetoricus et Oratorius* (1625), connects the latter, *laus regis*, with the demonstrative topics (44–45).

Consistent with what I have called the instability of the genre, the topics themselves are somewhat unstable: sometimes they appear to belong to both kinds of rhetoric equally, but more often they blend with other topics that belong to different kinds. Thus, *prius/nunc* (which might easily be understood in modern terms as a kind of "before/now" arrangement) and "procession" (which might be understood as a parade metaphor) are essentially demonstrative topics directed at the popular audience. However, *prius/nunc* naturally blends into related topics of "usurpation/restoration," and "restoration" into the topic of the "state physician," which not only introduces specific "ailments" but urges specific "treatments" too, and so becomes deliberative. "Procession" just as naturally modulates through another topic, "reconciled groups," to the topic of *parcere subiectis*, lowering the proud and relieving the distressed, a reconciliation brought about by force that the ruler is urged, deliberatively, to effect. The instability of the topics themselves accounts for the slipperiness of a panegyrist like Daniel, who seems to glide from one kind of rhetoric to another—from praise to advice, and from propaganda addressed to the people to advice to the king.

Although, as panegyric acquires pejorative connotations in the late seventeenth and early eighteenth century, few writers care to label their poems panegyrics (in the eighteenth century, no serious ones do), panegyrics (of a sort) continue to be written. These poems continue to exploit the tripartite relationship—formerly poet, prince, and people, but latterly party hack, patron, and party—that distinguishes panegyric proper (and improper). Sometimes such poems, like Swift's "Directions for a Birthday Song," varying the convention of the "painter-poems" as well as of panegyric, address, instead of the prince, the poet, who in turn is imagined "readdressing" his bad lessons to the prince—as if the prince were an untouchable, or "unaddressable," even in scorn, by a genuine poet. Still, if the mark of a genuine poet is to write a mock-panegyric, surely that involves some idea of what a real one is about.

The relationship of Swift's *Tale of a Tub* to panegyric in the above sense has yet to be developed, partly, I think, because panegyric is commonly thought of as poetry and poetry only, but mainly because the sense of it as a distinct kind of writing, a *genre* with a mirrorlike—perhaps one should say "fun-house mirrorlike"—relation to satire, a very major *genre* indeed, is still very recent.[6] The place of Marvell's *Rehearsal Transpros'd* in the panegyric tradition is even less established than *A Tale*'s, although the major themes of Marvell's satire include the relationship of praise to blame (or, as he puts them, panegyric and philippic), and of praise to advice. In the "Apology" of *A Tale*, Swift himself acknowledges a debt that becomes obvious in the body of the work. The major difference between the two works, I would argue, is that for Marvell in *The Rehearsal Transpros'd* the panegyric tradition is still alive in ways it definitely is not for Swift—ways that our enjoyment of Swift's satire depends on our noticing, and that would be missed without comparison to *The Rehearsal Transpros'd*. Both works demonstrate the increasing internalization of the addressee. This is apparent in versions of the king in *The Rehearsal Transpros'd*, and in the figures of authority (the Peter, Martin, and Jack) of *A Tale*—a development probably of no small significance to the novel. Increasingly, the old rhetorical panegyric is not heard but *overheard* or rather *overread*—the hearing by some vast national throng at some important public occasion gives way to the reading of a print-created public, a reading that is always private.

Numerous modern critics have remarked on the relationship of panegyric to satire, and to other traditionally more respectable branches of rhetoric. In *The Poetry of Limitation*[7] Warren L. Chernaik remarks that "Panegyric and satire, the poetry of praise and the poetry of blame, are sister forms" (175). He defends his statement with examples of the good contained in satire, out of a need to "present the norms whose violations it deplores," and says, "[T]hus satire abounds in visions of the good" (175–76). Garrison, in *Dryden and the Tradition of Panegyric*, quotes Shaftesbury's remark in *Characteristics* (1714) that "the Nerve and Sinew of modern *Panegyrick* lies in a dull kind of Satire; which the Author, it's true, intends shou'd turn to the advantage of his Subject; but which, if I mistake not, will appear to have a very contrary Effect" (34–35). Clearly Shaftesbury is talking about the unintended effect of bad modern panegyric rather than the generic similarity of even the best panegyric to satire, but what makes modern panegyric bad is ignorance of precisely this generic affinity and the failure to exploit it.

In *New Approaches to Eighteenth-Century Literature* Ralph Cohen and Ralph W. Rader discuss just this problem.[8] We have either had no notions of kinds, or too rigid ones. Cohen argues that "neoclassical forms were mixed and interrelated, dominated by didactic models."[9] Rader (42) uses the figure of the rabbit-duck to illustrate his point, remarking that "it is impossible to see it as both [rabbit and duck] at the same time, that our perceptive apparatus will not accept the ambiguity."[10] To me the rabbit-duck—lines on paper that the mind insists on seeing as either a rabbit or a duck but not both—could illustrate the trinity of history, satire, and panegyric. It could also serve as the emblem of the emblematic "painter-poems," or more generally of the way certain highly topical works seem to be polarized.

Most recently Leon Guilhamet, in *Satire and the Transformation of Genres*, has remarked how, as opposites, satire (or at least *demonstrative* satire) and panegyric evoke one another;[11] he says that "where satire is most intense, its opposite, panegyric, is always implied" (42). The role he assigns to satire as "mediator between the real and the ideal," with its "gaze squarely on the worst of what is real" (16), could with slight adjustment be assigned to panegyric, which also functions as a mediator between the ideal and the real, but with its gaze rather on the former than the latter. For Guilhamet great satire, in its exploitation and "transformation" of other forms and genres, is not the rabbit-duck but the Janus head:

> Although the Janus head looks to chaos in one direction as its object of attack, the second face gazes intently toward the golden age of genre, when order prevailed and Astraea presided over human institutions. (164)

Thus he regards the "painter-poems" as deliberative satires, based on Waller's "Instructions" but "de-forming" the deliberative oration, the course of action deliberated being the one implicit in Waller's contention that "Men that fight so deserve to rule the sea" (64). Guilhamet overlooks the deliberative capacity of panegyric itself and the fact that, as Isabel Rivers asserts in *The Poetry of Conservatism*, Marvell's satires were not wholly negative.[12] She writes that he

> tried to counteract the heroic courtly royalism that Waller and Dryden were creating by his support for a broader royalism based on the relationship between king and country. (102)

Rachel Trickett, in *The Honest Muse*, offers her own definition of panegyric as one of the three main kinds of writing in the eighteenth century (the other two being elegy and satire).[13] A panegyric is "a public celebration of virtue, nobility, and splendour, qualities which can be represented by a monarch, a hero, or a statesman whose private character might not bear a more intimate scrutiny" (16). Panegyric, she writes, is "radically affected by the changing ideas and circumstances of the age" (13).

In particular, the rise of the concept of "honesty," usually in opposition to or at least at the expense of "honour," challenged "the stock conventions of panegyric or even epic" (12)—especially "the virtues." She puts it in suitably Swiftian, sartorial terms:

> Suspicion of the outward trappings of virtue itself leads naturally to satire of the kind that tears away deceptive appearances from the reality, and it is as satirists that the Augustans are generally remembered. (12)

Oddly, she develops the same clothes analogy that, in *A Tale*, comes to stand, I hope to show, for analogy itself, and for a crisis of analogical meaning that threatens epideictic, since it must employ analogy in treating virtue:

> Honesty appeared to them above all as an unadorned virtue. In the same essay [*Essay upon the Original and Nature of Government*] Temple enumerates the effects on men of those embellishing graces which should accompany goodness, but he barely conceals his hint that they only too seldom do: "Eloquence, As it passes for a mark of Wisdom, Beauty of Goodness, And Nobility of Valour (which was its original) have likewise some effect upon the opinion of the People; but a very great one when they are really joined with the qualities they promise or resemble." (12)

Temple's polite language suggests that honor is not really an indication of virtue; the usual language about virtue has become counterfeit—"passes for a mark"—and everyone recognizes as much. The quotation suggests that real virtue somehow manages to show itself not by means of, but in spite of, its signifiers—almost without signifiers, which, as readers of *A Tale* should know, is impossible. Virtue can no more stand forth naked than Jack's Father's Will can stand forth coatless.

Still, the desire for the identity of signifying conventions and signified virtues seems to be at the heart of what is meant by the honesty that Temple evokes here. Honesty is in some ways a reactionary virtue, a blanket term for all the old virtues renewed—for prudence, temperance, justice, etc., redeemed from their tired old signifiers by a new one pretending not to be a signifier at all, while working on an even higher level of signification. Clearly, the challenge for panegyric is a *significant* one. Its conventional subject matter, "the good," "the noble," is challenged as counterfeit representation by a more intensely representational concept that purports not to be representational. Honesty begins with Jack—"suspicion of the outward trappings of virtue" (as Trickett describes the quest for honesty) (12)—and ends with Peter.

Analogy

Nilli Diengott, in "Analogy as a Critical Term: A Survey and Some Comments,"[14] deplores the fact that "theoretical discussions of analogy are almost non-existent" (227). She offers, besides the *literary* definition of analogy as "resemblance or similarity between two terms," complementary definitions from mathematics and the natural sciences. In mathematics, analogy "was used . . . to denote a geometric proportion of a four-part form—A is to B as C is to D. This formulation was based on a strict *equivalence* of ratios." In the natural sciences, "analogy is based on resemblance but never on identity" (228). Others[15] define analogy as "extended simile," making it, as Aristotle has it, a kind of metaphor "differing from it only in the way it is put."[16]

Charles O. Hartman, in "Cognitive Metaphor," describes something like a spectrum of analogy from metaphor to allegory. The main idea of his article is that metaphor, insofar as it is cognitive, is a kind of *compressed* analogy. He alerts us to the likelihood that any developments in analogy or analogical thinking must have serious implications for language and for our belief in its capacity to teach or tell us anything at all about the world. By the same token, analogy in panegyric has implications that go beyond political poetry.

In this book analogy is understood principally as "resemblance or similarity between two terms." I. A. Richards's terminology of tenor and vehicle[17] seems most helpful in describing analogical developments in panegyric and satire.

Samuel Daniel: The First Panegyrist in English

The complexity of panegyric in the late seventeenth and early eighteenth century was not a result of its decadence; it was always complex. The first English panegyrics by Drummond, Daniel, and Jonson were often obscure and contradictory, precisely because the king, whose character and rule they both reflected and reflected on, was conspicuous among their readership and, for all the ostensible directness of the form, could not be spoken to too directly, at least not without some risk. If at times we do not know for certain whether the poet is talking to the king, his muse, or himself, the confusion is deliberate.

In his discussion of the doctrine of cyclical recurrence in Daniel's works, Cecil Seronsy, describing society at the beginning of the downward trend, remarks "the small bit of evil that makes its appearance at the very height of felicity."[18] This aptly describes a troubling element of the "Panegyrike Congratulatorie." Here the "small bit," like a smudge of printer's ink on the horizon of Daniel's bright "day," might indeed be just that. Ironically, panegyric, an intensely "ear-oriented" kind of rhetoric, revives shortly after the invention of "eye-oriented" print. It does not take it long, with its clearly defined triadic relationships, its mediations and reconciliations, its invocation of spaciousness and vast national gathering, to become a factious, undifferentiated, solipsistic, and even claustrophobic (per)version of itself.

Daniel's poem is partly a bid for patronage. Rees, in her *Samuel Daniel: A Critical and Biographical Study*,[19] records that "There used to be a legend that Elizabeth had appointed Daniel poet laureate in 1599" (89). Though the legend appears to be untrue, it is nevertheless true that "the Queen was graciously disposed towards him." The poem can rightly be seen then, as an attempt to reconcile the English people with their new Stuart ruler, and the unofficial laureate with the new regime.

Though it was delivered to the king in public at Burleigh Harrington in Rutlandshire in 1603, there is some confusion over its date of publication. The folio in which it appears, dated 1601, is "evidently made up of earlier and later printed pieces." The poem itself seems to reflect this tension between rhetorical occasion and printed text, as if the poet were at times unsure of his medium.

Though the poem may have been a bid for patronage, it "does not descend to mere flattery,"as Rees points out (90). Rees discovers in the poem the very characteristics that Garrison, a decade later, picked out as establishing panegyric as a respectable genre. Thus, Daniel does not merely praise James for virtues he has, but "for the virtues he thinks he should have or acquire—a kind of anticipation of merit which is severe in its requirements and has a stern as well as a complimentary facet" (90). This "stern" side is Garrison's "deliberative function" of panegyric, the aspect of it that seeks to influence action. Beyond the deliberative nature of Daniel's praise, Rees notes Daniel's realization that "it is not now enough to rely on supreme personalities alone," and his corresponding emphasis on "good laws and good practices if England is to achieve her true and full greatness" (90) This equal emphasis on man and institution is typical of panegyric.

Analogous Structure: Versions of Kings and Poets

Daniel's concern about "supreme personalities" and their adequacy (or inadequacy) is expressed by the poem's meandering, self-reflecting structure. It is apt to confuse modern readers with its succession of stanzas, which are often joined only by a preposition, an adverb, or a conjunction (stanzas 14, 25, 55). However such "flaws" are arguably thematic, since one theme of the poem is the importance of succession and its tenuousness when it depends on one man (stanza 44). Moreover, by digressing from and then returning to his theme, by "reining himself in," Daniel is doing himself what he urges the king to do. He addresses his muse in a passage that, taken out of context, seems as if it *must* be addressed to the king (and must certainly have seemed so when the poem was spoken at Burleigh Harrington):

> Thou euer hast opposed all thy might
> Against contention, furie, pride and wrong,
> Perswading still to hold the course of right;
> And peace hath beene the burden of thy song:
> And now thy self shalt have the benefit
> Of quietnesse, which thou hast wanted long;
> And now shalst have calme peace, and vnion
> With thine owne warres, and now thou must go on.
>
> (stanza 53)

On one level the "contention, furie, pride and wrong" are the subject of *The Civil Wars,* which Daniel has been writing and which he hoped to complete under James's peaceful rule (the poem was, in fact, never completed). Various analogies are implied: between the actual civil wars and the civil wars in Daniel's book, between the end of the civil wars and the conclusion of the book, between the "Muse" bringing about this end in the book and James enabling it to do so by bringing it about macrocosmically in the state, and finally, between Daniel, the laureate, and James, the king, both laboring for similar ends in their respective, interdependent spheres. Significantly, this very analogy of the writer as vehicle for the king is at the heart of later satires like *A Tale of a Tub* and *The Dunciad,* or for that matter, *The Rehearsal Transpros'd,* in which Samuel Parker himself seems to become the tenor of his numerous vehicles of kingship.

The poem's double rhetorical function—of advice and praise—helps to explain its structure. What one part advises another praises and vice versa. The poem aims at an identification of advice and praise, an identification facilitated by reiterated praise of the king's advice to his son in the king's own *Basilikon Doron.* Praising the king for such advice involves repeating the advice to the king himself—a not-too-subtle reminder. The poem could be described as *mirroring* as it reflects James's advice to his son back to the father.

Not coincidentally, the mirror is an important motif in *Basilikon Doron.* James advises his son, "[L]et your owne life be a law-booke and a mirrour to your people; that therein they may read the practise of their owne Lawes; and therein they may see, by your image, what life they should leade."[20] Elsewhere he urges Prince Henry to be, in his person, "a lampe and mirrour to your company" (37).

But James is subjected to a kind of "diachronic" mirror that magnifies as well. Daniel's poem depicts him at the beginning of a new cycle of English (or rather, now, *British*) history, as not just image but a *fulfillment* too, of the line of his great ancestor, Henry VII. James's own interpretation of history appears from his book to have been cyclical:[21] we can apply past experience to the present because "such is the continuall volubilitie of things earthly, according to the roundnesse of the world, and revolution of the heavenly circles" (McIlwain, *Political Works,* 40).

One need only look at the Stuart family tree to anticipate how James's background could be adapted (as it was later in stanza 41) to the themes of circularity and unity stated in stanza 1. James's great-grandfather was Henry

VII of England, himself a "restorer" (he restored peace by defeating Richard III and marrying Elizabeth of York, thereby ending the War of the Roses) and founder of a dynasty. Thus, James can be seen to be merely coming into his own as Henry's successor. Henry's struggle against Richard is compared to James's struggles in Scotland. The point of such a comparison is not just to indicate that James is acquainted with "this great mysterie of government" (stanza 43) but also to depict him as the fulfillment of a pattern. The fact that Henry was not born a king while James was, is an instance of the difference-in-similarity that enables James to fulfill the pattern without actually breaking or repeating it. Once again Daniel wants to have things both ways; he wants to reconcile two mutually exclusive values, kingship by merit and kingship by inheritance. He does so by basing one on the other. That Henry built well is proved by the state's survival under bad princes (stanza 45). Under James the state will do much better, because he is the fulfillment of a reign based on merit, and because (in lines that anticipate Swift's mock-panegyric "Directions for a Birthday Song") he is king by both merit and inheritance:

> That hadst thou had no title (as thou hast
> The onely right, and none hath els a right)
> We yet must now have bin inforc'd t'haue cast
> Our selues into thy armes. . . .
>
> (stanza 47)

Swift's satirical version capitalizes on the difficulty of having it both ways:

> In him such virtues lie inherent,
> To qualify him God's vicegerent,
> That with no title to inherit,
> He must have been a king by merit.
>
> (lines 135–36)

Daniel seems to suggest that merit is really the key to kingship, and to cite James's own ancestor as a precedent, while overtly saying something else in the very next lines:

> None but a King, and no King else beside
> Could now haue sau'd this State from being destroid.
>
> (stanza 47)

Title amounts, in fact, to a panegyrical commonplace, one that is worked and reworked from Daniel to Churchill, where the use of the idea is subversive of it. The danger of the procedure of turning past rulers into analogical vehicles for the present is that it can underscore the discrepancy between vehicle and tenor, turning what should be a positive difference into a negative one. The analogies suggest the positives that James is not, and the negatives that he is.

Stanza 48 reinforces the circular motif by invoking the Platonic year. It "returns" with James about a hundred years after his grandmother, Lady Margaret Tudor, married James IV of Scotland:

> Thus doth th'all-working Prouidence retaine,
> And keepe for great effects the seede of worth,
> And so doth point the stops of time thereby,
> In periods of vncertaine certainty.
>
> (stanza 48)

With the return of Henry's heir to England, the *annus magnus* is complete; the golden age has begun (Erskine-Hill, *Augustan Idea*, 287). Much of the credit for bringing the Platonic year about goes to "learned Mourton," praised for his good advice in a passage ostensibly addressed to Margaret Tudor's grandmother, Margaret of Richmond (stanza 51). As a dispenser of good advice to a king, Mourton, archbishop of Canterbury and English statesman, is a precedent for (and version of) Daniel himself. Mourton seems to serve as a bridge to the conclusion (stanzas 52–59), which consists mainly of reflections on the poet's role as advisor and James's role as example. Advice and rule by example are nearly equated and valued as peaceful kinds of influence.

In stanza 53 the poet's role is described as "Perswading still to hold the course of right." The meandering and digressive structure of the poem necessitates at times a sudden "reining in" that becomes a metaphor for the "reigning" that the poet wants the king to do. It means to address the urgent problems. Out of their "humour of luxuriousnesse" (stanza 54) the people will be restored to "native modestie" (stanza 55) by James's example (stanza 57) and the example of his court (stanza 58). The "ship of state" and the "rule by example" topoi are neatly combined in the figure of James at the rudder. It is disappointing, but not surprising, to read that James's court was in reality "often rather seedy."[22]

Versions of Reality:
Topics versus Topicality

The poem begins conventionally by celebrating the occasion ("a greater day") with a circular motif for the peaceful union of Scotland and England. Terms like "Scot" and "English" are lost in the greater unity of "Great-Britaine" and the "mutual love" and "obedience" of every subject. Combined with a reference to the "wall of Adrian" (a former high-water mark of imperial sway now said to be exceeded), this amounts to an early invocation of "the Augustan idea."[23] There is, additionally, an element of the Christianized *pax Romana* that can be found in later works by Waller and Pope and traced back to its source in Virgil's *Aeneid*:[24]

> tu regere imperio populos, Romane, memento
> (hae tibi erunt artes) pacique imponere morem,
> parcere subiectis et debellare superbos.
>
> (6.851–53)

Curiously, this idea of restraining the proud and relieving the oppressed recurs often enough to suggest a disorderly society, if not one already disintegrating. The negative side of "imperial sway"—colonialism, "luxuriousness," and related vices—is treated more directly later (stanzas 34–35). The apparent allusion to Augustus in

> We shall not feare to haue our wiues distain'd
> Nor yet our daughters violated here
> By an imperiall lust. . . .
>
> (stanza 59)

is surprising, since Augustus was invoked positively in *Basilikon Doron* (Erskine-Hill, *Augustan Idea*, 108). Clearly that "mirror" is not held up to James uncritically; the poet differs with James when it suits him, and in a context where such difference would be noticed. This is the sort of detail about Augustus that contributed to the negative view of him in the eighteenth century; Augustus himself is one of those epideictic topoi that can be negative or positive—or both perhaps.[25]

The union celebrated in stanzas 1–3, an innovation in a sense, is actually less important than the *restoration* celebrated in stanza 4. The point may be that nothing James can bring to the English can be as much as the English themselves once were: "Glory of men, this hast thou brought to vs, / And yet hast brought vs more then this by farre." This restoration topic, which is demonstrative and addressed, as propaganda, to the people, is immediately followed by an idea intended to indicate the limitation of royal power, and which is therefore deliberative in function:

> God makes thee King of our estates, but we
> Doe make thee King of our affection,
> King of our loue: a passion borne more free,
> And most vnsubiect to dominion. . . .
>
> (stanza 5)

His internal rule over men's affections, stemming from the restoration described in stanza 4, is greater than any "imperial sway" alone, and cannot be imposed. While continuing to praise the people for this "affection," stanzas 6–7 develop the theme of limitation by hinting at what the people can do when imposed upon—with (for us) a kind of tragic irony:

> Time altred hath the forme, the meanes, and brought
> The State to that proportion'd euennesse,
> As 'tis not like again 'twill ever come
> (Being us'd abroad) to draw the sword at home.
>
> (stanza 7)

The *prius/nunc* pattern of stanza 8, which attempts to make the present ruler look good by contrast with the past, develops naturally from the preceding ideas of restoration, but leads to one of the contradictions mentioned above, because the previous ruler was still popular and still closely identified with current political and religious issues. Faithful to the conventions of the genre, Daniel clearly wants to depict James as better than the previous ruler and Elizabeth as nonpareil:

> This people, this great State, these hearts adore
> Thy Scepter now, and now turne all to thee,
> Touch't with as pow'rful zeale, and if not more,
> (And yet O more, how could there euer be
> Then vnto her, whom yet we doe deplore
> Amidst our ioy!) And give vs leaue if we

> Reioyce and mourne, that cannot without wrong
> So soone forget her we enioy'd so long.
>
> (stanza 8)

The difficulty of reconciling its conventions, its topoi, to its topicality (Cherniak, *Poetry of Limitation*, 127) can ultimately discredit the writer and turn a positive comparison into a negative.

After using lingering deference to Elizabeth as an indication of the fidelity of the English people, "true after death" (stanza 9), the poet can safely depict the outpouring of popular support for James in a series of "procession" topoi:

> It addes much to thy glory and our grace,
> That this continued current of our loue
> Runnes thus to thee, all with so swift a pace;
>
> (stanza 11)

The passage describes movement that in its steady continuity appears to resist change. What change there is, is implicit from the outset, and by it nothing is displaced ("Not as in motion put from out our place, / But in one course . . ."). The ceremonial procession or triumph here becomes a metaphor for change and the way it *should* happen. It is also a metaphor for space and order, both lacking in the greedy imperialism hinted at later:

> By which improuement we shall gaine much more
> Then by *Peru*, or all discoueries. . . .
>
> (stanza 35)

Rees's comments on the real "confinement" of Elizabethan society help dispel what seems to be a flattering misconception of its freedom, and also help explain why a preoccupation with place and space in public poetry quickly degenerates, in works like *A Tale of a Tub* that employ the themes and topoi of such poetry, into an obsession with displacement and confinement:

> It is a paradox of the age that while from one aspect it offered opportunity and adventure with a lavish hand, from another point of view the scope of action of some of its noblest spirits was strictly confined and controlled. (128)

In stanza 36 the poet suggests that if the king restrained the greed described in stanza 34, and based promotion on merit, there would be no need for people to leave the country; there would be "roome and place enough for all" (stanza 36). Daniel's idea is, essentially, that there is "place" for all so long as all are given it according to their merit; England is "crowded" and in need of colonies not from want of natural goods or physical space, but because of inequity. The rest of the section urges the king to prevent such inequity with the resources of the state:

> This golden Meadow lying ready still
> Then to be mow'd, when their occasions will.
>
> (stanza 39)

After digressing to discuss the "vile disnatur'd Vipers" (stanza 14) opposed to James's rule, the "procession" resumes as do the themes of reconciliation and unity. In stanzas 17–18 the restoration becomes medical, with James as doctor:

> The pulse of *England* neuer more did beat
> So strong as now: nor euer were our harts
> Let out to hopes so spacious and so great
> As now they are: nor euer in all parts
> Did we thus feele so comfortable heat,
> As now the glory of thy worth imparts:
> The whole complection of the Common-wealth,
> So weake before, hop'd neuer for more health.
>
> (stanza 18)

This may be meant to allude to a passage in *Basilikon Doron* where James urges his son to govern his subjects the way a doctor heals his patients: "by knowing what vices they are naturallie most inclined to . . . before he . . . begin[s] his cure" (McIlwain, *Political Works*, 22). When James discusses his problems with each of the three estates in Scotland he diagnoses the "naturall sickenesse" of the nobility as "a fectlesse arrogant conceit of their greatnes and power" (24). Concluding this section, stanza 19 offers a final flourish on the procession theme before the quieter section of instruction begins:

> Could'st thou but see from *Douer* to the Mount,
> From *Totnes*, to the *Orcades*, what ioy. . . .

Printed Words and Courts

Stanza 20 marks the beginning of a long passage on James's book:

> We know thee more, then by report we had:
> We have an euerlasting euidence
> Vnder thy hand, that now we need not dread
> Thou wilt be otherwise in thy designes
> Then there thou art in those iudiciall lines.
>
> (stanza 20)

Thus the king's own writings are invoked as a limitation on his conduct; however, it is really one thing for James to advise his son, and another for him to promise to abide by that advice himself. Daniel forces the point, since James makes no such promise in *Basilikon Doron*. Perhaps it would be fairer to say that Daniel assumes the promise, in order to advise it himself. By arguing (stanza 21) that it is the greatest glory upon earth to instruct a king, Daniel invokes a similar sanction for his own activity. The final lines of the stanza touch obliquely on the matter of succession, for which, in different ways, *Basilikon Doron* strengthens the people's hopes. Hope includes both expectation and desire; Daniel implies that without the desire for it, James's succession has little hope in the other sense, too.

The concluding couplet of stanza 22 introduces a series of stanzas (23–25) referring to *Basilikon Doron*, connected by the word "there":

> There we behold thee King of thine owne hart,
> And see what we must be and what thou art.
>
> (stanza 22)

The stress on place almost makes the book itself a microcosm of the court:

> There great *Exemplare, Prototipe*, of Kings,
> We finde the good shall dwell within thy Court;
>
> (stanza 22)

The passage could equally be read "in your book we find that the good shall dwell within your court" or "in your book we find the good that shall dwell within your court." In the next lines "there" is the court:

> Plaine zeale and truth, free from base flatterings,
> Shall there be entertain'd, and haue resort. . . .
>
> (stanza 23)

Daniel is as circumstantial about what else shall *not* be there as about what shall. Flatterers, self-seekers, favorites, monopolists, bribe-takers should not be there, but appear to have been at court recently. While it is still fairly clear, I think, what place Daniel means by "there," the court is consistent with other topoi discussed above in that it implies or even evokes its dark opposite. There is already present in this first panegyric the potential for transformation of praise to blame, for confusion of vehicle and tenor.

Still, for now the court of the book appears to be the vehicle for the real court, where the king will rule like the sun, a topos that introduces the important idea of "rule by example":

> There are no mightie Mountaines interpos'd
> Betweene thy beames and vs, t'imbarre thy light . . .
>
> (stanza 24)

Access to this court must be public and based on merit:

> There is no way to get up to respect
> But onely by the way of worthinesse;
> All passages that may seeme indirect
> Are stopt up now, and there is no accesse
> By grosse corruption. . . .
>
> (stanza 25)

When the corrupt have access to the king they may offer him bad advice and flattery, the subjects of the next stanzas, and deny *him* access too:

> The deeds of worth and laudable desarts
> Shall not now passe thorow the straight report
> Of an imbasing tongue. . . .
>
> (stanza 26)

Recalling the uneasy relationship of panegyric to print suggested above, it is surely significant that James is being bound, in these stanzas, less by his word than by his printed text. In the spoken poem, the printed word is binding; when the spoken poem itself is printed, the "binding" is reinforced in more ways than one. Print gives every reader a copy of James's word, as the poet is pleased to remind him:

> We have an earnest, that doth euen tie
> Thy Scepter to thy word, and binds thy Crowne
> (That els no band can binde) to ratifie
> VVhat thy religious hand hath there set downe
> Wherein thy all commanding Soueraigntie
> Stands subiect to thy Pen and thy renowne;
> There we behold thee King of thine owne hart,
> And see what we must be, and what thou art.
>
> (stanza 22)

James's "all commanding Soueraigntie" now becomes "subiect" to the printing press as well.

If in the above stanzas it is unclear whether the "there" referred to is the court depicted in *Basilikon Doron* or the actual court, a printed or a real court, the confusion is probably deliberate, the point being that the real court should resemble the printed one. There are, however, at least *three* courts involved here: the printed court of *Basilikon Doron*, the ideal court that resembles it, and the court implied by the vivid negatives of the stanzas. Ironically, the one Daniel says it is not is, obviously, the one it most *is*. While ostensibly using the same medium, print, to amplify James's ideal image, he reverses it. This could not be done so effectively, indeed would not be possible at all, were it not for print, which first makes the versions public, then gives them a permanence that enables reference and manipulation, various forms of response, and even attack. Finally, consistent with the peacefulness of his "rule by example," indeed by printed copy, Daniel invokes the "Nile" topos, with its emphasis on reciprocity and benign, calm power—a topos worth noting here if only for its very late, negative use in Swift's 1729 "Directions":

> Thus mightie riuers quietly doe glide,
> And doe not by their rage their powers professe . . .
>
> (stanza 32)

Some Conclusions

Jonson's almost exactly contemporary "A Panegyre, on the Happy Entrance of James, Our Sovereign, to His First High Session of Parliament in

This Kingdom" (1603),[26] uses as a precedent for "rule by example" both the king's book and Claudian's "Panegyric on the Fourth Consulship of the Emperor Honorius," in particular the speech of Theodosius to his son (a passage partially quoted by James in *Basilikon Doron*):

> The world shapes itself after its ruler's
> pattern, nor can edicts sway men's minds so
> much as their monarch's life;[27]

In Jonson's poem, Themis reminds James,

> That kings, by their example, more do sway
> Than by their power; and men do more obey
> When they are led than when they are compelled.
>
> (lines 125–27)

She urges him to be "as compassionate as wise" (108), just as Theodosius urges Honorius to be "kindly to his country" (319). In Claudian, Theodosius's speech is interrupted by the overenthusiastic Honorius, all set to slay tyrants, but James's similar interruption is much more muted, as suits one who never acknowledged the subject's right to rebellion, let alone assassination. Some of the muteness is no doubt due to the indirectness of Themis's speech, which makes the role of the poet, the relayer of the speech, all the more prominent:

> He owned their crowns, he would not so their crimes.
> He knew that princes, who had sold their fame
> To their voluptuous lusts, had lost their name.
>
> (lines 112–14)

Jonson seems to want to compare James's position here to that expressed in *Basilikon Doron* in which, even against a lawless tyrant, the rebellion of the subjects was "ever unlawfull on their part" (19). Not unlike Daniel's, Jonson's rendition of James's views is potentially subversive. Similar to these panegyrics, and typical of a new variation that reflects James's double crown, is William Drummonds's "Forth Feasting: A Panegyricke to the King's Most Excellent Majestie" (1617).[28] According to Garrison, it becomes the most influential of the "return poems" celebrating the annual trip of the Stuart kings to Scotland and back. With its paraphrases of Claudian and

Jonson, it reads "like an anthology of panegyrical topics" (131). These poems seem to anticipate later panegyrical poems like Dryden's "Astraea Redux," or, perhaps, Marvell's "Horatian Ode." I concentrate on Daniel's poem simply because I feel it contains nearly everything of interest that can be found in panegyrics of the period, and even anticipates many later developments within the genre.

The structure of the poem is thematic in that it reinforces the importance and the tenuousness of succession at the same time it emphasizes the need for control. It reflects on and qualifies imperial myths that were important to James and later central to the Stuart monarchy, and it generates important precedents for advice to the king that indicate considerable self-consciousness about the poet's function in panegyric. It is also an early instance of the topicality of the genre and how such topicality almost inevitably clashes with its topoi, its conventions, and commonplaces. However, it also illustrates that such conflict may be instructive, a warning to the king about how self-mythologizing can turn into satire when it fails to take reality into account. The contradictions in the poem between idealistic Platonism and un-Platonic reality reflect a potentially graver split in James's, if not Jacobean, mentality. Unresolved in the poem, such weaknesses are social rather than aesthetic.

The way the poem's topoi consistently evoke a topical reality at odds with their ideality, the uncertainties over precisely which court is described (the court in the poem, an ideal or a real one), or even which prince addressed, are typical of the potential for praise and blame to act as vehicles for each other. As the first panegyric in English, the poem is striking for its degree of self-reflectiveness. In its capacity to generate vehicles for itself (vehicles for a vehicle, in fact), in the tendency of those vehicles to obfuscate rather than clarify, and in obfuscating to blame rather than praise, it proves oddly prophetic.

2
Andrew Marvell's Political Poetry and the Panegyric Tradition

WHILE Marvell's *Horatian Ode upon Cromwell's Return from Ireland* challenges conventional panegyric, the "obvious source of unity [of which] is the figure of the monarch himself, who has both a ceremonial and a political role in the state,"[1] there is nothing here of the "union of ceremonial and political purpose" that Garrison says is at once "the greatest weakness and the greatest strength of the genre" (129). Indeed, Marvell can be seen to attack the genre precisely where it is weakest, in its emphasis on ritual and roles, which can potentially underline their "actors'" separation from reality and consequent powerlessness. In *The First Anniversary* Marvell can be seen to reunite ceremony and power in the figure of the Protector, vigorously appropriating many of the conventions of panegyric.

While these poems belong to the panegyric tradition simply by challenging it, they also belong to it in a more complicated way by fulfilling its potential, by realizing its capacity for reversal and conversion. They can change a good vehicle into a bad, and praise by blame and blame by praise. The consequent uncertainty about meaning helps obfuscate rather than identify the authority they assume. While it is very difficult to gather what effect these poems had on a seventeenth-century audience, some of that reaction is probably reflected in the contemporary critical disputes.

An Horatian Ode

The effectiveness of Marvell's attack is reflected in the controversy that still rages around the poem. Franklin G. Burroughs, Jr. remarks that "Marvell's 'Ode' has itself generated a kind of civil war."[2] With or without power, ceremony remains attractive; it may even be more attractive without power. This may partly explain the sympathy that critics have felt for Charles as "the *Royal Actor* born" of line 53 and the tendency of a group of critics, led by Cleanth Brooks, to construct an attractive figure out of scraps of ambiguity and allusion. Without ceremony, power is necessarily uglier; showing it to be so does not make Marvell less Cromwellian. Perhaps the real victim of the separation of ceremony and power is the reader.

Not all of the ambiguities cited by Brooks and his party have stood up. For example, critics have read the "Nor yet" and "still" of "Nor yet grown stiffer with Command, / But still in the Republick's hand" (lines 81–82) as adverbs of time, ominously implying that Cromwell might change at some *later* time; however, G. D. Monsarrat argues quite cogently, from Marvell's use of these adverbs elsewhere, that the lines mean only that "Cromwell has emphatically *not* "grown stiffer with Command" and that he is *always* "in the *Republick's* hand."[3]

The point of the allusion at the beginning and the end, to Lucan's *Pharsalia* is harder to determine. Clearly the "figure" alluded to is Julius Caesar, but it is unclear whether that figure is meant to help us understand Charles I, Charles II, or Cromwell, because the poem presents no current monarchical figure. The allusion is even further complicated by the different ways Caesar is viewed by different parties, and by the murky background of Marvell's quarrels with Lucan's continuator and translator, Tom May. In Lucan, Caesar is a villain. It is easy to see a parallel between Caesar's crossing the Rubicon after victories in Gaul and Cromwell's return to England after victories in Ireland, but Nicholas Guild suggests that the "Lucanian paradigm" fits neither Cromwell nor Charles I, but rather Charles II: "[I]nstead of Julius Caesar crossing the Rubicon at the head of an army of legionnaires to seize a crown and enslave his homeland, Charles crosses the Tweed at the head of an army of Scots."[4] This is an ingenious solution, but possibly too ingenious, since Charles II is entirely absent from the poem. To believe Guild, we would also have to believe that Marvell left the bearing of an important and potentially destructive allusion entirely up to circumstances outside the poem.

This brings us to another problem. Is the poem a celebration of a return or a send-off? Patterson sees the ode as "the celebration of a return from a significant journey or campaign . . . a Statian *sylva* poem,"[5] but it could almost equally be a *proempticon*, a congratulatory send-off. If the former, then the Cromwellian resemblance to Caesar seems emphasized; if the latter—if it is a kind of warm-up or even recruitment poem for Cromwell's imminent Scottish campaign—Guild's emphasis seems more appropriate.

In important ways Marvell's poem participates in the tradition it challenges. As an explicitly *Horatian* ode, it invokes "Horace's role as a counsellor to Caesar Augustus, personification of peaceful rule and cooperation between literary and political values" (60). Thus Marvell has a precedent for the poet as advisor, and the reader has a good indication that some of what follows will be advice disguised as praise. Additionally, Marvell may be seen to have invoked from the outset the "Lucanian paradigm," but from the standpoint of the ex-Republican poet of Octavian, Julius Caesar's nephew. Marvell writes as Horace after Philippi, without telling us who won. We do not even know who Caesar is, let alone Caesar's nephew, but it is relatively certain who the poet is.

Marvell/Horace writes in line 41 of "Nature that hateth emptiness"; it seems that the void created by the absent "monarchical figure" has been filled by the greater sense of the poet's role. There is a certain self-consciousness about his relationship to power; it is reflected in details from the title and in the different "Arts" that maintain power in line 120. Critics have remarked that in the alternating long/short lines "the reader moves back and forth between a firm centre and a faint periphery."[6] What this alternation does is alert us to the role of the poet, himself controlling and guiding as power ought to do but does not. This is, arguably, Marvell's sophisticated, metrical equivalent of Daniel's controlled digressions:

> Nor yet grown stiffer with Command,
> But still in the *Republick's* hand:
> How fit he is to sway
> That can so well obey.
>
> (lines 81–84)

Margoliouth points out the verbal resemblances between the beginning of Marvell's poem and Tom May's translation of Lucan's *Pharsalia*. In evaluating such echoes, it is wise to bear in mind Franklin Burroughs's warning about distinguishing allusion from mere "literary borrowing, in which no extrapolation from the original context is intended" (119). Burroughs goes on to find resemblances of both Charles I and Cromwell to Caesar—the first to the "assassinated" Caesar and the second to the "victorious" Caesar. A more general allusion may be to Horace's *Odes* 1.37, "The Fall of Cleopatra," which can be seen, in its ambivalent depiction of Cleopatra as "frenzied queen" and "no craven woman," as a (distant) model for Marvell's sympathetic depiction of Charles as accepting his enemies, if not approving of them. Elsewhere, it has been suggested, the pursuit of Charles to "Caresbrooks narrow case" (52) may owe something to Augustus's pursuit of Cleopatra: "chasing her with his galleys, as she sped away from Italy, even as the hawk pursues the gentle dove, or the swift hunter follows the hare over the plains of snow-clad Thessaly." Such an allusion would work to liken Charles to the imperial loser, Cromwell to the winner.

The purpose of the opening is clearly to advise action, which is seen as heroic (something that is not the case in the *Pharsalia*). The suggestion of J. M. Newton that the action might be "an almost suicidally desperate one, like joining other young Royalist hot-heads in an attempt to catch and assassinate Cromwell in London"[7] is very amusing. The action advised is actually the one praised in these lines:

> So restless *Cromwell* could not cease
> In the inglorious Arts of Peace,
> But through adventrous War
> Urged his active Star.
>
> (lines 9–12)

Cromwell's action is his successful waging of the Irish campaign against the opposition of members of his own party, in particular the Levellers, who urged peace. Michael Wilding suggests that the destructiveness of lightning can be seen as praiseworthy, because it refers to "his savage suppression of Leveller mutiny."[8] Wilding bases his reading partly on the word "Emulous":

> And, like the three-fork'd Lightning, first
> Breaking the Clouds where it was nurst,
> Did thorough his own Side
> His fiery way divide.
> For 'tis all one to Courage high
> The Emulous or Enemy;
>
> (lines 13–18)

"Emulous," he argues, would apply (in the sense of "envious") more to the rank and file than to other army generals, as has been usually assumed. At the same time, Wilding argues that "the objection to the Irish campaign is something consciously excluded from the poem" (6). It is quite possible that Marvell appears to exclude such objections only to those who know nothing about this campaign.

Whether such actions are praiseworthy or not, to blame them is "madness":

> 'Tis Madness to resist or blame
> The force of angry Heavens flame:
>
> (lines 25–26)

Patterson cites these lines as an indication and limitation of the "possibilities for epideictic" (63), that is, for praise *and* blame. Presumably, the poet is aware, and wishes us to be aware, that he is restricted to praise or, at the very least, statement of fact. The next couplet employs both:

> And, if we would speak true,
> Much to the Man is due.
>
> (lines 27–28)

The preceding lines of the poem allowed for the possibility that Cromwell might still be blameworthy, though backed by Heaven. These lines allow for no such possibility; taken together, they convey the sense that Cromwell is both backed by Heaven and by the virtuous. If it is madness to blame him for doing things when he is fated to do so, it is doubly madness to blame him when he is fated and good.

"The possibilities of epideictic" include, as usual, more than blaming, but more than praising, too. It is worth observing, in such lines of implicit advice, the strong sense of *both* possibility and limitation. Note that the limitation is urged without any diminishment of potential freedom to do something entirely different, though "mad." Although reason is invoked as something one must act in conformity with, there is no assurance in the poem, or even any indication that conduct is based on it. The elements of praise and blame are part of the "panegyric tradition," but the doubt that anyone follows good advice anyway and the certainty that no one has to are disturbing innovations that reduce the poet from orator to something like "commentator."

Exactly what Cromwell's controlling virtues are is commented on, with different emphasis, by John Wallace and Blair Worden. The former sees Cromwell's virtues as of the "the four cardinal varieties, thereby matching his character against a classical ideal."[9] Wallace translates Marvell's "reserved and austere" into temperance, "industrious valour" into fortitude, "wiser Art" into wisdom, and then is stumped for something he can translate into justice. Blair Worden seems to be on surer footing when he suggests that Cromwell's virtues are essentially Machiavellian (535). Worden remarks that "industrious Valour" sounds "distinctively Machiavellian," and that prudence (which both Cromwell's retirement and later conduct seem to indicate) is also a Machiavellian trait; indeed, the opening of the poem suggests "Machiavelli's challenge to the prince, to seize the *occasione* which enables him, through his *virtu*, to tackle *fortuna*" (538).

Above all, Cromwell's *cunning* is indicated in lines 47–52, which describe the escape of Charles (apparently planned by Cromwell) and introduce the execution. Marvell's cunning is indicated by the way, at the moment of the deed, attention is deflected away from Cromwell and onto the "bloody hands" (line 58) of the "armed bands" (line 57). According to Wilding, "[I]t is the lower orders, the rank-and-file soldiers amongst whom the radical element flourished, who are given the taint of blood" (12).

Wallace describes the lines immediately following as a section of *proof*, comprised of a *confirmatio* (57–80) and a *refutatio* (81–96).[10] Charles's acceptance of his fate is described, according to Wallace and others, so as to suggest abdication rather than deposition (82). The "bleeding head," like that discovered in the foundations of the Capitoline Temple at the start of the Roman Empire, is an omen of empire and moreover suggests that Cromwell, as the founder of another empire, is a kind of *dux bellorum*, a necessary and therefore allowable dictator (72). The praise of the defeated Irish is a convention of panegyric: the "praise by enemies." Wallace suggests that it is more than just a convention in that it happily coincided with the facts more than is usual (85). In any case, the execution, the conquest, and the praise of the conquered people all prove that Cromwell is fit to rule.

Lines 81–96 comprise the refutation. Wallace traces the concept expressed in 83–84 ("How fit he is to sway / That can so well obey") to Solon and Plato, but Wilding is better at identifying just what is being refuted: the lines comparing Cromwell to an obedient falcon are obviously intended to counter charges that Cromwell did *not* obey Parliament (7–8).

In the peroration (97–120), it seems that, just as Caesar (like so many other topics) can be invoked for good and bad, so can Hannibal:

> A *Caesar* he ere long to *Gaul,*
> To *Italy* an *Hannibal.*
>
> (lines 101–2)

The idea expressed in the final couplet ("The same *Arts* that did *gain* / A *Pow'r* must it *maintain*") is another commonplace (from Sallust), but typically one used by both friends and enemies of the Commonwealth—"with the royalist cause, as a reason for refraining from bloodshed before it was too late, then with the parliamentarians as a defence of their martial law" (Wallace, *Destiny*, 97).

First Anniversary

Garrison's idea that Marvell's *First Anniversary* emphasizes the positive, attractive strength of power and ceremony, while the Horatian ode emphasizes the weakness, is tempered by the fact that Marvell "does not return to the institution of monarchy" (136). Garrison sees Marvell returning to the panegyric tradition in terms of "the union of power and grace, of human and divine, of actual and ideal, although hypothetical" (138).

It would be simplistic to see Marvell reuniting, in "The First Anniversary," the themes he so pointedly sundered in "An Horatian Ode." It is more accurate to say that he appropriated themes and half-themes for use in the later poem, excluding the weaker from his portrait of Cromwell. Thus the disjunction between man and office, disastrous for a king and inimical to panegyric, is glorious for Cromwell because the office itself is somehow inferior; he exceeds kingship as he would, for that matter, any other traditional office. Kings enjoy succession, but in the poem succession becomes a metaphor for ineffectuality spreading over generations. Cromwell has no succession, but does not need any, because after him there will be nothing comparable left to do.

Clearly Marvell has not merely written a conventional panegyric to an unconventional man. Instead, he has written a kind of antipanegyric that, anticipating Swift in *A Tale of a Tub* (not to mention his own *The Rehearsal Transpros'd*), converts the very conventions of praise to blame, here monarchical praise to monarchical blame—to *satire*, in effect. Critics have often enough noticed the poem's demonstrative character as *praise*, but too seldom as *blame*, which is equally the function of demonstrative rhetoric. This has no doubt contributed to what I consider the *mis*reading of Wallace, who sees the poem as a deliberative piece urging Cromwell to become a king himself. The praise in the poem is also advice, but none of it pertains to kings, or to men becoming kings; the blame does.

Though this poem preserves the deliberative capacity of the genre, it is not to persuade a king to rule and a people to obey, but to dissuade a regicide from becoming king and his people from accepting him as one. The transformation of conventional positives to negatives and vice versa must be seen as pivotal in the development of panegyric and satire.

The poem begins with the image of a man drowning in time. He is everyone but Cromwell, who

> alone with greater Vigour runs,
> (Sun-like) the Stages of succeeding Suns:
>
> (lines 7–8)

Note the motif of the circle, encountered earlier in Daniel, but here obviously not a positive image of wholeness and perfection but a negative one of pointless, debilitating repetition. Cromwell's motion appears to be linear; one can imagine him cutting through concentric orbits like a meteor—or a knife. A. J. N. Wilson calls him "sun-like" in "his indefatigable vigour";[11] later, he is "sun-like" as Roman emperors are, "in his powerful beneficence to the nation which he protects and to which he gives light and heat" (268–69). Line 9 obviously glances at the restoration topos: "the Day which he doth next restore." But there is also a trace of the *prius/nunc* pattern, each day being a superior *nunc*. The important point is that patterns that previously took ages are now accomplished in days.

The comparison/contrast is narrowed in lines 13–44 from Cromwell and all other men to Cromwell and kings. The main basis of the comparison/contrast is time. The "heavy Monarchs" (line 15) who are "more Malignant then *Saturn*" are presumably heavy with dross (and ancient with decline). The god invoked here is not the Saturn of the age of gold but the Cronos who devoured his sons but could not prevent one of them (Zeus) from usurping him. The idea that by usurping Charles/Saturn/Cronos, Cromwell himself restores the golden age is hinted at in lines 11 and 12:

> *Cromwell* alone doth with new Lustre spring,
> And shines the Jewel of the yearly Ring.

Curiously, critics have not emphasized the ambiguity of the Saturn topic, an ambiguity that facilitates its use in either praise or blame. Such topics effect the transformation of panegyric into satire, while still invoking the ideal of praise (making for a sharper kind of blame). Thus Swift uses the Saturn topos satirically in "Directions for a Birthday Song"; an anonymous writer uses it panegyrically in "The Golden Age" (1702):

> Now banished Justice takes its rightful place,
> And Saturn's days return with Stuart's race.
>
> (lines 7–8)

The idea of the Platonic year, used by James I and Daniel (among others) to describe the inevitable achievement of perfection under monarchical rule, is here a cycle that brings about *nothing*. It finds kings "in the same Posture" (18) as they began. Lines 21–22,

> Well may they strive to leave them to their Son,
> For one Thing never was by one King done.

echo and parody Waller's "Upon His Majesty's Repairing of St. Paul's"—and suggest how much the "negative/positive" change was due to the "answer/response" of contemporary controversy:

> This work of cost and piety begun,
> To be accomplished by his glorious son . . .
>
> (lines 7–8)

Marvell engages Waller here. As Garrison remarks, "Waller celebrates an institution; Marvell celebrates a man" (135). Waller stresses the king's repairing the church instead of rebuilding it entirely; to him this is an indication of humility and lack of ambition:

> Ambition rather would affect the fame
> Of some new structure, to have borne her name.
>
> (lines 27–28)

This conservatism becomes a metaphor for religious conservatism:

> an earnest of his grand design
> To frame no new church, but the old refine.
>
> (lines 35–36)

Thus the ground of Marvell's debate becomes apparent. Cromwell has no such continuity with past policies and institutions, and it would be pointless to argue that he achieved what he did without destruction. It is obviously more useful neither to deny Charles his peaceful continuity nor to attribute it to Cromwell, but to equate it with inertia—to not deny the facts, but to alter their value, their polarity:

> They neither build the Temple in their dayes,
> Nor Matter for succeeding Founders raise;
>
> (lines 33–34)

The rebuilding of St. Paul's is, like the Saturn topic above, another example of the close relationship of praise and blame, the same subject being capable of either one, depending on how it is colored. No doubt this relationship of praise to blame, of panegyric to satire, is brought out more in contentious times. Marvell goes on to see, in the long reign of kings, at best not a desire to do anything positive but a desire to stave off judgment.

In their useless prominence (decorativeness without power, like ceremony without power) they are compared to the wooden heads on a viol. The comparison enables Marvell, developing his musical metaphor, to introduce Cromwell as a more effective musician, a true Amphion opposed to Waller's false one. Cromwell as Amphion, learning the music of the spheres, is also contrasted with kings in the way he moves—not in their slow orbits, but with a suggestion of violence in "cuts his way still nearer to the Skyes" (46)—and of Jovian usurpation, consistent with the earlier allusion to Saturn/Cronos.

Wallace, who wants to see the *First Anniversary* as an essentially deliberative oration urging Cromwell to become king, has to see the state Amphion builds in lines 49–116 (which Wallace says, rightly, comprise a kind of *narratio*) as "harmonious and constructed on sound principles. . . . Rhetorically, it was necessary to describe the Protectorate, a kingdom in all but name, as a flawless pattern of a commonwealth" (116). But this is "rhetorically necessary" only if Wallace is right about the deliberative intent of the poet; and he is not. Wallace perceives the element of *discordia concors* in the structure Amphion creates, but does not notice, as Nicholas Guild does, that it "is composed through the delicate balancing of mutually antagonistic forces, ready to fly apart the moment his fingers cease to play on the strings of the Instrument of Government":[12]

> And each the Hand that lays him will direct,
> And some fall back upon the Architect;
> Yet all compos'd by his attractive Song,
> Into the Animated City throng.
>
> (lines 83–86)

The state requires someone *more* than kinglike, and certainly more effective than any of the kings in the poem.

At line 99 there is a change, if not in Cromwell himself then in the perception of him. His being different things to different people(s), but only his real self to the English, is thematic; it is also, as A. J. N. Wilson writes of lines 389–90, an allusion to the way a Roman consul would be both a great man abroad and "one among equals" in Italy (270). The incongruity that Wilson himself sees in lines 99 and following, when the man who is the keystone at home becomes the mover abroad, may be accounted for as a flattering (at least to the English) inability to sway his countrymen the way he can the rest of the world. The next lines seem to reinforce the idea that what we encounter here are but facets of the same man:

> And in his sev'ral Aspects, like a Star,
> Here shines in Peace and thither shoots a War.
>
> (lines 101–2)

This is another revolutionary aspect of Marvell's panegyric. One sees how, with the rise of an individual like Cromwell, the old emphasis on reconciling public and private facets has been perpetuated—or rather subsumed into a preoccupation with facets of a character essentially private and inscrutable.

Consistent with his being different things to different people (in ways that rather reflect *their* limitations than his), for "observing" princes he becomes Polaris, a guide; though not exactly a prince himself, he acts as an *optimus princeps* to others, perhaps because princes can only understand him as another prince. Yet the poet would rather they merely took Cromwell's lead in following the "Son" whose harbinger he is. While not directly addressing or advising a prince, Marvell advises princes; sometimes he briefly addresses them directly, doing nearly what a panegyrist does, but with the rudeness of one who is not himself a subject:

> Unhappy Princes, ignorantly bred,
> . . . .
> If gracious Heaven to my Life give length,
> . . . .
> Then shall I once with graver Accents shake
> Your Regal sloth, and your long Slumbers wake:
>
> (lines 117–23)

The above introduces the millenarianism that is "derailed" by Cromwell's coaching accident at line 159. Rhetorically, lines 117–58 comprise a kind of *divisio*, a "statement of theme" (Wallace, 137). Till he can urge on other princes to "chase the beast" (124) the poet will "Hollow far behind" (125) Cromwell as he hunts it alone. Marvell's own golden age, the conditions that would have to be met to achieve it, and the circumstances that tend to prevent it, are all described in lines 131–58. Wallace sees Cromwell as beyond doubt the man intended by the phrase "with highest Pow'r" (132). I think it should be noted, though, that Cromwell already has such power; lacking are grace and obedience. These lines must surely be addressed to the people, perhaps the more headstrong among the Puritans; they perform an essentially demonstrative function common in panegyric. Time is both imagined defeated at the start of the section ("For-shortned Time its useless Course would stay") (139) and undefeated at the end, largely because of sin. Nature is compared to a ship that the captain is always just about to bring to land and always prevented from bringing there, either by stormy seas or, if it is right to look ahead to the "mate," a mutinous crew.

The lost captains of line 158 introduce Cromwell, whose old and "Saint-like" mother (161) is presented as a remnant of the world her son wants to restore. The coaching accident, implicitly (if mysteriously) due to the people's restiveness, enables Marvell to imagine Cromwell dead, and so sing his praises while he is yet alive. The ploy works to refute possible charges of flattery, since we "speak as of the Dead the Praises due" (188). Marvell, by wanting to pretend that he is praising a dead man, inadvertently suggests the ulterior motives of praising a live one. Cromwell's fall is likened both to the Fall of Man and the Crucifixion, and thereby proves his importance. The imagery of the sinking ship in lines 210–14 connects Cromwell and the nation to the captains and their ships in lines 157–58. However, this is all only a "worst scenario"; in reality, as lines 215–20 affirm, Cromwell has been rescued like Elisha.

The idea that "We only mourn'd our selves" (line 219) when we mourned for Elisha, because Elisha went to a "better place," introduces what Wallace designates as the *refutatio*. The principal charge to be denied is that there was "something in it," that is, in power for Cromwell. Lines 225–26,

> For to be *Cromwell* was a greater thing,
> Then ought below, or yet above a King:

seem to anticipate Pope's "Just less than Jove, and much above a King" in *Imitations of Horace*, Ep. 1.1.186. Wallace wishes to interpret these lines as signifying that Cromwell *should* become king because "to be Protector is at once to be both inferior to, and yet 'above', that is, to command more arbitrary power than, a king" (130). This is inconsistent with the foregoing, since after the description of kings Cromwell could hardly be said to be inferior to them in any way; moreover, the nature of the Amphionic state argues rather *for* special power than *against* it. Cromwell is not power hungry in becoming ruler, because he was greater in himself. He is not designing but rather fit for some greater purpose that drives him:

> an higher Force him push'd
> Still from behind, and it before him rush'd . . .
> (lines 239–40)

Last, but by no means least, Cromwell neither wanted nor wants to become king. What he does in giving up his "privacy so dear" (223), Wilson suggests, resembles more the noble republican Roman's renunciation of *otium* for *industria*.

The comparison to Gideon at line 249 is crucial, because it suggests a role for Cromwell other than kingship. It is hard to imagine that Gideon could be cited as anything but a *good* example for his refusal of the crown for himself and his sons. Steven Zwicker argues persuasively in "Models of Governance in Marvell's 'The First Anniversary'" that the role Marvell has in mind for Cromwell is not that of king but "similar to that of biblical judge: a figure like Samson, Gideon, and Jeptha who defends an elect nation and punishes its enemies, ruling without crown as Protector of England."[13] It is arguable that through the citation of Noah in line 282 "Marvell emphasized his intention of proposing Cromwell as a replica of Noah the king" (Wallace, *Destiny*, 134), but he could equally be seen as Zwicker sees him, as "another example of governance without kingship" (10). Coming where he does, after an extended "ship of *state*" metaphor in which "some lusty mate" (line 273) invokes the context of an argument *against* tyranny, it seems unlikely that Noah would be functioning as king; however, like several topoi cited above, "Noah" can work both ways (as just patriarch to argue against kings, or as patriarch-king to argue for them, especially to circumvent Nimrod, who was both the first king *and* a tyrant).

Noah and the "*Chammish* issue" (line 293) form a bridge to what Wallace describes as a passage of digression and diatribe against the Fifth Monarchists (293–324). Significantly, they are characterized by a fierce ambition for a king:

> Rejoycing when thy Foot had slipt aside;
> That their new King might the fifth Scepter shake,
> And make the World, by his Example, Quake:
>
> (lines 296–98)

Wallace has trouble accounting for the violence of the diatribe "in a panegyric unless it is related to their threat to step into Cromwell's shoes" (137). I would only observe that Dryden's panegyrics contain similar violent passages and that, once again, Wallace's argument seems to have him in a bind. When Cromwell represses the Fifth Monarchists at the end of the passage, he does so not as king but as captain. This connects him with the other captains at line 158 and the "lusty mate" at 273, as more a usurper than a king:

> But the great Captain, now the danger's ore,
> Makes you for his sake Tremble one fit more;
>
> (lines 321–22)

At the beginning of the peroration, popular consternation at Cromwell's accident is compared to the consternation of the first man at the first sunset. I do not agree with Wallace that the passage should be read as "an account . . . of the utter blackness into which England had been thrown in 1649 and her subsequent recovery under Cromwell" (135). Nicholas Guild's objection, that "Cromwell could be ranked among the 'Owls and Ravens'" (252), seems to preclude Wallace's own desire to interpret lines 341–42 as meaning that "Cromwell, the second sun, should make the monarchy rise again in himself."

The praise by a European king that follows in lines 349–94 is an example of "praise by enemies," like the praise the Irish bestowed on Cromwell in the "Horatian Ode." The restoration and reconciliation he praises Cromwell for are precisely what, in a different context, he should as king be praised for himself. As Wilson noted, the king perceives Cromwell as a barbarian might have perceived a powerful Roman: with perplexity about his being so great abroad yet only one among equals at home:

> Abroad a King he seems, and something more,
> At Home a Subject on the equal Floor.
>
> (lines 389–90)

The "Maturity with Hast" (line 382) that the King praises Cromwell for seems to echo the Augustan maxim *festina lente*. If so, it is consistent with much of Cromwell's description, which according to Wilson tends to transform the Protector into a kind of Horatian "*vates*-statesman" (260) who has not just a vision of order but the means to implement it too. The final address to Cromwell as "Prince" (line 395) should probably be taken in this spirit, "Prince" meaning simply *princeps* or "first citizen." The allusion to Cromwell as "the *Angel* of our Commonweal" (line 401) suggests to Zwicker that "the model finally appropriate to the Protector is neither king, nor prophet, nor even judge, but Christ as the instrument of salvation" (12).

Marvell's subversion of panegyric in these poems is thorough; that it does not appear to be exhaustive is partly due to events, and to his own and other poets' further exploitation of the genre after the Restoration. Marvell's poems show how the polarity of the same things, the same topoi, can be altered and reversed, thereby creating new virtues (and new vices) in the vehicle of the old. Such panegyrical topoi and formal arrangements will continue to be used to present analogous but contrasting, and even conflicting, figures of authority in the 1660s and 1670s, in the "Painter-Poems" and *The Rehearsal Transpros'd*. What went before might well have been the (already sufficiently ambiguous) last word, but the complexity of this development makes it a mere interlude (perhaps one should write *interregnum*) by comparison. Because under the pressure of events the meaning of panegyric becomes just other panegyrics, or panegyrists, this complex development comes to be seen as an abuse of analogy, of the relationship between vehicle and tenor, between who or what means and what is meant. Panegyric, standing for the means of presentation if not *signification* itself, becomes itself a metaphor for obfuscation and obstruction.

3
"Competing Versions": The "Painter-Poems" and *Annus Mirabilis*

SATIRE and panegyric are siblings; that is, they are branches of epideictic rhetoric, of which the subject is "praise and blame," the end "the honourable and disgraceful," and the time "the present" (Aristotle, *"Art" of Rhetoric*, 33–37). As already remarked, epideictic rhetoric can easily become deliberative, intended to influence action, by a change of phrase from nonprohibitive to prohibitive statement, and just as easily praise can become blame (and vice versa), according to which term we adopt.

Satire and panegyric are also topical and therefore controversial. For this reason, too, each tends to evoke its opposite, as each addresses an extra-literary third element—not simply history, but more precisely the contemporary, common knowledge or understanding of events.

For the period we are discussing, such events were those of the Second Anglo-Dutch War, declared officially on 22 February 1665 and officially concluded at the Peace of Breda on 21 July 1667. Major battles of the war include the Battle of Lowestoft on 3 June 1665, with its inconclusive ending thanks to the intervention of Henry Brouncker; the illegal, embarrassing, and above all, unsuccessful "Attempt at Bergen" on 2 August; the Four Days' Battle from 1 June to 4 June 1666, with its nearly disastrous division of the fleet; the St. James's fight of July 25; and the humiliating destruction of the British fleet at Chatham on 13 June 1667. This war has been described as "the clearest case in [British] history of a purely commercial war . . . a war of which the purpose was simply to take by force material places and things, especially ships."[1] It is hardly surprising that it is paralleled by equally important parliamentary and administrative developments that are reflected in the period's literature.

Waller's "Instructions to a Painter" and Marvell's "Second Advice," which introduce the *ut pictura poesis* technique into modern political satire, represent the beginning of the subgenre of "painter-poems." These poems, with *Annus Mirabilis*, respond not just to the events of the Second Dutch War, but to each other; paradoxically, while participating in the panegyric tradition, they contribute to an analogizing tendency that stresses the incapacity of language to describe "transcendentals" like the Good and the Bad, and that separates it from life. Waller's "Instructions" is answered by Marvell's satirical "Second Advice," that poem by Dryden's panegyrical *Annus Mirabilis*, and that poem by the satirical "Last Instructions." Versions of events rapidly become versions of versions; in I. A. Richards's terminology (*Philosophy of Rhetoric*, 96), vehicles about events become vehicles about vehicles, or simply put, vehicles become tenors in a collapse of meaning that, by "Last Instructions," is both political and epistemological.

I would like to offer one preliminary suggestion, inspired partly by Rader and Cohen's articles in *New Approaches to Eighteenth-Century Literature*. Cohen notes that in the early eighteenth century "the development of a comparative, historical consciousness underlies the didactic shift, the discovered relations between observations of nature and historical introspection" ("On the Interrelations," 42). Rader says generally of twentieth-century criticism that "because literary works can be held to mean nearly anything, they seem in effect to mean nothing at all" ("The Concept of Genre," 81). He argues, persuasively I think, that our understanding of literature derives from "a comprehensive inferential grasp of an author's overall creative intention in a work, which allows us to eliminate in the act of reading any potential incoherencies and ambiguities which cannot be resolved within our appreciation of the coherence of the whole" (86). He uses the figure of the rabbit-duck to illustrate his point that "it is impossible to see it as both [rabbit and duck] at the same time, [because] our perceptive apparatus will not accept the ambiguity." Much of Waller's hyperbole, I think, is deliberate ambiguity that, consistent with Rader's point, we do not accept; rather than leave it ambiguous praise, we make it blame.

Cohen's point about the rise of "historical consciousness" suggests, I think, some of the relatively new factual constraints under which Waller and Marvell wrote, imposed partly by the rise of dissent through political unrest, partly by new attitudes to knowledge. Rader's idea about the nonambiguous way people read may be less true of some "readings" than others, but it must certainly be true of the way a contemporary audience would have read *these* poems. They read them in a climate of heightened "historical consciousness," not to say intense political partisanship.

Panegyric

In numerous ways, Marvell's "Painter-Poems" and Dryden's *Annus Mirabilis* participate in the panegyric tradition described by Garrison. All of them, of course, employ the convention of advising another to do what the writer is doing himself. This is itself a panegyrical topic, a variation of the poet's traditional advisory role; the connection is still appreciated, decades later, by Swift in "Directions for a Birthday Song."

Consistent with what Aristotle says is most appropriate to panegyric, Waller's "Instructions" seeks "to magnify, making the duke of York a superior Achilles and the battle of Lowestoft (in reality rather inconclusive) a second battle of Actium."[2] Insofar as it is a *deliberative* panegyric, it attempts to show not just that the English rule the sea, but that they ought to: "Men that fight so deserve to rule the sea" (64). It is a good example of what Chernaik calls Waller's "central formula: topical detail treated in epic manner, with a strong element of praise" (127). According to Patterson, Waller had "in effect been advising the king of the war's acceptability."[3]

Each of the "Painter-Poems" ends with a section addressed to the king. Lines 331–40 of the "Second Advice" are intended to discredit Waller as a flatterer, and to characterize his "Instructions" as an attempt at reconciliation with Charles after his poem to Cromwell. The panegyrist has to convince the king and the public to accept his praise and advice over everyone else's. Marvell prepares the reader to reject Waller's and accept his own advice to the king. He uses the sun topos to argue that the men whom he attacked in the foregoing section are merely "swarms of insects" (345) engendered by Charles's warmth. In fact, he attacks Waller's use of such topoi while asserting his own right, and greater capacity, to use them himself. Thus he parodies Waller's comparison of the king to Minos (and of England to Crete) but extends it, too, making Clarendon a "State-Daedalus" (349), a would-be usurper, or at least the father of a would-be usurper (Anne Hyde). Like the traditional panegyrist, Marvell both praises the king for the heavenly descent of his "Race and Pow'r" (361), and advises him to rule by "its pattern" (362). This is a variation on "rule-by-example," the king's own heavenly origins becoming an example to himself, as he should be to his people. The final lines warn that kings are as subject as anyone else to the contingency the "Second Advice" shows so much of: "Kings are in War but Cards: they're Gods in Peace." Marvell not only substitutes his praise for

Waller's, but his advice, too. Marvell's praise is itself contingent on Charles pursuing a policy the opposite of that advocated in the "Instructions."

Dryden's *Annus Mirabilis*[4] abounds with panegyrical topics. In the "Transitum" to the Fire of London, the king appears in the ruined, burning city like the sun itself, the traditional topos of a king:

> Now day appears, and with the day the King,
> Whose early care had robb'd him of his rest;
>
> (lines 949–50)

Significantly, he is distinguished less by the trappings of power than by the obvious sign of mercy, tears:

> More then his Guards his sorrows made him known,
> And pious tears which down his cheeks did show'r;
>
> (lines 957–58)

Conventionally, he combines power and clemency:

> The wretched in his grief forgot their own
> So much the pity of a king has pow'r).
>
> (lines 959–60)

The reciprocity of mutual trust, *alterna fides,* between king and city is the basis of grief, and the grief in turn perpetuates the reciprocity:

> He wept the flames of what he lov'd so well
> And what so well had merited his love.
>
> (lines 961–62)

His power is demonstrated differently in stanzas 242–47, in a way that suggests the Virgilian ideal, *parcere subiectis,* another commonplace of panegyric:

> He chears the fearful, and commends the bold,
> And makes despairers hope for good success.
>
> (lines 967–68)

More important, throughout the poem Dryden *advises* as much as he praises. He praises the citizens but makes that praise contingent on their acceptance of his main thesis, that the Second Dutch War was "expensive, though necessary" (48). He holds up to the city an image not of what it is but of what he wants it to be; similarly, he holds up to the king himself an example for him to be and for his people to obey.

The most telling exploitation of panegyric in the "Third Advice" occurs in the duchess of Albermarle's speech. The duchess, punning on her former trade, says she will "make a shift" to do without the duke's "nuptial gift" (321) till he has exacted revenge from the Dutch; in the meantime, she gives him very specific advice about running the fleet. Significantly, she also gives him advice about what to advise the king:

> Tell the king all, how him they countermine;
> Trust not, till done, him with thy own design.
>
> (lines 339–40)

Albemarle has to look after the spiritual well-being of the men, too. When the duchess wishes that her husband could be divided like his command, to rule "one half of him the sea and one the land" (354), she seems to be urging him to act as a kind of surrogate king, or at least to be implying that he could act as one. Her advice to the duke how to run the navy is easily expanded into advice to the king how to rule the kingdom. In particular, her advice "Cherish the valiant up, cowards cashier" (326) seems to be yet another variation on the Virgilian ideal of *parcere subiectis et deballare superbos* (*Aeneid* 6.853), relieving the oppressed and lowering the proud.

In "Last Instructions," Marvell seems to go one step further, from replacing advice to the king with advice to the king's general, to replacing the king himself with one of his own ministers, Clarendon. In what is arguably the fulfillment of these poems' analogizing tendency, Clarendon becomes a kind of King of Night, analogous to Charles and his parliament's day; the great "outdoer" of Waller's "Instructions" becomes the great "undoer" of the navy, and (potentially) of the realm.

Waller's "Instructions to a Painter"

Waller's "Instructions to a Painter"[5] appeared on the Stationers' Register for 1 March 1666. The poems's chief device is its chief weakness: amplification. Chernaik says that the panegyrist tries to gloss over what the satirist tries to expose, to indicate that all is right, but at least some of Waller's contemporaries automatically interpreted his glossing as an indication of something wrong. Lady Ranelagh suggests that for some people Waller's panegyric was already satire:

> I know his calling as a poet gives him license to say as great things as he can, without intending they should signify any more, than that he said them . . . and the less the subject he speaks of, or the party he speaks to, deserves the great things he says, the greater these things are, and the greater advance they are to make towards his being admired, by his poetical laws.[6]

She in fact indicates a problem with *ethos*, with the impression the panegyrist's own character makes on the reader. This is exploited by Marvell in his attack on Parker, which also focuses on hyperbolic language. Clearly one problem with such language is that, not having any relation to its ostensible subject, it may be taken—indeed perhaps has to be taken (if it is to be taken for anything)—as a reflection of the writer's own egotistical personality. However, Waller's vanity would actually count on our noticing his divergence from the truth. In this regard he resembles the poet of Swift's "Directions for a Birthday Song"—the greater the liar, the greater the poet.

> Thus your encomiums, to be strong,
> Must be applied directly wrong:
> A tyrant for his mercy praise,
> And crown a royal dunce with bays:
> . . . .
> For princes love you should descant
> On virtues which they know they want.
>
> (lines 115–28)[7]

Marvell (or whoever the writer of the "Second Advice" is) makes Waller's literary lying look dangerous by quantifying it and connecting it to something real: the wasteful habits of Stuart government. Extravagance becomes an extraliterary matter of dollars and cents, and human life.

After instructing the painter to do the nearly impossible,

> First draw the sea, that portion which between
> The greater world and this of ours is seen.
>
> (lines 1–2)

the poet then orders the painter to do the really impossible, to "draw" qualities like expectation, which (he seems to know) cannot be represented by anything but poetry:

> Draw the whole world expecting who shall reign
> After this combat, o'er the conquer'd main.
>
> (lines 5–6)

Additionally, the painter has to draw especially unpainterly subjects, like "gallantry" (9) or "hope and courage" (15), meaningless without poetic explanation:

> Make Heav'n concerned and an unusual star
> Declare th'importance of th'approaching war.
>
> (lines 7–8)

This, incidentally, anticipates the deliberate inappropriateness of Swift's treatment of virtue in the "Stella" poems. Waller's technique is no more than a novel way of indicating that the duke was brave, etc., without actually saying so. Swift's unusual procedure of describing virtue quantitatively in Stella's "Birthday Poems," for example, jolts us into the realization that virtue is not a quantity but a quality. Waller's emphasis, however, is consistently (nauseatingly) quantitative: the duke outdoes the wind at making sails swell, and the sound of cannon when it comes to terrorizing; he is indeed something of a Restoration nuclear deterrent.

At lines 65–76, treating the poor strategy of blockading the Dutch fleet between Texel and Vlie, the panegyrist *forces* topical events into an ill-fitting heroic mold. Because the English cannot get at the Dutch to slay them, the Dutch must die ignobly in bed (presumably long after the English would have run out of provisions). Because the Dutch are also engaged in a war against Spain, the English, by cutting off trade, are said to "invest" (74) the provinces, and thereby "outdo" the Spanish. Such passages suggest the underlying economic motives of the war, and offer another clue why Waller's treatment of it failed. Heroic "outdoing" is strangely at odds with Waller's palpable awareness of economic forces; a heroic treatment of, say, the Gulf War could scarcely be more likely to fail. This kind of discrepancy between amplified, heroic treatment and quantified, modern warfare may also result in a grave problem of ethos for the poet; while wishing to seem generous, he seems rather mean and hypocritical, like Homer with a balance sheet.

The forced return of the fleet to port is glossed over by the idealized treatment of the duchess's visit in lines 77–90—the sort of thing the sea gods have not seen since the birth of Venus. The subsequent Dutch attack on the Hamburg merchant fleet, exposed as a result of the bad English strategy, is treated as a fluke, a last gasp before inevitable defeat. But note how bathetic is the idea of the fleet racing out to encounter the Dutch, half-victualed. The suggestion of mismanagement is unmistakable. Waller tries to color it as rugged surmounting of obstacles, but the obstacles seem unnecessary. Dryden, as we shall see, tries to solve similar problems in *Annus Mirabilis* by adopting as his principal motif a phoenix, which actually seems to require disasters, mismanagements, obstacles, etc. This gives them and "outdoing" a kind of sanction.

Consistent with the "outdoing" topics, when the English finally encounter a significant portion of the Dutch fleet, that encounter is likened to Actium, when the stake amounted to all the known world; the modern confrontation is greater, however, as is the surface area of the modern, colonized world.

Waller's hyperbole describes the Hague and even Amsterdam trembling at the "cannons' roar" (265) as the duke advances. Though the Dutch can keep off the sea, we are supposed to believe they are afraid they cannot keep off the duke (275–76). The poet breaks off to remember the painter, but also (in a good example of the painter convention providing a convenient distraction) to forget the battle, to avoid its actual inconclusiveness. Lines 287–310, in which the poet apologizes, but also excuses himself, on the grounds of poetry's superior expressiveness, provide a way out. The main section of the poem then concludes with a schematic picture of the king in Parliament as a young Augustus. But one should note the seeds of future satire, which Waller has obligingly sown, in the picture of the Commons "Pouring out treasure to supply his fleet" (306).

In the concluding section addressed to the king, brief but important as the climax of the poem, the poet addresses Charles directly through a version of the inexpressibility topos, similar to the outdoing topoi:

> His club Alcides, Phoebus has his bow,
> Jove has his thunder, and your navy you.
> But your great providence no colors here
> Can represent, nor pencil draw that care
> Which keeps you waking to secure our peace,
> The nation's glory, and our trade's increase.
>
> (lines 315–20)

Note, in the last line, the telling revelation of what this "outdoing" has been for. Charles is himself the last in the series of "outdoings" that comprise the poem and, more than anything else, characterize its structure. On increasing scale, James's attributes outdo the elements, the duchess of York outdoes (or nearly outdoes) Venus, the Battle of Lowestoft outdoes Actium, Opdam outdoes Phaeton; on ever grander scale, poetry outdoes painting, and Charles outdoes poetry.

"The Second Advice to a Painter"

The satiric stance of the "Second Advice" and its relationship to Waller's "Instructions" are both summed up in the first word: "Nay." If you want to draw what Waller wrote, Marvell says, don't listen to *his* instructions, but to *mine*. The distinction between the poet's telling and the painter's drawing enables Marvell to suggest that the fight Waller wrote about and the fight his (Marvell's) painter draws are one and the same. Waller's consistent amplification, besides highlighting his own heroic treatment, has adumbrated the lower factual level that he started from, or even implied one below that. Marvell uses the events "behind" Waller's poem, that element of common knowledge that both poets had to address, to subvert it, and to corroborate his own "advice." In a sense, he has merely substituted for Waller's incredibly elevated tenor a credibly reductive one, and even suggested that, thanks to Waller's ineptness, their tenors are really the same. Waller's poem, intended to be a vehicle for transcendent good, easily becomes a vehicle for transcendent bad.

Since Waller's object was clearly not to "write" events the way Marvell implies he did—by writing a true story at odds with his own idealizing tendencies—the "Courage" Marvell tells us it took to write thus may be seen as a form of stupidity, precisely that form which fails to be aware of genre. "Courage" also has other meanings here, none of them kind to Waller. One, which has implications for the literariness of the battle, is that Waller has courage only for writing about wars, not for fighting them. Another, also related to the important literary analogizing of the "painter-poems," is that what is foolish to *write* is mad to *do*.

Also associated with "courage," and closely related to Waller's generic obtuseness, is the mock-heroic. In the examples that follow, such as "Allin tilting at the coast of Spain" (8)—one wonders if Marvell means "trembled"

(4) in the sense of "with laughter" or in the sense of "with fear." Allin "stemming... Herc'les Pillars with his prow" (10) is an Ariostoan figure, at sea in more ways than one. He is the same Allin described by Waller (55–64) as a falcon. There his action is as inflated as here it is deflated; there the emphasis is on destructive action, here on its wasteful aftermath:

> how two ships he left the hills to waft
> And with new sea-marks Dover and Calais graft;
>
> (lines 11–12)

Allin's deliberate destruction of the enemy ships seems indistinguishable from the destruction, even by accident, of English ones. The common denominator is wastefulness, with no one the better for it. The lines that refer to the City's replacement of one ship, accidentally blown up, with another "gift," could refer just as well to the ships Allin sank:

> Blow one ship up, another thence does grow:
> See what free cities and wise courts can do!
>
> (lines 17–18)

In the world Marvell describes, what lasts is what is built not to last: it is either something replaceable or, like the china that outlasts plate, too cheap to be bothered with. Marvell seems to allude to a scene in a City comedy:

> So some old merchant, to insure his name,
> Marries afresh, and courtiers share the dame;
> So whatsoe'er is broke, the servants pay't,
> And glasses prove more durable than plate.
>
> (lines 19–22)

This is a world, like ours, of "planned obsolescence," where the transitory—trash, really—acquires a kind of permanence if only because it can be replaced with still more trash. This is the logical consequence of Waller's insistent "outdoing" topics in which "the subject is shown not only as equal to the heroes of antiquity but as excelling them in their own sphere" (Chernaik, *Poetry of Limitation*, 139). The principal consequence of "outdoing" is exhaustion, a feverish impermanence of values and (significant for panegyric) of virtue, as bad in its way as the material impermanence Marvell describes.

The reason for the obsolescence and the transitoriness, as also perhaps for Waller's panegyrical "outdoing," is greed. By selling offices in the navy (from that of high-ranking officers to that of lowly boatswains), Coventry has made himself as important as a point on the compass, something that "pilots" have to learn along with more conventional, less political points about navigation. Of course, one result of this is that the navy will end up with pilots who are better at navigating Coventry than navigating the sea. Marvell does what all satirists do: he presents the targets of his satire as unnatural, but such presentation is especially damaging here because it places them out of touch with the natural element they are supposed to know and "rule." The scale of Coventry and his officers' unnaturalness is underlined by his becoming himself an unnatural North Pole:

> Pilots in vain repeat the compass o'er,
> Until of him they learn that one point more.
>
> (lines 33–34)

What Coventry attracts, or wishes to attract, is gold; worse, he is himself more attracted than attracting: like any mercenary, he would be a singularly inconstant "point." The commodities of lines 37–40 become increasingly unnatural and venal (making me suspect that they are an earlier example of the "commodity fetishism" Laura Brown describes in *The Rape of the Lock*). They range from the relatively natural "raw goods" of "Muscovy" (line 37), through the baser "iron and copper" (38) of Sweden, to the "war" (38) of Munster, "prize" of Ashley, "customs" of Warwick, and "pay" of Carteret (39). Finally they reach a climax in the wholesale selling of the fleet by Coventry. The harmfulness of such unnatural "outdoing" is now made obvious.

Consistent with the idea of the navy as merely an extension of Coventry's greed, the sails that swelled in Waller with the duke's "extraction" and "glorious mind" (19) here have nothing to do with the duke (who is treated as a dupe anyway), but everything to do with Coventry's combination of greed, wealth, and girth. The sails swell like Coventry's purse and stomach, with tackling for purse strings (42), and Coventry pulls the strings in more ways than one. Later, in lines 113–20, the "burden" of the navy, both financial and physical, is seen as an extension of the burdensomeness of Hyde and Paston:

> First, let our navy scowr through silver froth
> The ocean's burden and the kingdom's both,

> Whose very bulk may represent its birth
> From Hyde and Paston, burdens of the earth:
>
> (lines 113–16)

These lines parody Waller's

> A greater force than that which here we find
> Ne'er pressed the ocean nor employed the wind.
>
> (lines 101–2)

The unnaturalness of the burden is wondered at by "porpoises" (121) and "sea fowl" (123), to whom it is unnatural in other ways:

> Let shoals of porpoises on ev'ry side
> Wonder, in swimming by our Oaks outvied,
> And the sea fowl, at gaze, behold a thing
> So vast, more strong and swift, than they of wing. . . .
>
> (lines 121–24)

Oaks should not swim; ships should not fly. "Outdoing" is now seen in its worst light as an arrogant violation of nature, as man mistaking his own nature. Marvell takes the same physical detail that Waller does, but finds a more realistic, reductive analogy for Waller's idealistic one.

Lines 45–52 treat the same events covered by Waller in lines 65–76 and 91–96: the unsuccessful blockading by the English of the Dutch fleet in Texel and Vlie, and the capture of the English merchant fleet. Marvell shrewdly places the events together, showing what disastrous consequences this poor strategy had. The causal relationship is asserted, as if the English perversely (or traitorously) willed their own capture:

> Hedge the Dutch in only to let them out.
> . . . .
> That the blind Archer, when they take the seas,
> The Hamburg convoy may betray at ease.
>
> (lines 46–50)

Note how these events may be colored, highlighted or denigrated. In Waller the capture by the Dutch is seen as the end of the beginning of Dutch sea power, in Marvell as the beginning of the end of British sea power.

The different order of the events reflects the different aims of the poets.

Waller violates chronology, de-emphasizing the causal relationship of the two events by separating them with the lines on the duchess's visit to Harwich (77–90). The corresponding lines in Marvell (53–108) come after the linked events, and are much more elaborate than Waller's version, perhaps because Marvell's point is that the duke and his men are better at courtship than at fighting.

Now the duchess's "glorious train" (81) becomes a "triumphant tail" (55) and the idea of the birth of something glorious, Venus, out of the sea (83–84) becomes the return of something inglorious, a land crab, to the sea (57); evolution becomes devolution. Now the navy, which is depicted majestically "spreading" (79) its sails to Harwich, is described doing a "caracole" (60), a dance step suitable for a courtier but probably not for a sailor, let alone a whole fleet. Waller's "outdoing" becomes sheer extravagance, at odds with his classicism:

> One thrifty ferry-boat of mother-pearl
> Sufficed of old the Cytherean girl.
>
> (lines 63–64)

The allusion to the whole visit as a "Sea-masque" (66) equates it with more extravagance, the dangerously self-flattering art-form of the Stuart court, and suggests that the war may be a symptom of the same wasteful vanity. It also connects Waller's poem to an unsavory tradition of court panegyric:

> Yet navies are but properties, when here
> (A small sea-masque and built to court you, dear)
> Three goddesses in one: Pallas for Art,
> Venus for sport, and Juno in your Heart.
>
> (lines 65–68)

The lines depicting the duchess as "three goddesses in one" are another satiric version of Waller's "outdoing" topoi, here reduced to the kind of mere quantitative overkill used by Swift in his own mock-panegyric "instructions" for a panegyric, "Directions for a Birthday Song," to evoke the vulgarity of the Brunswicks:

> Six thousand years hath lived the goddess,
> Your heroine hardly fifty odd is.
> Besides you songsters oft have shown

> That she hath graces of her own:
> Three graces by Lucina brought her,
> Just three; and every grace a daughter.
>
> (lines 161–66)

The quantitative aspect of the visit is continued and combined with tawdriness in the idea that "this naval scene" (70) is a payment "with interest" to the duchess for the meanness of her secret marriage to the duke. The visit becomes a belated nuptial, parodic of Antony and Cleopatra's and equally inauspicious. Marvell depicts the duchess of York as "a lecherous and greedy Cleopatra."[8] Cleopatra, as Erskine-Hill explains, could always be depicted this way, thanks to Octavian's propaganda against her (*Augustan Idea*, 6); she is typical of the topics of this kind of poetry, in that she can be depicted *both* ways. The main point of the comparison is waste, reported in such financial terms as make it mean and repugnant, the opposite of "heroic":

> Never did Roman Mark, within the Nile
> So feast the fair Egyptian Crocodile,
> Nor the Venetian Duke, with such a State,
> The Adriatic marry at that rate.
>
> (lines 71–74)

Lines 75–76 glance at the "inexpressibility" topos, which Waller used to great effect in "Buckingham's Death." But here the inexpressibility has less to do with emotional intensity than fickleness: "For love, alas! has but a short delight" (77). Finally her passion is inexpressible principally because it is fleeting and spurious.

The painter resumes his brush at line 109 where Marvell alludes to Michelangelo's *Last Judgment* as a standard of the terrible. Patterson remarks that the painting was itself "motivated by political disillusionment following the Fall of Rome" (139). This would make allusion to it here function in nearly the same way as the allusion to Nero above, to suggest that the navy, if not the whole society supporting it, is doomed. Patterson also suggests that the allusion "responds to the challenge of Leonardo, who had declared the poet incapable of representing 'a bloody battle'" (139). Waller responded to Leonardo's challenge, especially the concept of the *paragone*—the hierarchical relationship of the arts with painting superior to poetry in terms of expressiveness—by asserting that

> though you draw armed heroes as they sit,
> The task in battle does the Muses fit.
> They, in the dark confusion of a fight,
> Discover all, instruct us how to write,
> And light and honor to brave actions yield,
> Hid in the smoke and tumult of the field.
>
> (lines 289–94)

Marvell's position, as one would expect of a satirist, is that the reality of war can be expressed by no art; and this is a position consistent with his satire on art and artifice throughout. To the satirist war is inexpressibly *bad*:

> The noise, the smoke, the sweat, the fire, the blood,
> Are not to be expressed nor understood.
>
> (lines 207–8)

The gallant in lines 135–54 blames Noah for inventing ships and wine, because his means of salvation seems likely to be our undoing, or at least the gallant's. Patterson remarks that, in Marvell's *First Anniversary*, "we find the same ambivalent typology of Noah as originator of shipbuilding and viniculture put to deft and positive use a metaphor for a great head of state" (140). Clearly Noah is another topos that can work equally well in satire and panegyric. The savior may become the destroyer of the race, or the race itself may become so corrupt that its earlier salvation becomes, retroactively, the beginning of the end.

The explosion, which in Waller occasions the Phaeton simile, is here described in terms of a dance, like the duke's own ships "caracoling":

> Monsieurs like rockets mount aloft and crack
> In thousand sparks, then dancingly fall back.
>
> (lines 169–70)

The shooting of the duke's companions is, like the duchess's visit in Waller, displaced in time; that is, in the poem it follows the destruction of Opdam's ship. This is done in order both to give Opdam his own and to avoid suggesting, as Waller does, that the explosion and the rage of the duke at the death of his companions are somehow connected. Both poets manipulate events in time, placing them in or out of chronological sequence, to score a point. The goodness or badness of events is entirely a matter of presentation; or certainly it must have seemed so to contemporary readers.

Waller attributes the "victory" to English courage:

> The Dutch elsewhere did through the wat'ry field
> Perform enough to have made others yield,
> But English courage, growing as they fight,
> In danger, noise, and slaughter takes delight:
>
> (lines 227–30)

Marvell attributes it to chance, the contingent nature of war:

> Now all conspires unto the Dutchman's loss:
> The wind, the fire, we, they themselves, do cross . . .
>
> (lines 233–34)

But that the Dutch do not lose *worse* is due to the duke, and to the faulty chain of command that lets a hanger-on like Brouncker give orders. Brandishing his sword so as to distract the compass, he reminds one of earlier mock-heroic figures like Smith and the Dutch captain, who "wave their bright swords glitt'ring in their hands" (210):

> he then first draws his steel,
> Whose virtue makes the misled compass wheel:
>
> (lines 241–42)

The duke takes a nap and Brouncker orders the navy to stop the pursuit, allowing the Dutch to escape. The events are not stated directly, probably because the poet did not really know, but the depiction is loose enough to fit the reality. Brouncker's "corrupting" the compass with his shiny coward's sword is neatly consistent with the other corrupt, unnatural compass above:

> The constant magnet to the pole does hold,
> Steel to the magnet, Coventry to gold.
>
> (lines 35–36)

Finally, the principal beneficiaries of the war are the duchess herself and men like Arlington. For the nation it has achieved nothing:

> Thus having fought we know not why, as yet,
> We've done we know not what, nor what we get:
>
> (lines 317–18)

Annus Mirabilis

Patterson explains that Dryden's poem was written sometime in late 1666, partly as an answer to Waller and Marvell. She describes it, not inaccurately, as "a piece of royalist propaganda which directed its attention to the two most distressing events of 1666: the division of the fleet under Monck and Prince Rupert, with its disastrous consequences in the Four Days' Battle, 3–6 June; and the Great Fire of London, 2–6 September" (144).

For its heroic treatment of events, Dryden's poem is as indebted to other poems, in particular the "painter-poems," as to the events themselves. Reading it in the context of the poems it answers and is answered by raises questions about literary success and the way we determine it. Since the success of a rhetorical poem depends on its persuasiveness, it is appropriate to consider whether it persuaded anyone when it was written.

Dryden himself seems quite confident of literary success, so far as it goes; however, it is not really the point. In the "Account" addressed to Sir Robert Howard, where Dryden is at pains to state his thesis that the war was just,

> For I have chosen the most heroic subject which any poet could desire: I have taken upon me to describe the motives, the beginning, progress, and successes of a most just and necessary war.... (50)

there is already the paralleling of literature and life that is noticeable in the "painter-poems" and that characterizes mock-panegyrics like *MacFlecknoe* (and later, parts of the *Rosciad*). Thus there is a parallel between the suffering of London's citizens in the dedication and the rather trivial, purely literary suffering of Howard:

> [S]ince you are to bear this persecution, I will at least give you the encouragement of a martyr: you could never suffer in a nobler cause. (50)

Somehow reading the poem has become Howard's "war effort." Dryden's intention is presumably to *praise* Howard (though one can never be too sure about such things); unfortunately, he inadvertently *blames* him and *insults* the citizenry by classing their very real hardship with Howard's mere inconvenience. If reading the poem is Howard's "bit," then writing it is Dryden's:

> The former part of this poem, relating to the war, is but a due expiation for my not serving my king and country in it. (50)

The effect of such parallelism is to seal literature off from life and consequently to undermine its persuasive or propagandistic power: as everyone knows, parallel lines never meet. Dryden will be mocked for this in *The Rehearsal*, in which he himself becomes a metaphor for the kind of egotistical, solipsistic writer who cannot keep his praise from accidentally becoming satire, because it is all self-praise and founded upon a very silly notion of self.

Dryden is at pains to deflect charges made in the previous "Painter-Poems" that the war was a burden to the nation; he argues that in fact "greatness of arms" is rather a "support" than a burden (52). Even this praise of English warriors may be diverted to the king, since only the subjects of the "best of kings" (52) can be praised without offending the king himself.

Note that for Dryden a historical poem, which *Annus Mirabilis* is, by definition cannot be a satire, since its "proper wit" ought to "consist in the delightful imaging of persons, actions, passions, or things" (53). Probably the quotation from Ovid that he applies to Virgil—*materiam superabat opus*—expresses his own ideal of the right relationship between events and literature. In fact, Virgil becomes a kind of literary screen for Dryden with which he can filter out much of the lowness of his material. His use of "the proper terms which are us'd at sea" has a surprisingly similar effect, since while it flatters the readers (and the writer) with the impression of *actuality*, it draws them away from what is being described to the *way* it is being described. It is a kind of "antiflattery" device, a flattering defense of a flattering technique.

Dryden's self-conscious artistry explains why the art metaphor, so negative in "Second Advice," is positive here; it is implicitly a sanction for Dryden's own idealizing. It draws the reader away from the messiness of what is actually occurring, and gives events the sanction of what happens in art:

> These fight like Husbands, but like Lovers those:
>   These fain would keep, and those more fain enjoy;
> And to such height their frantic passions grows,
>   That what both love, both hazard to destroy.
>
> (lines 109–12)

Still, such procedures tend to backfire, by making the battle so unreal that it seems mock-heroic, or so unreal that we dismiss it entirely, replacing it (as Marvell does Waller's version in the "Second Advice") with cynical educated guesses. The danger is illustrated by Dryden's negative use of the same metaphor in the next section, "War Declar'd by France," where it suggests the powerlessness of Louis to act:

> And threat'ning *France*, plac'd like a painted *Jove*,
> Kept idle thunder in his lifted hand.
>
> (lines 155–56)

The sense of powerlessness is not entirely absent from the first quotation; moreover, the reader is quite capable of reading some of the powerlessness of the second back into it.

If Dryden's workmanship was intended to surpass its material, some of the material by implication must have been unworkable. The Battle of Lowestoft is described perfunctorily compared to its treatment in Waller and Marvell. It comprises only five stanzas (stanzas 19–23). The victory is seen to be owed to the king through his brother, the duke of York. Lawson's death is treated as a sacrifice that cements England's special relationship with the sea; however, there is no buildup as there is in Waller, nor mention of the failure to make the victory decisive. Still, the "shatter'd" Dutch ships are described escaping, and the reader might well wonder *how* and *why*.

Similarly, in "The Attempt at Berghen" (stanzas 24–38), although there is no direct indication of the sordid negotiations between Tiddeman and the governor of the port, it is nevertheless clear that the attempt is a failure:

> And though by Tempests of the prize bereft,
> In Heaven's inclemency some ease we find;
> Our foes we vanquish'd by our valour left
> And only yielded to the Seas and Wind.
>
> (lines 117–20)

Dryden's concentration on such details obscures for us whether the attempt was successful or not, even makes it irrelevant; one can only wonder how it affected his contemporaries.

The description of the Four Days' Battle corresponds to sections in the "Third Advice to a Painter," which indeed may have been a reply to it. Notice how the controversial division of the fleet, treated in so many lines in the other poem, is here reduced to three words, as if the stated action were normal before a war: "Our Fleet divides" (213). After reading the "Third

Advice," it should occur to the reader to wonder why. That it might not is due to the poem's tacit but powerful endorsement of a pattern of success built on failures; it does not address or seek to address considerations of necessity. When the phoenix is one's main motif, one will not be too concerned about prevention.

In the "Second Day's Battle" Dryden tries to present Albemarle in the best light by imagining him bearing up under the mistaken assumption that the advancing ships are Dutch. The line comparing the intensity of the fighting to "only" a civil war may be the wryest in the whole poem. The fighting is inconclusive; Dryden has to make the best of it and make not being defeated seem as good as victory:

> not to be o'rcome was to do more
> Then all the Conquests former Kings did gain.
>
> (lines 319–20)

The imperial theme is invoked again when Albemarle is compared to Caesar (352), but negatively, even for the English, since he is not the victorious but the *assassinated* Caesar. The Dutch are politically stigmatized as assassins, perhaps appropriately in that they were *Republicans*. Dryden even makes the best of "making the best of it," by making such presentation of his hero a validation of his own character, by making it effectively an "antiflattery" topos:

> Let other Muses write his prosp'rous fate,
>   Of conquer'd Nations tell and Kings restor'd
> But mine shall sing of his eclips'd estate,
>   Which, like the Sun's more wonders does afford.
>
> (lines 357–60)

John Dryden stands by his hero (like the narrator of *A Tale*, perhaps).

It is interesting that Albemarle's ship is the ark on the second day, and Rupert himself the "New Messiah" (454) on the third; the Four Days' Battle has been accommodated to the Resurrection, complete with typology. The futility of Rupert's mission and the unnecessariness of the division in the first place are glossed over by making the lack of achievement a virtue, proof of his subordination to duty (the duty of returning, when he never should have gone away in the first place):

> To rescue one such friend he took more pride
> Than to destroy whole thousands of such foes.
>
> (lines 463–64)

Ironically, Dryden pretends to make himself, or rather have his hero make, the very distinction between the appearance and the substance of virtue that he frequently exploits in his poem:

> Heroique virtue did his actions guide,
> And he the substance not th'appearance chose;
>
> (lines 461–62)

Clearly, as Aristotle remarked, the same thing may be made to appear either virtuous or wicked. But just as clearly, when the thing is as controversial as the events of the Second Dutch War, it retreats into the unknown, where it assumes the characteristics of our worst suspicions.

"The Third Advice to the Painter"

The "Third Advice" resumes where the "Second Advice" left off, with Sandwich's mission to Spain and the duke's love—not for the duchess but for the wife of Sir John Denham. The allusion may be meant to qualify the idea, near the end of the "Second Advice," that the only benefit of the war had been to provide the "Duchess' closet" with "triumphant checkstones" and "shell" (325–26). For all we know, she may not have benefited either.

The comparison of Rupert and Albemarle to dice is another indication of the contingency of war, like the very last line of the "Second Advice": "Kings are in war but cards: they're gods in peace" (368). Their "linked mane" (13) suggests a two-headed beast, probably meant to be continuous with the monstrosity and abnormality described in the "Second Advice." Likewise, the description of the news of them "like chain-shot, tearing fame" (14) and the magical way they are supposed to quell United Provinces by being "united gen'rals" (17), seem meant to develop ideas that go back to Waller's original "Instructions," in particular Waller's use of "Fame" (162) and the equally magical near-conquest of the Dutch after the Battle of Lowestoft.

Rashly, Albemarle ignores the warnings about chance in the "Second

Advice" and, in his overconfidence, is likened to Samson. His arrogance is expressed in another "outdoing" topos, combined with a "name" topos. Mistakenly, he,

> swoll'n with sense of former glory won,
> Thought Monck must be by Albermarle outdone.
>
> (lines 39–40)

Here the topos is more ambivalent, because in his new "aristocratic" status Monck clearly outdoes something, namely himself, that was good already. Nicholas Jose remarks that "he (Albemarle) has been corrupted by his new title and his association with the court,"[9] but that corruption is by no means total. The duke's mistakenness—and I think this is an important indication of the way we are to take not only him but his common wife, too, later in the poem—is less in himself than in his acceptance of false values, in particular false heroism, associated with the court. The paragraph concludes:

> Little he knew, with the same arm and sword,
> How far the gentleman outcuts the lord.
>
> (lines 41–42)

The description of the battle (43–94) is mock-heroic but curiously muted. The object of the satire is more the battle than the principal combatants, who appear less responsible for it than the court and possibly the king. Ruyter mocks by asking

> if he thought, as once our rebel nation
> To conquer theirs too by a declaration?
>
> (lines 45–46)

The reference to *Iter Boreale* implies a poetical battle behind the real one:

> This said, he the short period, ere it ends,
> With iron words from brazen mouths extends.
>
> (lines 49–50)

The author's consciousness of his own contribution to such "battles" may account for a gentler or more ambivalent use of the arts in the section; one is at least more aware of skill here:

> He plays with danger and his bullets trolls
> (As 'twere at trou-madam) through all their holls.
>
> (lines 59–60)

The mainly decorous gods of Waller are replaced by a more realistic Victory, who out of impatience lets Albemarle's ship be wounded "Achilles-like" in the heel, or keel (reminding one of the comparison of the duke of York to Achilles in the "Instructions"). Albemarle's sails are shredded, appropriately for the husband of a seamstress, into lace. Albemarle himself is compared to a lowly "old bustard" that is yet not despicable because it refuses to yield. The simile is negative and positive; it destroys "Albemarle," but it restores "Monck."

The things Albemarle's rage is contrasted with become more serious, and historical: the Rump (which Albemarle himself suppressed), Charles I, and (possibly) Archbishop Laud. Jose may be right that the poet is hinting at the need for a *second* Restoration (192). The subsequent command to the painter to "draw curtains" (106) over such shame is really a kind of *occupatio*, pretending not to say something while drawing attention to it. Typically, the painter is asked not to describe Albemarle's buttock wound, while the poet describes it for us:

> But most with story of his hand or thumb
> Conceal (as Honor would) His Grace's bum. . . .
>
> (lines 123–24)

The conflation of story and picture suggests again that the poet, while ostensibly referring to the painter, is really addressing other poets. The convention allows him not just to juxtapose literary lies with the truth (thereby exposing it all the more), but also to take the reader with him behind the curtain in the artist's studio where the lie is made, or behind the "Homeric mist" (160) where the truth is hidden. The emblematic Jonah and Perseus are typical of such lying mystification (and of panegyrical amplification), since while they gloss over a weakness they simultaneously draw our attention to it and, for all their irrelevance, retain a potentially damaging connection to the truth. The painter convention, as it drifts synaesthetically into a metaphor for writing, contributes to the literary analogizing of these poems and to the sense of literature itself as a cover-up, even a *multilayered* cover-up. Such literary lies contribute to the greater lie of the state that the Four Days' Battle was a victory; the literary punishment will be the dearth of paper after the Fire of London, or, anticipating *The Dunciad*, silence.

The poet bids the painter to interrupt his work to paint the duchess: "Paint thou but her, and she will paint the rest." Her speech is not a sudden violation of the painter convention but has, in fact, been anticipated by the references to painting as a telling or story. When we are introduced to her she has herself just been interrupted by the news of Albemarle's defeat while she is doing something related to pictures, namely, "nailing up hangings" (174), . (I wonder if there is, in her reception of the news, a burlesque of Waller's poem about the way Charles I took the news of Buckingham's death.) She is common, smelly, and dirty, but not stupid; indeed, her want of refinement is apt to be positive in poems attacking court corruption, and it is.

It is hard to agree with Wallace that she is "presented as so lewd and ignorant a woman that her hostile narrative about the government might appear to be discredited before it began" (*Destiny His Choice*, 154). Wallace similarly misreads the gallant's speech in the "Second Advice," to which the duchess's is similar, by failing to appreciate that the gallant's criticism is all the more effective for coming from within the court party. Wallace's misreading or sheer failure of appreciation stems at least partly from a desire to discredit Marvell's authorship of the poem through faulting its technique. The technique is more effective than Wallace, with his case against major authorship, is willing to allow. His misreading also reflects a curious interjection of his own hindsighted opinion about the conduct of the Dutch war. He maintains the duchess's speech is unsound politically as well as technically:

> If Marvell was the author of the *Second* and *Third Advices*, and Professor Lord has argued that he was, then not only was his rhetoric much inferior to what it became a year later but he was guilty of an appalling error in policy. It was precisely the belief of government and people alike that the Dutch war could not continue, coupled with the lack of funds, that led to the failure to put out the fleet in 1667 and the consequent invasion of the Thames by the Dutch warships. (155)

Evidently Marvell's advice may not disagree with Wallace's.

Patterson's reading of the duchess is, I think, truer:

> Yet despite this unpropitious portrait, which has led both seventeenth- and twentieth-century readers to misinterpret her role, the duchess's very coarseness has a special appropriateness to her task. Originally a common

> seamstress, and still a "Presbyterian Sibyl," she is doubly an outsider whose exclusion from Cavalier and Anglican circles gives her a necessary distance, while her connection with Monck gives her credibility. (153)

Patterson argues that in the course of her speech she is "transformed, by her own performance, from a grotesque figure with animal connotations to a prophetess" (156). It is at least arguable that the duke is transformed along with her. The duchess is yet another example of the strangely equivocal quality of the topics and subject matter of panegyric and satire. Her speech comprises the entire second half of the poem, except for the "To the King."

Before faulting the division of the fleet she faults the division of the command between her husband and Prince Rupert. She describes the ambitious courtiers, divvying up her husband's command before he is known to be dead, as cannibalizing a living body; none of them wants her, though none can inherit Albemarle's command without her. She argues that most of them are hangers-on, who preferred easy exile to the harder business of running the country. Most are not even men:

> What, say I men? nay, rather monsters! men
> Only in bed, nor to my knowledge then.
>
> (lines 229–30)

She hints that the duchess of York's father, the earl of Clarendon, planned the naval war as a means of raising his daughter's dowry and suppressing dissent. To remove the duke of York from danger and protect his father-in-law's dynastic ambitions, Albemarle is sent to war in the hope that "George might now do less than both" (274). When it became obvious that Rupert should be recalled (the duchess alleges), the courtiers waste time worrying about their penmanship and then, after all their extravagance and greed, send the message "third class"; she protests that, had it been an official document conferring rights or privileges on themselves, it would have been processed immediately—sent "special."

From lines 355 to 434 the duchess accompanies her husband in vision as he fights Ruyter and brings his fleet home. Her speech allows the poet both to praise the English in typically chauvinistic lines like

> Fire out the wasps, George, from their hollow trees,
> Crammed with the honey of our English bees.
>
> (lines 383–84)

and to deplore the waste of war in lines like

> Plant now Virginian firs in English oak;
> Build your ship-ribs proof to the cannon's stroke;
> To get a fleet to sea exhaust the land;
> Let longing princes pine for the command.
>
> (lines 403–6)

There is, as in the "Second Advice," no way to prevent Dutch waste from becoming English; the flames burning the Dutch fleet also ignite London. The blame is for those, like the earl of Clarendon, who

> first begot this war,
> In an ill hour, under a blazing star.
>
> (lines 423–24)

Albemarle's reuniting of the fleet to bring it home is, in some sense, what the king should do for the whole nation. The duchess's advice to her husband is essentially reiterated in the section addressed to the king. After Albemarle brings the fleet home, the king should abolish it, because it has become a source of division in more ways than one. If there is to be a fleet, it must not be allowed to become an instrument of factious policy; if it is, it will prove a liability, a Trojan horse to Troynovant.

"The Last Instructions to a Painter": Further Divergence

"Last Instructions" is dated 4 September 1667, but was not published until 1689. Patterson suggests that the "very specificity" of the date must carry some weight: Marvell is known to have spoken in the House on 31 October in defense of Peter Pett, so that "Marvell's intentions in 'Last Instructions' were clearly to remove the blame for the Chatham disaster from military administrators like Peter Pett" (158).

The "Last Instructions" is, if anything, more explicitly a reply to Dryden than even the "Third Advice"; moreover, it replies in ways that, while continuing to exploit the traditional topoi, perhaps inadvertently draw poetry ever deeper into a distorted mirror of Charles's kingdom. Parallelism, specifically the *paper* sort, is one of the principal themes of the poem. Even its heroes are essentially *mock*-heroic ones (even, I will argue, "*new*-heroic"), conspicuous for the way they conduct paper battles in Parliament according to rules of order, speeches, procedures. The parliamentary in-fighting, of which we get a great deal, *parallels* (when it doesn't utterly supplant) the real fighting. The villains would all be better at paperwork of a different sort, involving money, credit, usury. We should not be surprised, therefore, at the number of puns, of words that draw our attention to other words rather than to things. After so many "competing versions," our attention naturally attaches more to the versions themselves than to the events depicted.

Here is no room for the sort of deliberate flattery described by Italian theorists like Lomazzo; there is no room for the flatterer either, since to describe things as they are, one must resemble them oneself. This amounts to a curious handling of the problem of ethos, the proof derived from the impression of the speaker's character; perhaps because the satirist is always open to the ad hominem charge of nastiness, Marvell faces it head on by accepting it, and by shifting the blame to society.

As well as vertically between writer and subject, the chain of resemblances extends horizontally to the likenesses between the things themselves—I should say people: St. Albans, Clarendon, etc.—and what they do. This kind of analogizing, between what they do and what they are, between what they do in one sphere and what they do in another, is clearly related to the reductive physical parallelism we have encountered earlier. Such an analogizing tendency argues, I believe, for the common authorship of these poems as much as their common painterly emphasis pointed out by Patterson.

It seems, ironically, more than sheer luck that the painter's talent here must depend on lucky strokes. In the episode of Protogenes and his dog, for example, by a lucky stroke the painter simulates the dog's slaver when he dashes his sponge against the canvas; and surely it is no mere coincidence that one of the first subjects this painter has to depict is Henry Jermyn, earl of St. Albans, a notorious *gambler*. What St. Albans does is take advantage of occasions that for others would prove disadvantageous. Thus, for instance, his great size, his large posterior in fact, recommends him to the Queen Mother and becomes the basis of his "diplomatic" skill, his "Plenipotence":

> He needs no seal but to St. James's lease,
> Whose breeches were the Instrument of Peace;
>
> (lines 41–22)

"Plenipotence" is one of the many puns in the poem that, as suggested above, tend to turn it into a distorted mirror of events. In the burlesque version, St. Albans' penis, which accounts less than *fat* for the fullness of his breeches, parallels his diplomatic authority; both are spurious. This pun will occur again, for the men the English send as their "plenipotentiary" ambassadors to the court of Louis XIV are little more than codpieces. St. Albans's "plenipotence," the only authority he has, is a reminder of what Stuart diplomacy tends to be based on. His belief that such "bedroom politics" signifies "the golden Age was now restor'd" involves a pun on "restoration" as a renewal of the organ of sex—an idea of the Restoration that Jose would appreciate (Rochester, too)—and a pun on "golden," since for men like St. Albans the Restoration is mainly a chance for more wealth. This connection of men to events through physical characteristics (which involves the reduction of both men and events to the lowest common denominator) is consistent, of course, with the connections made earlier between Coventry's great girth and the "burdensome-ness" of the navy, and between Arlington's split nose and the division of the fleet.

In the portrait of Anne Hyde, duchess of York, more punning connects Anne to negative aspects of her society. She is a kind of Archimedean virtuoso or projector (also, as a friend of the duchess of Newcastle [50] a bit of a bluestocking), and often as naked as Archimedes was when he discovered how to test a crown for gold. Her experiments include her marriage to the heir, the duke of York (an experiment on a crown), the renewal of lost virginity ("How after childbirth to renew a Maid" [54]), and the (apparently successful) poisoning of her rival, Lady Denham.

The two portraits of royal whores provide a background for the mock-heroic parliamentary debate depicted in lines 105–306. They prepare us, structurally, for the excise bill (131–46), which is itself only another (but newer and so greater) "whore of State" (150). The portraits of the mistresses, the excise, and the Royal Society all seem to indicate the same problem with the Lady State: "Britannia" has been supplanted by something else. Rule is based on whatever it is these and—looking ahead some lines—Frances Stuart represent. It should surprise no one that a member of the court party, married to a whore, defends (even votes for) another.

The description of the supporters of the excise occasions more punning that, combined with mock-epic treatment, continues to draw us into an unreal, parallel world. Thus "pays" (172) is shown to sound like what it deserves, "dispraise" (171), because it refers to bribery; in this world a *paymaster* is really a *bribe*master. Thus Prodgers's name, by happy accident, sounds like what he is, a procurer, a pimp. The playing on "Bulteel's" name is similar. Clearly the punning, based on accidental resemblances, reinforces the *contingent* nature of the subject matter, as does the initial depiction of the House of Commons as a gamblers' den (which, as the resort of men like St. Albans, it was).

The punning also reminds us that the parliamentary battle is mainly a war of words over what to call things. Thus a "thrifty Troop of Privateers" (195) may be those seeking to enrich themselves by means of *private* bills, or legalized pirates, or *both*, insofar as those who introduce private bills into the House of Commons are no better than pirates. The mock-heroic treatment is even retroactive, affecting the flavor of the battles of the previous advices. Such a host, we are told, exceeds even that of the Four Days' Battle, although it is "from all Gun-shot free" (230).

That the heroes who resist the court party's excise bill are *also* treated mock-heroically suggests to me the author's desire for a kind of fair-mindedness that is clearly absent from the court. Thus Sir Richard Temple,

> conqueror
> Of Irish cattle and Solicitor;
>
> (lines 255–56)

seems to have defeated the actual cattle of the cattle import bill. Seymour,

> that with spear and shield
> Had stretched the monster Patent on the field;
>
> (lines 257–58)

seems to have slain the Canary Patent itself. Whorwood, who tried to impeach John, Viscount Mordaunt, is said to have "pierced" him through his armor, like the giant of a romance. Though treated mock-heroically, underlying such events are important concerns that, as they affect the royal prerogative, have some bearing on panegyric. According to Paul Seaward, the Irish Cattle Bill "declared illegal imports to be a 'nuisance'"; moreover,

> the declaration that imports were a "nuisance" implied that they were self-evidently wrong, and against natural law; laws against such *mala in se* could not, it was accepted, be dispensed with by the king's prerogative. The addition hinted at a concern that the king might allow some individuals licences to import cattle contrary to the Act when it was passed.[10]

Underlying the Canary Patent are equally important questions of rights and prerogatives: "The limitation of the trade in the Canaries to members of the company, and the rules limiting membership made it a monopoly, they claimed, in contravention of the Common Law and of a statute of 1606 which prohibited the creation of any monopoly of trade with Spain and Portugal; the king might dispense with neither, as they guaranteed the subjects' fundamental rights" (285). Even Mordaunt represents a serious concern, since "the charges against [him] smacked of something grander, the military's disregard for the rules of law, of the constitution, even of common decency" (287). Significantly, Waller, called "trumpet-gen'ral" because he has only one register for all rulers, is sufficiently impressed by *this* battle to tell the truth for once, or at least to swear to do so:

> Old Waller, trumpet-gen'ral, swore he'd write
> This combat truer than the naval fight.
>
> (lines 263–64)

The lines also carry some suggestion that this, the parliamentary "paper war," really is the fight; certainly, it is the one that Waller, and Marvell himself for that matter, really knew. By showing us what he knows Marvell introduces something new, less mock-heroism than a new kind of heroism; for all their mock-heroic presentation, underlying the episodes is something genuinely heroic, a true English victory.

Naturally, Marvell seems to encounter some difficulty with the depiction of virtue in such a setting. When he does attempt it most seriously, it is in a series of balanced antitheses that unfortunately remind one of Pope's portrait of Addison. The antitheses have a neutralizing effect that suggests the neutralization, if not neutering, of virtue itself; virtue, when it does appear, appears too poised to do anything:

> A gross of English gentry, nobly born,
> Of clear estates, and to no faction sworn;
> . . . .
> To speak not forward, but in action brave,
> In giving gen'rous, but in counsel grave;
>
> (lines 287–92)

The moment of victory, since it must be a matter of parliamentary procedure, is really nothing, less even than the writing of it. The writing is analogous to the parliamentary "fight," as the latter is analogous to the real one (whatever, wherever, whenever *that* is):

> See sudden chance of war! To paint or write
> Is longer Work and harder than to fight.
> At the first charge the enemy give out
> And the excise receives a total rout.
>
> (lines 303–6)

Rather than making "the good" more convincing, such analogizing, by its very excessiveness, makes it fainter.

Lines 335–72 depict the chancellor Clarendon's joy at the prorogation in terms of an elaborate analogy that allies him with the forces of darkness, and with the very things that portend most evil to kings, themselves conventionally identified with the sun:

> So, at the sun's recess, again returns
> The comet dread and earth and heaven burns.
>
> (lines 347–48)

Inversely, the sitting of Parliament is likened to day, to sunlight; everything good that has been done by Marvell's patriots during Parliament's "day" may now be undone by Clarendon and his friends during the "night" of its prorogation. Clarendon himself becomes a kind of demonic, parody-king, a king of the night because without a parliament:

> See how he reigns in his new palace culminant,
> And sits in state divine like Jove the fulminant!
>
> (lines 355–56)

This is Marvell's analogy-making at its most serious, and the seriousness is effected by his exploitation of topoi traditionally associated with kings in panegyric. The advice and the warning to Charles could not be more explicit.

At last, forced to write an order recalling Parliament, like the gallant in the "Second Advice" who wishes ships had never been invented, Clarendon wishes that he had never learned to write. This amounts to a kind of desperate self-betrayal since, as indicated by the confusion over the pun on *Candy* (as both the island off the Essex coast where the Dutch are reported to be and the island in Busenello's poem where the English wished the Dutch were), what he and his fellow courtiers *really* want to do is turn reality into the literary idealization of Busenello's and Waller's poetry. His continuing mistakenness is revealed by his thinking that now *not* writing will make any difference. He is in grave self-contradiction, as a man who depends entirely on written arrangements, especially with the bankers of lines 491–506.

The whole episode of the Dutch invasion and the burning of the fleet at Chatham is the work of Clarendon's "night" described above; hence, the appropriateness of the poet's cry "Black Day accurst!" (735). The depiction of the king disturbed at night by visions of a distressed nation and visitations from his assassinated father and grandfather powerfully connects this night to Clarendon and his noxious, nocturnal rule. The main body of the poem ends with the king, in the morning, resolved to remove Clarendon.

Conclusions and Hypotheses

Marvell's satire succeeds as Waller's panegyric cannot, for two main reasons. First, even without reference to public information outside the poems themselves, the satire is simply more credible in this case. Waller's consistent amplification is not connected to anything or anyone ethical, so it is relatively easy for Marvell to attach it to something unethical—that is, to greed. Once this connection has been made, it is hard to unmake it, just as it is impossible, once Marvell "paints" it, to see "outdoing" as anything other than a matter of wasted pounds and shillings. This bad ethos, which has already implicated the "outdoings" as wasteful, greedy events, is reinforced by a consistent strategy of validation or, since this is mainly a satire, invalidation. By this means the poet of the "Second Advice" appears as natural as the poet of the "Instructions" seems unnatural. Trees should not swim, and courtiers should not fight, or give orders, or set themselves up as navigational "points"; moreover, no one can be trusted who thinks that they should, as Marvell suggests Waller does.

Second, panegyric tends to evoke its opposite. There is not so much an ambiguity, because that implies something vague and even untidy, as there is a neat convertibility to the topics and figures of satire and panegyric, as if they amounted to a common store and one might draw upon either as a branch of epideictic rhetoric. One is reminded of Leon Guilhamet's metaphor of the Janus face. Thus, amplification easily becomes diminution, and vice versa, just as, in the case of the duchess's visit, evolution becomes devolution; Venus, emerging from the sea in Waller, returns to it in Marvell as a crab. Similarly, in the gallant's speech, Noah, the savior of the race, becomes the destroyer, Christ becomes the Anti-Christ, and the new beginning merely a protraction of the old ending.

Far from being entirely negative (or satirical, for that matter), these poems reveal, as Isabel Rivers puts it, "the proper relation between king and commons" (119). The disagreement between critics like Wallace and Patterson (and myself, for that matter) about precisely what some of the positives are, underlines a problem with epideictic poetry, with panegyric and satire, especially when they are conspicuously present within the same poem. As Aristotle suggested, panegyric can at any time become satire or vice versa; perhaps it is inevitable than when the two are juxtaposed they will change roles more than once. No doubt the frequency of such alternation was controlled for contemporaries by their awareness of certain facts in conjunction with what the poet was *advising*; it may be controlled for us today by a knowledge of history in conjunction with a sense of what that advice must have been. In slightly later works, like Marvell's *Rehearsal Transpros'd* and Swift's *Tale of a Tub*, where praise and blame seem attached to no policy or (at most) to a policy of inaction, such alternation dazzles the reader, till it dazes him or her.

That literature is not only blamed but punished in the "Third Advice," and that the silly paper villains of the "Last Instructions" are villains precisely because they want to turn events into the literature that is written about them, suggests a different response to literary "treatments" like *Annus Mirabilis*, and a qualification of Jose's statement that "Underlying much of the political poetry of the decade . . . is the suspect assumption that the end of poetry is to give form and persuasiveness to a fiction and that the fiction itself is enough" (166). Such an assumption seems to have been made and rejected somewhat early on.

4
The Rehearsal Transpros'd:
The Panegyrical Paratext (1)

READING the important critics of *The Rehearsal Transpros'd*, Marvell's polemical refutation of Samuel Parker's religious absolutism, is to revolve a Jamesian cube of reality. All disagree, while none entirely succeeds at refuting the others. Each tends to delineate a different line of argument, and no particular line of argument does justice to this exceedingly dense and complicated text.

John M. Wallace is perhaps the most conservative of Marvell's critics, and in depicting Marvell's career as a moderate loyalist he not surprisingly emphasizes the moderate, pragmatic arguments of *The Rehearsal Transpros'd*. Naturally, he stresses decorum at the expense of irony and satire, and occasionally misses the subtlety of Marvell's complex rhetoric, as when he sees Marvell's version of Parker as the megalomaniacal Bayes as merely a foil for the prudence of the king. More recently Patterson, Anselment, and Chernaik stress the more "literary" aspects of the text. Of these, Patterson is hardest on Marvell for what she sees as a ultimately a failure of decorum (she accuses Marvell of "muddled decorum" in the first part), perhaps even a failure of moderation or of the attempt to define any viable middle ground, as he simultaneously refutes Parker and works towards a theory of Christian polemic at odds with the very means of such refutation. Anslement, in placing *The Rehearsal Transpros'd* in a tradition of religious ridicule, chronologically between *Smectymnuus* and *A Tale of a Tub*, tends to be most positive about Marvell's successful defense of a middle position in a suitable style — "between jest and earnest." Chernaik sees him as developing out of the constraint of animadversions, adopting impersonation and a literalization of metaphor sometimes approaching allegory—a way of writing that anticipates and occasionally rivals Swift's best work.

The work that Marvell was most immediately refuting was called *A*

Preface to Bishop Bramhall's Vindication, but in *The Rehearsal Transpros'd* "paratextual" elements, like prefaces, titles, title pages, and so forth, figure prominently in a discussion of praise and blame, as part of the panegyrical strategy by which Marvell discredits Samuel Parker's praise of, and advice to, Charles II. In their opportunistic praising and unrelatedness to what they "signify," prefaces, titles, names, and even letters become a metaphor for the meretricious vehicle for the Good. In this respect they are like the prefatory pieces of *A Tale*, one of whose major themes is the disjunction between tenor and vehicle, which eventually causes a collapse of meaning, in particular the meaning of important transcendentals like the Good. In particular, the abuse of the relationship between poet and prince, so clearly articulated in panegyric, is treated as a specific form of the abuse of the relationship between that which means (the poet, or, in a sense, the vehicle) and that which is meant (the king, or, in a sense, the tenor). Marvell's political satire has epistemological implications. Marvell's use of panegyric is part of the larger issue of arbitrary signification, an issue obviously related to the issue of form and content, which Patterson, for example, articulates differently as a concern for the way "form could actually invalidate content" (177), and for the proper way, in the light of contradictory scriptural precepts, to "answer" a fool.

Printing

Consistent with his paratextual and literary emphasis, Marvell revises the myth of Cadmus sowing the dragon's teeth. The dragon's teeth become not soldiers, but type. This emphasis on printing as a very mechanical and somewhat reductive kind of writing helps Marvell to reduce Parker's language to its elements, and then endow those elements—letters, suffixes, and so forth—with a seemingly independent life. Just as the initials of John Owen's name are extended into the entire alphabet (against which Parker has a grudge), so when Parker criticizes Owen's comments on Arminianism and Socinianism, Parker is seen to have a grudge against all the other "isms." Marvell argues that schism, which hard-liners like Parker are responsible for, creates "ism": "[L]et *schism*, if you please, rhime to *-ism*" (78). Marvell finds Parker similarly obsessed by another suffix, "ness," both in a word that has to do with his political and religious absolutism,

"Categoricalness" (86), and in his use of it to "translate" or "transpose" certain key Christian concepts: "[O]ur Author translates Joy to *Chearfulness*, Peace to *Peaceableness*, and Faith to *Faithfulness*" (87). The suffix effects yet another corruption when attached to "symbolical": a passage on "Symbolicalness" (91) in Parker's "Preface" is likened to "the Bill of Fare, not at the *Ordination-Dinner* at the *Nags-head*, but of the *Excusation-Dinner* at the *Cock*" (92). The "nesses" become a linguistic means for the establishment of what amounts to a parallel, or rather parodic, *non*-religion. Suffices and prefixes resemble prefaces as a kind of small scale, arbitrary abuse of signifier over signified. They also tend to draw us away from "reality," while maintaining enough reference to it to warn us against Parker: "nesses," for example (a note explains), are also "the 'collar of ss' [that] was worn at that time by the two chief justices and the chief baron of England" (349), something that Parker is seen as wanting to wear himself as magistrate.

Parker's defense of "the Magistrates power of instituting significant Ceremonies" with the analogy of the "Sovereign Authority" taking upon itself "to define the signification of words" (102) actually backfires, weakening his argument that such power is not great. As Marvell explains, the power to determine such "signification" is so great that one of the most powerful rulers ever, Augustus Caesar, "was used to fly from a new word though it were single, as studiously as a mariner would avoid a Rock for fear of splitting" (103). Not only is the meaning of a word important, but even the meaning of a syllable: "The difference of one Syllable in the same word hath made as considerable a Controversy as most have been in the Church" (103).

This returns us to Marvell's earlier emphasis on the suffixes "ness" and "ism," and to the motif of transposition, since "the transposition only of a letter a, another time in the name of a Goat, by some call'd *Crabe*, and by others *Cabre*, was the loss of more men's lives than the distinguishing but by an Aspiration in *Shiboleth* upon the like occasion" (103). Marvell's attitude to language is intensely conservative, and no doubt intended—if it is fair now to speak of *Marvell's* intentions, after he has spoken so freely of Parker's—to effect a "transposition" of his own, making himself the conservative and Parker the radical "innovator." As an "innovator" Parker should leave religious matters alone, while devoting his time to a common project among contemporary linguistic innovators, the "Universal Language"—so that "in time the whole World might come to be of his Parish" (105).

Headings and Titles

Marvell gives us a "works also writ by the author," like that just after the title page of *A Tale*. A similar list of works by the same author is given again later (40), but it is more a list of *children*; Marvell speaks of Parker's works as being "regularly *spawned*" (40). His *Defence*, written after the king's "Declaration," is spoken of as "his second Child" and allegorized as a tyrannical usurper like Richard III: "It was a very lusty Baby, and twice as big as the former, and (which some observed as an ill sign, and that if it lived it would prove a great Tyrant) it had, when born, all the Teeth, as perfect as ever you saw in any mans Head" (62). The time it took him to write it is seen as a sort of gestation period, the length of which partly accounts for the size; its railing content is its "cry" (63). Parker's own "maturation" becomes largely a matter of pagination, as Marvell traces the development of his thought from page to page, and book to book.

The importance that Marvell himself attaches to titles can be seen in his later treatment of the phenomena. He treats the title page of a rather obscure book on the Book of Common Prayer and Christian burial as "an *Emblem* how much some of them do neglect the Scripture in respect to their darling Ceremonies" (137). Parker is imagined to be "present" at Marvell's reading, and he "wakes Up" when Marvell does, at the title page: "*A Preface shewing what grounds there are of fears and jealousies of Popery*" (117). The continuation of the title, "*a Consideration what likelihood, or how much danger there is, of the return of Popery into their Nation*," actually changes the sense of it from "there are grounds" to "there are no grounds" (117). Marvell remarks that without its second part it has no relationship to the contents of its book. The public aspect of the title, and the fact that only the first part of the title will enjoy this aspect, makes it especially dangerous: "[N]o man can look at the wall, no man can pass by a Book-sellers stall, but he must see *A Preface showing what GROUNDS there are for FEARS and JEALOUSIES of POPERY*" (118). Clearly, the first part of the title functions as a little disjunctive preface.

Elsewhere the title is identified with the signifier that enables us to recognize a thing (or *not* to), in this case nothing less than the English Civil War: "But Men are all so weary, that he would be knock'd on the head that should raise the first disturbance of the same nature. A new War must have, like a Book that would sell, a new Title" (112). Like the preface later, the title comes to stand for the arbitrary relationship of vehicle to tenor, an arbitrariness that we (poststructuralists) might recognize as linguistically correct but which is here identified with absolutism.

One of the things that, after Parker becomes "a madman in print" (31), contributes to his "Vain-Glory" is seeing "his Title page was posted and pasted up at every avenue next under the Play for that afternoon at the Kings or the Dukes House" (31). It is while "taking the opportunity at once to piss and admire the Title-page of his Book" (32) that Parker is brained by "*J.O.*'s" book and driven mad as a result; he is likened in this regard to King Charles VI of France, who was driven mad when his page dropped a lance on his head. "*J.O.*'s" book is in turn likened to the lance: thus, once again and in a place where one would not expect it, literary, even paratextual aspects of polemical disputes like that between Parker and John Owen find a historical analogy that is mock-heroic. The mock-heroic analogy is further developed in such expressions as "*Ink-shed*" (37), as when Parker/Bayes seems to have a grudge against every letter of the "*Latine Alphabet.*"

Prefaces

Marvell's first quote is not from the main body of Parker's *Defence* but, typically, from Parker's paratext, the "Epistle to the Reader." The point of the quote is to fault the conventional language common to such prefatory pieces, a language parodied effectively in *A Tale*:

> *But if this be the Penance I must undergo for the wantonness of my Pen, to answer the impertinent and slender Exceptions of every peevish and disingenuous Caviller; Reader, I am reformed from my incontinency of Scribling, and do here heartily bid thee an Eternal Farewell.* (Rehearsal Transpros'd, 3)
>
> *When every little Would-be-wit takes Pen in hand, 'tis vain to enter the Lists, &c.* (A Tale, 45)

Marvell turns a conventional complaint into the very fault Parker objects to in the "confessions" of the Non-Conformists; later, Swift sees in it the hypocrisy of the "fat unwieldy fellow" in Leicester-Fields who complains about crowding when he is himself the worst offender. In Marvell, the fact of the ensuing preface is made to testify to Parker's hypocrisy; it is his first broken promise, "his Promise to write no more" (4).

The language Marvell quotes from "The Preface" is remarkably anthropomorphic, as if the bishop's *Vindication* were a human being, but one now rather out of fashion:

> *The ensuing Treatise of Bishop* Bramhall's *being somewhat superannuated, the* Bookseller *was very solicitous to have it set off with some Preface that might recommend it to the Genius of the Age, and reconcile it to the present juncture of Affairs.* (4)

Marvell immediately exploits the latent sartorialism of the passage,

> A pretty task indeed: That is as much as to say, To trick up the good old Bishop in a yellow Coif and a Bulls-head, that he may be fit for the Publick, and appear in Fashion. (4)

He designates Parker a "Preface-monger" (4). The sartorialism—fashion—neatly ties in with Marvell's later criticism of Parker as an arrogant modern, condescending to his betters in worse ways than writing prefaces for them, and with satire on one aspect of "fashion," ceremony in the church. In both Marvell and Swift the preface naturally becomes a metaphor for "empty gestures," which makes its use in religious ridicule all the more important; the preface can be seen, generally, as a kind of formalist abuse, at the same time that Parker's "Preface" can be seen as specifically advocating such abuses in religion but also turning them into absolute requirements for anyone wishing to belong to the state church. When one Matthew Parker, formerly archbishop of Canterbury, successfully rebuts Samuel Parker's position, the latter's solution (Marvell supposes) will be to write yet another preface: "Now Mr. *Bayes*, I doubt you must be put to the trouble of writing another Preface against this Arch-bishop" (116). Archbishop Parker had written in favor of tolerance for those opposed to ceremonies that were not ordained by Scripture; Samuel Parker's imagined response to this moderation about ceremonies is to write another "ceremonial piece," another preface; one imagines Parker's prefaces encrusting other men's works the way the ceremonies defended encrust Christianity.

The Bookseller gets the better of Parker: "[T]he Bookseller I see was a cunning Fellow, and knew his Man." He hires him as a young priest, his preface becoming the altar on which the bishop's *Vindication* is sacrificed "to the Genius of the Age" (4). While this ties in with the theme of preferment, since Parker would do much worse than sacrifice a preface to advance himself, it is also part of the analogical technique of *The Rehearsal Transpros'd* to let Parker's crimes remain for the most part literary ones while illustrating their potential harmfulness with analogies from politics and history. Another pertinent example is his later comparison not to a paratextual but to a genuine pagan priest under Caligula who really does sacrifice a lot more than prefaces.

Praise and Blame

In the narrow form of paratextual "valorization," it is unsure whether Parker praises the bishop more by prefacing him, or the bishop praises Parker more by being prefaced by him. Very likely Parker gains more from the bishop. The problem with the paratext—the arbitrariness of its relation to the text—establishes a pattern, the reversed relationship between the praiser and his subject, which has serious implications for panegyric, for Parker's relationship with the king when he addresses him, and (for reasons mentioned above) for meaning generally. Again, the paratext provides the cutting edge of Marvell's satire, a double-edge in fact, reinforcing the connection to the burlesque of Buckingham's play on the one hand and to the serious rhetorical concern with panegyric on the other.

After the preliminaries that Marvell, alluding to *The Rehearsal*, calls the "Dance" (10), he proceeds to discuss Parker's failure in his "Preface" to praise or "recommend" the book prefaced—to do what Gérard Genette calls "valorize the text." Here the business of panegyric and "valorization" are similar; Parker praises both a man *and* a book in his "Preface," and though the man is not a king, he is, as bishop, a figure of considerable authority nonetheless. In Parker's fulsome language, he emerges as rather *more* than king. The element of advice, so important a part of panegyric, remains, but is now directed exclusively to the living, reading audience.

Marvell first informs us that he had been disposed to accept Parker's praise because he esteemed the bishop and his work. Wanting to like the bishop, or liking him already, he wishes in retrospect that he had never got acquainted with Parker's version of him, the effect of which is to make him like the bishop a little less than before. Marvell says he would rather "live and enjoy [his] own Opinion, than be so treated" (11). Parker's praise is so conditional, so qualified, that it indicates an almost chronic inability to praise without condescending to, patronizing, and even insulting not only his subject but his subject's entire era.

This is essentially a problem with ethos, which intensely concerns Marvell. Somewhat circularly, Marvell imagines that by a man's words he can discern his character, by which he can in turn interpret his words: "I marked how your Answerer look'd when he spoke of the day of Judgment" (90). Part of Parker's problem with religious ridicule is that his ridicule seems discontinuous with serious language; Parker, at least according to Marvell, cannot be humorous and serious at the same time: "Here it is that after so great an excess of Wit, he thinks fit to take a Julep and resettle his Brain, and the Government. He grows as serious as 'tis possible for a madman, and pretends to sum up the whole state of the Controversie with the Nonconformists" (92).

What Marvell usually exploits to undermine Parker's praise is just more of the same conventional language: "[H]e was, as far as the prejudice of the Age would permit him, an acute Philosopher" (11). Parker is made to pay dearly for his parenthetical expression, which Marvell terms somewhat uncharitably "a malignant remark" (11) that "infuses" itself "into the Praises of him whom he most intended to celebrate" (11).

When Parker's praise is not thus undermined for being too conventional, Marvell argues it is "at best very ridiculous" (11) because of its fulsomeness. Thus Marvell says, speaking of Parker's "great Elogy of the Church of *England*": "I find on either side only the natural effect of such Hyperboles and Oratory, that is, not to be believed" (123). He accuses Parker of using the fulsome "language of a lover" in writing of the bishop, though he cannot believe (he says) that Parker is so desperate "that he should make a dead Bishop his Mistress" (13), if only because he could not conceivably be in love with such a grotesque (even if it is his own creation, *and* a *self*-image): "[I]f the Bishop were alive, he would be out of love with himself" (13). The "Preface" becomes "like those frightful Looking-glasses made for sport" (13), reminding one again that to praise convincingly, as in the "painter-poems," one must demonstrate one's ability at blame as well; in fact, one must demonstrate competence in the epideictic mode generally, which includes both praise *and* blame, panegyric *and* satire. Unfortunately, the things Parker praises the bishop for are improbable or undesirable or both. We are told, for example, that Bramhall had "a mind large and active enough to have managed the Roman Empire at its greatest extent" (12) or that "he finished all the glorious Designs that he undertook" (11), one of them being reconciliation with Rome. The effect of such praise is to "diminish always the Person whom they pretend to magnifie" (12).

Bramhall himself had wanted to suppress the book to which Parker had attached his preface (20). Thus, the imprudence of his design to reconcile Anglicanism with Rome is really more Parker's than his. To put it differently, Parker imprudently attempts to praise the bishop by drawing attention to something in the "Preface" that the bishop himself knew would have the effect of blame, at least in his own lifetime. Again, as with "*J.O.*," the motive, even more than the judgment, is suspect. Far from seriously wanting to praise Bramhall, he finds the best way to praise him is to gloss over some of his more imprudent schemes: "[T]he Author's end was only railing" (20). Thus Marvell shifts his ground from asserting that Parker's fault is in the fulsomeness of his praise to asserting that it is in the fulsomeness of his blame; either way, the fault is a failure to demonstrate a general competence in the epideictic mode at *both* praise and blame. Without *both* a kind of uncontrollable alternation sets in. Parker's "praise" of Bramhall is now seen to have been motivated by a desire to blame "Forreign Divines and the Nonconformists" (20); naturally, since this "praise" is motivated by a desire to blame, some of it comes out as blame. In this respect, he resembles the Bayes of *The Rehearsal,* who "prefers that one quality of fighting single with whole Armies, before all the moral Virtues put together" (21).

When it is not undermined by its own virulent nature, or fulsomeness, or sheer inappropriateness, Parker's praise may still excite envy, as panegyric does in *A Tale*. Swift compares praise to "a pension paid by the world" (*A Tale*, 47); Marvell compares it to an estate, here one that no one wants to see "engrossed and monopolized" or "suddenly got" (12). Too much praise, like a sudden large windfall, raises too many questions about the recipient and the giver. All this criticism of Parker's praise is centered around the paratext and his handling of certain paratextual functions, preparatory to debunking Parker's ability to praise in a more serious context.

The particular man whom Parker wishes to *blame* is John Calvin; he is the one (there had to be someone) he praised Bramhall in order to rail at: "Poor Mr. *Calvin* and Bishop *Bramhall,* what crime did you dye guilty of, that you cannot lye quiet in your Graves?" (23). Consistent with Parker's failure at praise and blame, Marvell says he can't tell "which of you two are most unfortunate" (24). The problem is partly one of ethos, of always suspecting the author of a sinister intention; it extends beyond epideictic to matters of veracity. Praise and blame always reflect the praiser-blamer's character; naturally, a failure of one or the other suggests a character defect. A transposition of praise and blame is inseparable from a transposition of good and bad, right and wrong: "For, though an ill man cannot by praising confer honour, nor by reproaching fix an ignominy, and so they may seem on equal terms; yet there is more in it: for at the same time that we may imagine what is said by such an Author to be false, we conceive the contrary to be true" (24). Unable to control the "transposition" of praise and blame, Parker loses control of all others, like sacred and profane, Scripture and romances (29,30).

Marvell's language is itself "transpositional," but *intentionally* so, and with Marvell conspicuously in control: "I saw that he pursued *J.O.* if not from *Post to Pillar*, yet from *Pillar to Post*" (39); "[H]e had so confounded the Question with differing terms and contradictory expressions, that he might upon occasion affirm whatever he denied, or deny whatsoever he affirmed" (47–48); "[A]s I am obliged to ask pardon if I speak of serious things ridiculously; so I must now beg excuse if I should hap to discourse of ridiculous things seriously" (49).

Marvell uses Parker's little allegory of the "Bramble" (Calvin) on "*the South side the Lake Lemane*" (24) to show how his praise becomes blame and vice versa; the "Bramble" is intended to be blamed, but its description as "*both Pope and emperor too of the greatest part of the Reformed World*" is all too close in wording to the praise of Bishop Bramhall as one who "might (like *Caesar*) *manage the Roman Empire at its utmost extent*" (17): Parker's praise and blame are so nearly identical that Marvell's comment seems not unfair:

> [A]s smiling and frowning are performed in the face with the same muscles very little altered; so the changing of a line or two in Mr. *Bayes* at any time, will make the same thing serve for a Panegyrick or a Philippick. (24)

In his penchant for railing, Parker resembles the "lightning" of Bayes's prologue in *The Rehearsal*. Marvell draws an analogy between Parker's reduction of religion to morality and his reduction of discourse to "railing" (72). As with previous analogies, the literary matters are the reality (or tenor) while others, here religious matters, are only *potentially* so. Parker quotes Lord Bacon as a precedent for railing, but Marvell quotes the same man against it. Parker attempts to use Christ, writing that "*Christ was not only in a hot fit of Zeal, but in a seeming Fury too and transport of Passion*" (76), but Marvell rejects this precedent too, passing on to other points in Parker's argument—for example, that railing is expedient. Using the example of two scolds, he argues that "she that rails most has the least reason" (76). The literary quarrel finds its analogy in something a bit ridiculous but earthy, like Marvell's reduction of diplomacy in the "painter-poems" to a Skimmington Ride.

Marvell mimics Parker's own voice in a feigned diatribe against printing that, anticipating the Hack's praise of satire in *A Tale*, is really a panegyric; while the satire overtly depicts printing as the enemy of progress, it is by implication its friend. Parker himself is depicted as allied with the reactionary forces of darkness, and likened to a little monkish censor:

> 'Twas an happy time when all Learning was in Manuscript, and some little Officer, like our Author, did keep the Keys of the Library. (4)

Parker really opposes not so much the press as the *freedom* of the press:

> But now, since Printing came into the World, such is the mischief, that a Man cannot write a Book but presently he is answered. Could the Press but once be conjured to obey an *Imprimatur*, our Author might not disdain *perhaps* to be one of its most zealous Patrons. (4–5)

The Patronage Analogy: The Addresser as Client

An essential part of Marvell's strategy in *The Rehearsal Transpros'd* is to challenge Parker's role as Charles's panegyrist on the grounds that Parker is an especially undeserving client, that he is constitutionally unable to praise, and that his advice is dangerous because it reflects the wishes of a pathologically ambitious man. To follow Parker's advice would be to effect the transposition of tenor and vehicle on the political level: to turn Charles into his client Parker and Parker into his patron Charles. In discrediting Parker, Marvell necessarily reexamines what ought, and what ought not to be, the relationship between writer and patron (in this case the greatest patron of all, the king).

The idea of patronage is invoked early and ironically in *The Rehearsal Transpros'd*. Parker is chastised for describing himself as "none of the most zealous Patrons of the Press." Parker is depicted not only as a *reluctant* literary patron, but a *hypocritical* one, too; despite his reluctance he continues to publish, and as a Protestant priest he remains indebted to printing for the contribution it made to the Reformation.

Almost immediately, in one of the many reversals (transpositions) of the piece, Parker is shown to be more *client* than patron. Wondering what could be the "closer" and "more comfortable" thing that Parker protests he is more interested in than writing, Marvell offers three suggestions: "either his Salvation, or a Benefice, or a Female" (6). Each of Parker's works may be "transpros'd" or, in some fashion, translated into the benefits of patronage: "a Prebend for his first Book, a *Sine-cure* for his second, and for this third a Rectorship, although it were that of *Malmsbury*" (6). Malmsbury is a keen stroke since, as the town of Hobbes's birth and part of Parker's "take," it indicates a connection between Parker's views and his ambitions: Parker will be Hobbesian so long as it gets him Hobbes's town, but it will *only* get him Hobbes's town, a territory considerably smaller than what he is after.

The subsequent account of Parker's search for and attainment of patronage comprises a kind of "progress poem" in prose, but a Swiftian progress in which advancement is synonymous with regression. Thus Parker's becoming chaplain to Gilbert Sheldon, the archbishop of Canterbury, in 1667 is the beginning of the end: "From that day you may take the date of his Preferments and his Ruine" (30). The means by which he ingratiates himself with the archbishop are but a version of the way he would ingratiate himself with the king; that is, they are a perversion of the panegyrist's conciliatory means, because they exploit faction while the panegyrist strives for unity and, worse, turn the writer himself into yet another patron analogous to, but considerably less than, the real one (and with a following that is all "infinite below"): "For having soon wrought himself dexterously into his Patrons favour, by short Graces and Sermons, and a mimical way of drolling upon the *Puritans*, which he knew would take both at Chappel and Table; he gained a great Authority likewise among all the domesticks" (30). Ironically, but consistently with all the other transpositions of the piece, the pro-establishment, absolutist Priest comes to resemble the dissenting orators with oratorial "machines" in *A Tale*. The vehicle can corrupt the tenor to such an extent or, in the words of Patterson, style can negate content

Just as Parker will play the rake or the divine for preferment, so in his later career he will reverse his position, arguing now for absolute authority and now for the right of conscience. Parker's early career (starting, really, with the betrayal of his parents) and his relations with his patron then encapsulate his later career and his relations (or would-be relations) with the king. The sorts of reversals necessitated, apparently, by Parker's ambition and consequent unprincipled accommodations with authority are more of the many profoundly analogical "transpositions" of *The Rehearsal Transpros'd*.

After stating Parker's argument in *Ecclesiastical Polity* (48–60), Marvell remarks that even in an age of degrading patronage when many people will do almost anything for preferment, Parker would have to enforce his measures himself, as "Hangman General": "For I know no Gentlemen that will take any of them out of his hands, although it be an age wherein men cannot well support their quality, without some accession from the publick. . . . So that Mr. *Bayes* must either do it himself in person, or constitute the chief Magistrate to be his Deputy" (60).

Marvell's "history" of Parker's publications resumes on page 61, with Parker not getting the preferment for *Ecclesiastical Policy* that he thought he deserved: "I do not find that the *Ecclesiastical Policy* found more acceptance than could be expected from so judicious a Prince" (61). Marvell shows Parker balked at court as in the church: "[A]s he got no Preferment that I know of at Court . . . so he mist no less of his aim as to the Reformation of Ecclesiastical-Government upon his Principles" (62). Marvell presents Parker's dilemma as another absurd transposition of the right relationship between client and patron: it is not Parker who falls into disgrace with the king, but the king who falls into disgrace with Parker; it is not Parker who feels the king's displeasure, but the king who is to feel the effects of Parker's. Consistent with Parker's apparent usurpation of his hoped-for patron's role (it is typical of Parker's solipsism that in him the client-patron relationship collapses into one self-preferring client-patron or patron-client), the book he writes in a fit of pique inspired by nonpreferment, the *Defence of Ecclesiastical Politie*, resembles the usurping "tyrant," Richard III: "It was a very lusty Baby, and twice as big as the former . . . if it lived it would prove a great Tyrant" (62).

Marvell continues to use ideas of preferment and patronage to depict Parker as what kings most should dread, a usurper. Thus, Parker not only becomes the king's patron, but a fickle one at that (perhaps because, as a pseudopatron, what he gives is always conditional on getting what he wants): "[H]ow dangerous a thing it is for his Majesty and all other Princes to lose Mr *Bayes* his favour . . . now that they will not do as he would have them, when he had given them Power and Instructions how to be wiser for the future, He casts them quite off like men that were desperate" (64). Parker's about-faces for the sake of preferment, his "transposition" of the natural relationship between patron and client, and his ideological reversals from

Ecclesiastical Politie to the *Defence of Ecclesiastical Politie* are all structurally similar, and combined with the "transpositions" wrought on *The Rehearsal* they are largely responsible for what (considerable) unity the work has.

Great churchmen are depicted almost as types of Parker, whose antitype could potentially "fulfill" them by bringing even worse disasters upon the state than the recent civil war. Thus, Robert Sibthorp, who published in 1627 a sermon called *Apostlelike Obedience: Shewing the Duty of Subjects to pay Tributes and Taxes to their Princes* in 1627, seems to conform to the pattern already established: "[H]is being a Man of a low fortune, conceiv'd the putting of his Sermon in Print might gain favour at Court, and raise his fortune higher" (127). Sibthorp is in turn supported by another rising man, Bishop Laud: "Bishop Laud, who was in this whole business, and a rising Man at Court, *undertook an answer*" (127). Roger Manwaring is cited as yet another clergymen who got preferment by recommending a policy of absolutism. All these men contributed to the tensions that led to the civil war, and their similarity to Parker, especially in terms of patronage and preferment, implies that his writings and policies could lead to the same sort of national disaster.

Marvell develops these themes into still more variations on the idea of patronage in *The Rehearsal Transpros'd: The Second Part*. The lapse of time between Part One and Part Two is made a factor in Parker's "progress" as client. When Parker apologizes for the time it took him to write his *Reproof*—he pleads physical infirmity—Marvell accuses him of an egotism that violates the correct relationship between the writer and his patron or prince. Plutarch and the Dutch historian Lieuwe Van Aitzema write circumstantially about the health of their respective monarchs, Alexander the Great and the Prince of Orange; Parker writes about his own health, collapsing the distance between writer and prince, or writer and subject.

The way Parker collapses the relationship between writer and prince is seen as typical of the way Parker would collapse other literary relationships: "Has he been an Author? he is too the Licenser. Has he been a Father? he will stand too for God father. Is he then to be married? he asks his own Banes in Print." These collapsed *literary* relationships provide, in turn, a literary vehicle for the way Parker would collapse relationships in the state. He would seek power the way Nero did: "He could not be contented with the *Roman Empire* unless he were too his own *Praecentor*" (150). The literary vehicle tends to make Parker ridiculous at the same time the political one suggests that were he not so ridiculous, he would be very dangerous indeed.

While the immediate tenor of Marvell's analogizing is Parker's writing, since that is what he is animadverting to, the reader is always aware of the danger that at any moment this tenor, consistent with all the other bewildering transpositions of the piece, could in turn become just another vehicle for Parker's politics. Consequently the reader wants to participate in Marvell's fanciful depictions. It is as if comparing him to Caligula (for some fault of style) were an almost magical way to prevent him from ever becoming Caligula.

The other answerers to the first part of *The Rehearsal Transpros'd* are accused of writing solely from a motive of preferment, with the "Arch-Deacon" as patron: "[T]he more hungry starvelings generally look'd upon it as an immediate Call to a Benefice, and he that could but write an Answer, whatsoever it were, took it for the most dexterous cheap, and legal way of Simony" (171). This precipitates a literary "succession crisis" like the ones in *MacFlecknoe* and (later) *The Dunciad* (and later still, among the judges in *The Rosciad*) among the "Pretenders" (172) to Parker's role. Marvell's wonder at the number of his answerers prompts him to liken Parker to a prince for the way princes "have sometimes been perswaded by their Servants to disguise several others in the Regal garb, that the enemy might not know in the battel whom to single" (174). Thus, once again, a literary activity is illustrated by a political or military one that could itself become a reality if the literary one did not remain uppermost; keeping it uppermost depends, of course, on accepting—and agreeing with—Marvell's wit. Marvell consistently offers both literary and political versions of strife; the reader must want as badly as Marvell does to make the literary version the reality, but this is conditional on accepting Parker as a literary *buffoon*. Wonder at the identity of his answerers prompts Marvell to draw yet another analogy between Parker and his dwindling incarnations and the soul in Donne's "Progress of the Soul"—significantly, another "progress poem" used to evoke "the Progress of so great a Prince."

In conclusion, Marvell's treatment of patronage and preferment in *The Rehearsal Transpros'd* is a striking example of the use of analogy to illustrate panegyrical relationships, as a literary vehicle for a political tenor. Subsequently, this literary vehicle becomes the tenor of political vehicles, mock-heroically evoking both the absurdity of Parker's abuse of such relationships (whether between poet, prince, and people or between client, patron, and party) and the serious danger of such abuses. The analogizing is multitiered and profoundly disturbing, a kind of epistemological quicksand. Because political matters stand for literary matters that in turn stand for political matters again, one participates in the humor of the piece only at the high cost of becoming serious again, of appreciating how easily political vehicle becomes tenor, or reality.

Sometimes the analogy is general: Parker's relationship with his first patron, for instance, is analogous to every succeeding one; until he is stopped, his following will only get larger and worse, as will the faction by which it grows. Sometimes it is a matter of manner, as when Parker's recording his own ailments is seen as collapsing the relationship between writer and subject or patron and, therefore, analogous to the way Parker would collapse offices in the state. Finally, the analogy may even be between what Gerard Genette would call "paratext" (the details of Parker's title page, for example) and Parker's imaginary, Hobbesian empire. Such analogizing seems to develop out of tendencies remarked in the "Painter-Poems" and before. If anything, the tendency is more developed here, with Marvell insisting on the political vehicle of the analogy all the more (although aware that its literary tenor only becomes a vehicle that "stands for" politics after all) as men like Parker threaten, by their writing, to make such politics the tenor, the reality.

Another aspect of the increased literariness of Marvell's analogizing is the containment, within his own polemics, of his enemy's argument. The multiple versions of men and events that were to be found in different works (such as the "painter-poems") have now been internalized and developed into literary techniques focusing on one important aspect of the client/patron relationship that remains to be examined in detail: the versions of the king (or, for that matter, of kings) in Marvell's work, which are not so much Parker's versions as they are Marvell's version of Parker's versions.

The Patron: Versions of the King

Marvell presents early in *The Rehearsal Transpros'd* two conditions, one of which must be met by a Parker patron: "[I]f you have a mind to die, or to be of his Party, (there are but these two Conditions) you may perhaps be rendered capable of his Charity" (11). They illustrate a basic malfunction of Parker's praise: that it is always *self*-praise, and therefore disqualifies him from writing panegyric, which requires that he address his praise to some significant "other."

As remarked above, Parker's praise (or *self*-praise) reflects what Parker would like to be himself (at one point in the second part, Parker is compared to "Mountebanks abroad, who after a deal of Scaffold Pageantry to draw audience, entertain them by decrying all others with a Panegyrick of their own Balsam" [168]). Thus, if the versions offend us, if the praise seems more like blame, the fault is in Parker's character, which is *megalomaniacal* as well as virulent.

The third problem with Parker's versions, besides his egotism and nastiness, is attributable to what we have already noticed in the "painter-poems": the similarity between satire and panegyric as kinds of epideictic rhetoric, by virtue of which one can easily become the other. What Marvell remarks of Parker's prose panegyrics is really true of anyone's *including* Marvell's: "[A]s smiling and frowning are performed in the face with the same muscles very little altered; so the changing of a line or two in Mr. *Bayes* at any time, will make the same thing serve for a Panegyrick or a Philippick" (24). Parker's fault is in not realizing the danger and in running unnecessary risks.

When Parker comes to advise Charles, these versions of kings and rulers become, potentially at least, versions of Charles, too. Marvell, himself a would-be adviser, counters these with his own more attractive versions, many of which are inseparable from advice. Marvell's indication of what Parker should have done *assumes* that the king is doing what *he* should do (Marvell would have known or at least *suspected* the contrary): "[H]e [Bramhall, in fact, standing for Parker standing for the king] should in the first place have contrived how we might live well with our Protestant Neighbours, and to have united us in one Body under the King of *England*, as Head of the Protestant Interest, which might have rendered us more considerable, and put us into a more likely posture to have reduced the Church of *Rome* to Reason" (16).

Thus Marvell counters Parker's megalomaniacal version of kings—and specifically of Charles himself—with the truly praiseworthy (to *Marvell* at least) version of him as "Head of the Protestant Interest." Marvell's version should remind one of how easily the prohibitive slides into the nonprohibitive, and how easily Marvell's wishes—"the king *should* be Head of the Protestant Interest"—seem to have been realized in an attractive fiction that he himself does not believe. As well as allowing for the deliberative function of panegyric, one has at least to entertain the possibility that Marvell, for some of his audience, is being ironic in such statements. For that matter, one ought perhaps to make more allowance for such a possibility whenever praise is used deliberatively. Again and again in *The Rehearsal Transpros'd*, the reader has to wonder whether a version of Charles is functioning as deliberative panegyric or irony or, if possible, both.

After playfully speculating whether the "J.O." of Parker's preface could have been a former schoolmaster, Marvell seriously concludes "the King was the Person concerned from the beginning" (43), thus deflecting Parker's wrath from his enemies to his hoped-for patron. The version begins with the relation of Charles's "Declaration of Indulgence" just prior to his restoration. Marvell depicts this positively as "the last Advice left Him by his glorious Father" (43), thereby promoting his own implicit advice regarding the present "Declaration." Marvell praises the king for "consummate Prudence and natural Benignity" (43), on the condition that he promote religious toleration. Upon his restoration, Charles is both a man of peace and a man of his word ("to royal and generous minds no stipulations are so binding as their own voluntary promises" [43]), but is thwarted by the clergy, by men like Parker whose "Animosities and Obstinacy... have in all Ages been the greatest Obstacle to the Clemency, Prudence and good Intentions of Princes, and the Establishment of their Affairs" (44). The king is obliged, therefore, to wait for a "better season," which unhappily coincides with Parker's *Ecclesiastical Policy*, in which (according to Marvell) "he doth all along use great liberty and presumption" (44).

Curiously, while skilfully urging his own implicit advice, Marvell faults Parker for meddling, with his advice, in state affairs; he faults Parker for doing what he does better: "who, while his Prince might expect his Compliance, doth give him Counsel, advises him how to governe the Kingdom, etc." (44). Marvell stresses his own reluctance even "to mention Kings and Princes . . . lest by reason of my private condition & breeding, I should, though most unwillingly, trip in a word, or fail in the mannerliness of an expression" (49); one must think, again, that Marvell is being at least *slightly* ironic. Finally, this version of the king is of a man conspicuous for virtues of generosity, patience, honesty, and prudence—all contingent, however, on his resisting Parker.

A recurrent version of the king is of a shrewd man always able to see through Parker's advice—to Marvell's. Thus, Marvell depicts Charles as *knowing* that all Parker's flattery and advice have an ulterior motive: "He knows it's all but that you may get into the Saddle again; and that the Priest may ride him, though it be to a Precipice" (51); moreover, he depicts him as feeling a satisfaction with limited power that he probably never felt, but which Marvell indirectly advises him to: "He therefore contents Himself with the Power that He hath inherited from his Royal Progenitors Kings and Queens of *England*, and as it is declared by Parliament" (51).

Ironically, in yet another version, Charles is depicted as following Parker's advice, with consequences that still tend to thwart Parker. He follows Parker's advice "that Princes should be more attentive and confident in exercising their Ecclesiastical Jurisdiction" (73), only to contravene Parker's other advice by issuing the "Declaration." More seriously, he gives Charles all the credit: "I rather believe, he never deign'd to read a line in him, but what he did herein, was only the result of his own good understanding" (73).

Charles is finally just too *princely* to follow Parker's advice; that is, he is a genuine member of a body of men depicted as (for want of a better word) *naturals* at government. Thus Charles shares their common lore or *statecraft*, almost as if he were the member of a select society. "Princes have always found that uncontrollable Government over CONSCIENCE to be both unsafe and impracticable" (93). It is remarkable, yet typical of the way he attacks Parker for doing what he only does better, that Marvell presumes so far as to tell princes what their wisdom is (which implicitly tells them how to be wise) a few pages after faulting Parker for presuming to advise princes what to do. Actually, he avoids the pitfall of appearing to presume to advise his "betters" by simply ignoring the facts, by *assuming* that his advice is their wisdom.

In the most pointed section of the first part, that wisdom appears to be a product of bitter experience, especially bitter for Charles, who lost both a father and a grandfather (Charles I and Henry IV) by assassination, as a result of following "bad advice": "His Majesty, whose Genius hath much of both those Princes, and who derives half of the Blood in his Veins from the latter, will in all probability not be so forward to hearken to your advice as to follow their Example" (108). There is a kind of "rule-by-example" at work here, not the *good* example of the *optimus princeps* but rather the "bad example" of the way princes really have been *(pessimi princepes?)* and the consequences their folly has had for them and their kingdoms.

Charles's predecessors are turned into *examples* for him to be instructed by, in a way that James would have found both familiar and shockingly strange, while Marvell pretends that he does not really need such "royal instruction." Curiously, the princes Charles is *not* related to serve as more positive examples: Augustus is the example of a ruler who (unlike Parker when he compares determining ceremonies in the church to defining words) had the good sense to "fly from a new word though it were single, as studiously as a Mariner would avoid a Rock for fear of splitting" (103). Closer to home, Elizabeth I of England serves as an example of a good ruler with good laws who is nevertheless maligned, just as the bishop was, retroactively, by Parker's "favour" (113).

With understatement (perhaps), he admits that he himself has not *always* had such faith in princes, but that "a little while, or sometimes many years after, [he has] found that all the men in the world could not have contrived any thing better" (108). Knowing the widespread suspicion of the king's intentions among Marvell and his party, it is hard to know how to take such a remark; for that matter, it is hard to know how to take Marvell's depiction of Charles as a member of a "select group" of men versed in the mystery of government, since membership in *that* could, by Marvell's own examples, indicate at least as great a penchant for absolutism and other follies as for wisdom and prudence.

Later, it becomes even harder to resist the possibility of irony, to separate Marvell's praise in *The Rehearsal Transpros'd* from his blame in other works. Patterson points out, for example, the apparent parody of *First Anniversary*, "For one Thing never was by one King done" (21), in Part Two: "I will not say what one Prince may compass within his own time, or what a second, though surely much may be done" (234).

In this positive version of Charles as "born" king, Parker himself necessarily appears as an amateur or dilettante (which is, interestingly, what Charles himself tried to appear as), meddling in state affairs where he has no business, to very bad effect: "the disturbance of all Government, the misrepresenting of the generous and prudent Counsels of His Majesty, and raising a misintelligence betwixt Him and His People" (169). The last "bad effect," the separation of the king from the people, is precisely opposite to the effect the panegyrist should have, or any writer seeking the king's interest.

The negative versions of Charles are generally versions of Parker himself, from Bishop Bramhall in his *Preface* to the men of Parker's party who would be "the onely hard-hearted and inflexible Tyrants" (111). They are also grotesques of Charles as he would be if he followed Parker's advice. The curious thing about them is that they are often closely related to the *positive* portraits. They are another good illustration of the similar topoi of panegyric and satire, and of the way similar things, by virtue of their treatment, emerge as praise or blame.

On one level, since *all* these versions, negative *and* positive, are really his, Marvell seems mainly to be demonstrating, even at the expense of belief, his sheer epideictic competence. Since the negatives and positives are of the same thing, he alerts the reader, by means of this almost alarming writer's virtuosity, to the difficulty of coming to any final, true judgment of what constitutes "the good" or "the bad." This, I think, tends to preclude Charles II from being, as Anselment claims he is, "the satire's vision of true civility" (116). The proliferation of versions is also partly a problem of analogy, since the vehicles, positive and negative, appear to be responding to one another, to something like opposite polarity, more than to their respective tenors; moreover, by virtue of their neat, mathematical correspondence, they ultimately cancel one another, leaving us without means of presentation or even cognition, but with the strong sense of some definitely different but rather elusive reality.

Thus, the king who in Marvell's positive is the head of the Protestant interest, in Parker's negative version resembles the head of the Catholic interest, or at least the Grand Inquisitor: "like the Governor in *Synesius*, busied in his Cabinet among those Engines whose very names are so hard that it is some torture to name them" (60). The real torturer, Marvell reminds us later, is Parker himself, who would "put all Princes upon the Rack to stretch them to his dimension" (92). Presumably princes would have to be tortured before they would assume such powers voluntarily.

Obviously related to this version of Charles as head of the Catholic interest is the version of him as the pagan king of a foreign country, Madagascar. The implication is that, if Charles became the sort of king that Parker wants him to be, he could no longer be king of a (presumably) civilized country like *England*. For arguing that it is "safer to give a Toleration to mens Debaucheries than to their Religious Perswasions" (55), Parker becomes a decadent Roman emperor and, in that capacity, another version of Charles should he adopt Parker's absolutist position. *Debauchery Tolerated* is the name given to the first act of Parker's (or Bayes's) mock-heroic "play" in Part One; in Part Two Parker issues, in the imperial fashion "of our Princely Grace and Favour" (277), a decree (rather like Peter's in *A Tale*) granting "License to all manner of Vice and Debauchery" (277). This version of a debauched ruler granting debauchery to all, which Charles clearly must realize if he adopts Parker's policy, is oddly close to one historical version of Charles himself.

The above are all related to the version of Charles as Parker's fool, as the ridiculous clown that he becomes in Parker's hands as Parker reverses himself and "strips and disrobes them [kings] again of all those Regal Ornaments that he had superinduced upon them" (64); in this version of kings we have Charles as he would be if he had followed Parker or, more important, let Parker determine his power for him.

Just as Marvell praises Charles for belonging to the race of kings who, sometimes at the cost of hard experience, know (or would have known had they survived their experiences) how to rule, he is seen in Parker's version as praised for belonging to a race whose members did *not* know how to rule; consequently, Charles is by inference a born *misruler*. In Marvell's version (of *history*, in effect) Charles is ranked among distinguished Protestant rulers like Henry IV of France and James I and Charles I of England; in Parker's version (also a version of *history*) he would be ranked among Parker's positives (really negatives), such as the notorious *Bloody* Mary; "[U]pon her death there came in an iron Age" (305), Marvell writes, using Parker's persona, and then comments: "[A]ccording as great Princes or eminent Prelates are more or less ceremonious, so must they be ranked in your Calendar" (307).

The relatedness of the above, all really Marvell's versions, illustrates the similarity between satire and panegyric suggested by Aristotle, and the possibility that the same thing may by a turn of phrase (or some other technique of presentation or treatment, like what we encounter in the "painter-poems" and *Annus Mirabilis*) be praised or blamed. The head of one interest in panegyric remains the head, but of the opposite interest in satire; the man of virtue becomes the man of vice; the wisdom of experience merely confirms the habit of folly; the "born" king is a "born" king still, but kingship itself has changed. Marvell takes pains to turn Parker's "lines" into philippic, but his own can just as easily be changed; finally, he seems neither to *frown* nor to *smile*, but to *leer*.

5
From Cheated Sight to False Light: Analogy from Swift's "Odes" to *A Tale of a Tub*

THERE is a change in the perception of the ideal and the transcendent as we move from Swift's "Odes" to *A Tale*, from panegyric to satire. Perhaps it is reflected in the difference between line 147 of "Ode to Dr William Sancroft"—"false mediums [that] cheat our sight"—and the line "Artificial *Mediums*, false Lights, refracted angles, Varnish, and Tinsel," from page 172 of the "Digression on Madness" in *A Tale*. Insofar as the panegyrist accepts the existence of the ideal, he will understand the problem of transcendence in terms of *cheated* sight: there is something there, you just cannot see it. The satirist will tend to discount the ideal and treat the problem of transcendence differently: there is *nothing* there and *that* is what you cannot see.

The perception of the ideal (negative or positive), in any absolute sense, is impossible; we require some kind of *analogy* to approximate it. Swift's analogies succumb to gravity; they tend to illustrate vice rather than virtue. Edward Rosenheim identifies this problem in the "Ode to Sancroft," and describes Swift's attitude as "perverse Platonism":

> For Swift, on the contrary, human "knowledge" as it appears in this ode is the product of an active distortion and inversion of Truth—to such a degree that our "truth" resembles its original only enough to foster our deluded belief in our own wisdom.[1]

The analogies that should help us to understand transcendent virtues like "truth" either don't work or work in reverse, by illustrating falsehood and vice.

The entire "Ode to the King" may be regarded as one of Swift's unsuccessful vehicles of the Good, since rather than the goodness of William III (which it is clearly intended to convey as its tenor) it suggests a chasm between such goodness and the man himself. While the poet's function is to confirm the king's "delight of doing good," which is "fixed like fate among the stars," the problem is how that "delight" gets translated on earth. The first lines of "Ode to the King" say,

> Sure there's some wondrous joy in doing good;
> Immortal joy, that suffers no allay from fears,
>   Nor dreads the tyranny of years,
> By none but its possessors to be understood:
>
> (lines 1–4)

It is hard not to translate "joy in doing good" into joy in plain *winning*, especially when Swift seems to translate it thus, a little later in the same strophe: "What can the poet's humble bays / . . . Add to the victor's happiness?" (8–11). The empty pageantry of the first strophe already suggests the divorce between the ceremonial thing that kingship ought to be—in theory or "among the stars"—and the gritty, bloody reality, a split that panegyrists (according to Garrison and others) have traditionally tried to mend.

There is also, as John Irwin Fischer argues, a split between two versions of William that divides the poem itself: "The subject of the first is a king who is beyond death, fear, and even time itself, but who is unknowable. The subject of the second is a king whose deeds and character are significant precisely because they are referable to a providential design that is not only beyond his control but beyond his very understanding."[2] A problem with transcendence has fragmented even the subject of Swift's poem.

Part of the tension, which leads Fischer to read the ode as *two*, is between the apparently permanent nature of the "joy in doing good" (by which the poet means, essentially, the *thesis* that we always derive joy thus) and the nature of William's enjoyment of such joy, which is clearly impermanent and dependent on "*valour*," but which also *seems* to be more permanent than it is, coming as it does in contrast to a passage about transitory pomp. It is as if Swift would have us take (or *mistake*) for an ascription of permanence to William what, upon examination, is really an ascription of permanence to his *thesis*.

In the "Ode to Dr. William Sancroft" the problem of transcendence is treated explicitly as one of analogy. Swift asks Truth in the second strophe, "But where is even thy image on our Earth?" (17) and suggests why men can't see it:

> foolish man still judges what is best
> In his own balance, false and light,
> Following opinion, dark, and blind,
>
> (lines 54–56)

That the problem is analogical becomes explicit in Swift's obvious embarrassment at his own analogy between what the Jews did to Christ and what Sancroft's contemporaries did to him (the effect of which is to make Sancroft Christ):

> And though I should but ill be understood
> In wholly equalling our sin and theirs,
> And measuring by the scanty thread of wit
> What we call holy, and great, and just, and good,
> (Methods in talk whereof our pride and ignorance makes us use)
> And which our wild ambition foolishly compares
> With endless and with infinite;
> Yet pardon, native Albion, when I say
> Among thy stubborn sons there haunts that spirit of Jews
> That those forsaken wretches who today
> Revile his great ambassador,
> Seem to discover what they would have done
> (Were his humanity on earth once more)
> To his undoubted master, heaven's almighty son.
>
> (lines 121–34)

There are, in fact, at least two Sancrofts. The regular one "moves too high / To be observed by vulgar eye" (149–50) while the irregular one only appears so because of our own "cheated sight" (147). The tendency in this poem is for the worse to prevail.

While the two poems just cited address the difficulty of analogy, the "Ode to the Athenian Society" makes it nearly identical to the difficulty of interpretation. The elusiveness of the poem's transcendent tenor may in fact be its meaning. John Irwin Fischer sees in the poem an illustration of "the human dilemma that what is perfect in itself is necessarily blank to us" (21). In panegyric, the poet occupies a middle position between the ideal and the real, but in this poem the poet replaces the real with his own pleasant—and wildly far-fetched—imagination of it. What we end up with is a solipsistic version of a public form in which the effort to translate transcendence is supplanted by subjective daydreaming. That the almost *necessarily* nebulous Athenians, really a group of Grub Street hacks led by the notorious journalist, John Dunton, have replaced some significant figure like a king, is manifest from the number of panegyrical topics addressed to them: the "sun" topic for the renewal of learning in lines 22–24, the restoration topos, with its *prius/nunc* pattern, and the "Nile" topos, with its idea of the limitation of monarchical power.

The first strophe of Swift's poem is complicated by the fact that, while the whole may be regarded as one vehicle, it contains arbitrarily designated sections of tenor and vehicle. In a twenty-one-line analogy the "::" (or "so" in a construction "as the sun is to day, *so* the moon is to night") is stated precisely in the middle at line 11. In the designated vehicle, lines 1–10, we have vital heat, flood, mountain, universal rain, primitive sailor; in the tenor, lines 11–21, we have learning, household, sacred ark, philosophy, and dove/muse. The gist of the tenor is that after turmoil (war) learning revives, helped by philosophy; the vehicle uses the story of the resettling of the waters after the flood and the landing of the ark on Ararat. In fact, both sections of the strophe should be designated vehicles, for a tenor that is nowhere stated and never clear. As if Swift himself were doubtful of the tenor, he *laminates* it with vehicles that fail to convince us—not only of the *good* that is there, but that there is anything there at all.

The country looks "As if the universal Nile / Had rather watered it than drowned" (42–43). The Nile in turn provides an important, pivotal connection to analogical cruxes that seem to be at the center of the poem, insofar as it has one. In Swift's day the most interesting thing about the Nile, besides the fact of its regular and benign flooding, was considered to be the obscurity of its source. Thus it can be seen as connected to the young poet's "wild-excursions," his sometimes prurient curiosity, the rather cynical and debunking curiosity of the vulgar "crowd" (87), and the consequently necessary obscurity of the "Athenians," all of which are developed in the third and subsequent strophes.

There Swift remarks that praise and blame are different effects of the same cause: "want of brains" (85). Apparently we cannot even understand ill-natured wits by their effects. In the fourth strophe, the "wits" themselves can, on a more important level, see no relationship between effects and cause: "Do own the effects of Providence, / And yet deny the cause" (109-10). What Swift points to, I think, is ultimately the problem of understanding a transcendent (in his case a "cause") by its effect or, in our terms, a tenor by its vehicle.

Just as the "wits" deny major causes, they deny minor; thus, in the fifth strophe they will fail to see any relationship between the Athenians and their effects, between them and their magazine, and will "deny you to be men, or anything at all" (120). From God as cause to John Dunton seems too great a leap for the latter not to act as a reductive analogy of causation. The fears about atheistic "wits" in the fourth strophe may well represent the tenor of the poem, and the cynicism of such "wits" about the Athenians in the fifth strophe may be the vehicle for such ideas, but it is very easy for the two to be reversed, and either way the discrepancy between the tenor and vehicle, between skepticism about God and skepticism about rather nebulous "Athenians" (who are after all only Grub Street hacks), is too great not to be damaging. One *effect* of the discrepancy is to bring *analogizing* itself into disrepute, and indirectly to *deny* that a cause, at least an *important* cause, can be deduced analogically from its effect—any more than a tenor from a vehicle, the tenor of this poem especially. In the process of attempting to solve the problem analogically, Swift actually indicates its insolvability—an indication that is itself a kind of solution—by means of the poem's tenorless vehicles, which are themselves causeless effects. Swift finally appears to settle for something like agnosticism in the sixth strophe:

> But as for poor contented me
> Who must my weakness and my ignorance confess
> That I believe in much, I ne'er can hope to see;
> (lines 132–34)

He turns from rage at what others see to "contentment" at not seeing anything himself but believing regardless. But the nagging problem remains: our attitude to the "Athenians" and our attitude (if that is the word) to God have become inextricably, hopelessly confused.

From Panegyric in the "Odes" to *A Tale of a Tub*

Panegyric, in the rhetorical and generic sense elaborated by Garrison and others since the mid-70s, remains one of the least explored aspects of *A Tale of a Tub*. Although when the word is used it usually connotes just praise, here we are interested in the way the sections of *A Tale* repeatedly exploit conventions common to the genre. An awareness of these conventions, thematic and formal, and of the way they are exploited helps us to account for certain currents of solipsism that come to a head in his "Section IX."

The dedications to Somers and Prince Posterity reproduce the triadic arrangement, common to panegyric, of poet, people, and prince. In the first piece the poet is supplanted by the Bookseller (in several senses, since the Bookseller seems to have the writers entirely under his control), the prince by Lord Somers, and the people by the reader; in the second, the poet becomes the Grub Street Hack, the prince Posterity, and the people the faction of moderns the Hack is promoting. We have already seen how Swift reproduces some of the conceits of the earlier odes (in particular of the "Ode to Temple") in the first dedication. The Bookseller refers to the topics of praise as "an old beaten Story" (25) but lists the typical virtues anyway, by means of parasepiopesis (stating something while pretending not to). His initial anxiety over whom DETUR DIGNISSIMO refers to seems to be a variation on the anonymity we get in "Ode to the Athenian Society." The prince of the second dedication is strangely absent, a prince in a perpetual nonage. The "Epistle Dedicatory to Prince Posterity" may in fact be a parody of a royal instruction treatise, as it offers *A Tale* as a "faithful Abstract . . . intended wholly for your Service and Instruction" (38). This idea is alluded to again in "Section I," when the Hack refers to his "History of Renard the Fox" as the "*Apocalyps* of all State-*Arcana*" (68).

The second dedication is notable for the way the conventions of panegyric are systematically violated to discredit the Hack. The other violations are all tributary to the violation of ethos, the proof that depends on our impression of the moral character of the speaker and that, as Aristotle indicates in his *Rhetoric*, helps to convince us that what the speaker praises is really praiseworthy (17). The Hack's very language tends to undermine ethos; he frequently uses words that are traditionally to be avoided or at least to be used more cautiously in panegyric: "before the next *Revolution* of the Sun" (33) and "What *Revolutions* may happen before it shall be ready" (36) are typical slips of this sort. Elsewhere he refers to the "murderers" of the moderns as authors, thereby deflecting some of the blame onto himself, as the most conspicuous modern author present. Worse, he continually states things negatively—modern works are "never-dying" rather than "always-living"—and in defending himself he usually just states his enemies' case (his own kind of parasepiopoesis, perhaps). The violation of the reconciliation topos in the Hack's partiality to a faction (the moderns, or just modern poets) can be seen as a further strike against his character. The depiction of time as a tyrant, or rather a usurping *maître de palais*, reminds us of similar ideas in the "Ode to the King." The attempt to depict one's rival adviser as a usurper, while advising the prince oneself, is common to panegyric; but the attempt here is frustrated from the beginning. The hopelessness of the Hack's position can be seen moreover in his desiring to obtain from his prince the very thing, perhaps the only thing, the poet traditionally has to confer—fame, immortality.

The conventions of panegyric—and their violations—can be traced throughout the body of *A Tale*. In "Section I" the people of the triadic arrangement become "the crowd." The poet is represented by the ladder—"a symbol of faction and poetry"—which is clearly a violation of the reconciliation topos. The poet is also depicted as a kind of usurper "climbing up by slow Degrees" (62). The confounding of *meum* and *tuum* attributed to such poets is precisely what Marvell (a good panegyrist) accused Parker (a poor one) of doing in his *Ecclesiastical Politie*. In "Section III" the Hack writes a mock-panegyric to critics, invoking the traditional topics to praise the true critics, who are distinguished by their inability to praise. Peter, in "Section IV," is referred to as the "hero of the play," and in "Section VI" as a hero who "by gradual steps" rises to a throne. We are reminded of the uneasy combination of the heroic and the panegyric introduced by Cowley and continued by Swift himself, especially in "Ode to the King." Clearly Peter is a kind of king, and the description of his adventures comprises a kind of mock-panegyric in prose.

Analogy in *A Tale*

Of course, not all of the problems with analogy in the odes need be problems for satire, which in treating the "bad" also uses analogy; if analogy is approximate or irresistibly reductive, so much the better. Brian Vickers indicates that Swift's earlier works reflect the influence of a seventeenth-century tradition in which writers like Bacon figured prominently. For example, Vickers compares typical Baconian analogies, like "it is in praise as it is in gains" (Essay, "Of Ceremonies"), to Swiftian imitations like "It is with *Wits* as with *Razors*" (1): The beginning of the analogy, says Vickers, "is formal, and the reader thinks it is going to continue seriously—he begins to assent to the proposition—and then the trap springs" ("Swift and Bacon," 103).

Unlike such analogies, which Nilli Diengott would call explicit, the main analogy of *A Tale* slides almost immediately into identification; man is not like a suit of clothes, he *is* a suit of clothes. This fact, and Swift's comments on St. Paul's "allegories" and how they are wrongly converted into "articles of faith" (IX, 262; 66), suggests that what Swift most dislikes about analogical language is the ease with which it slips from comparison to identification. The clothes analogy clearly works on the order of identification between microcosm and macrocosm, between man and the world. Vickers says in "Analogy Versus Identity"[3] that this is the very mistake that Aquinas and like-minded thinkers (including, much later, Bacon himself) wanted to avoid. "Man has 'some' similarity with the world and, therefore, is called a microcosm; but he [Aquinas] does not say that man is, strictly speaking, such a microcosm."[4] After all, "the peculiar Talent" of the modern, writes the modern author of *A Tale*, is "fixing Tropes and Allegories to the *Letter*, and refining what is Literal into Figure and Mystery" (189–90), or, in other words, confounding analogy and identification. There is another sense to this passage, which is that the tenor of analogies tends to become just other vehicles (i.e., "letters") rather than the tenor they are supposed to help us understand (i.e., "the spirit"). According to John Clark, this is the essence of knave in the knave and fool configuration in *A Tale*; the modern knave is an allegorist, or analogist, of the letter or vehicle rather than the tenor. Consequently there is really no distinction between knave and fool in *A Tale*.

Deborah Baker Wyrick, in *Jonathan Swift and the Vested Word*,[5] calls the clothes analogy in *A Tale* "the book's root metaphor" (31). She sees in it "the problem of how and by whom or what an investiture—the word as the clothing of thought, or feeling, or intention—is given meaning" (20). Surely this remains a problem that extends beyond the scope of particular religious and social disputes over materialism and preferment (though still a part of these). Moreover, a narrow attack on materialism would not account for or even be consistent with Martin's acceptance not just of clothing but even of "corrupt" clothing in order to have any clothes at all.

Wyrick's indication in the analogy of the role of intention in determining meaning on an abstract textual level remains pertinent on other levels. Where Martin "draws the line" in preserving the coat on one hand, and ridding it of corruptions on the other, depends entirely on good faith, on his good intention to preserve a meaning that is never entirely disinterested. He must decide what the tenor of the coat is, deliberately distorted vehicle that it is. The reader must do exactly the same thing when he comes to the clothes analogy or any other part of *A Tale*. He must establish through his conscience and his judgment a tenor for this vehicle "encrusted" not just by Swift but by generations of not-so-disinterested critics. The temptation, for the "latest" critic, is no less than it was for Jack: to hate the encrusting vehicles more than he loves their tenor.

If, as Wyrick puts it, "Swift's lyrical tableau of investiture" lacks "satiric bite" (32), an opinion she shares with Edward Rosenheim and Kathleen Williams, it must be both for the reason she gives, that "the metaphor of investiture serves the concept of authoritative order" that Swift believed in, and because the bad that is the target of the satire is inseparable from the good that is not.

Authority, as Wyrick argues (supported by critics like Michael Seidel), is also paternal, and this suggests another connection with panegyric. The problems with worldliness, preferment, institutionalization, and meaning, to name but a part of the tenor of the clothes analogy, arise from the death of the first authority, God. His absence, the uncertainty (to say the least) surrounding those figures like Peter and Jack who attempt to fill it, and the resulting confusion and vertigo of *A Tale*, are all presented in terms of the corruption and even violation of the conventions of panegyric, especially of its tripartite relationship (now between writer, authority, and readership). Clark suggests that it is surely no coincidence that analogical disorder occurs in the context of the loss of authority in *A Tale*; such disorder can be seen as one consequence of "The revolt of the Renaissance and Reformation against medieval authority."[6]

The frenzy of Jack, trying to get at the tenor in the very act of destroying the vehicle, hating his brother's usurpations more than loving his father's authority, appears then to be a metaphor for the danger that continually confronts the reader (no less than the preferment-seeker): the risk of irreparably separating vehicle from tenor, of meaningless vertigo, or, to use the book's own phrase, "perpetual turning." At its most agreeable such disjunction seems merely a product of the "playfulness" remarked on by Rosenheim, when a fiction "gleefully expanded, loses its analogical dimension and acquires the character of robust comic fantasy."[7] At such moments the tenor is no longer a particular satiric target, Rosenheim suggests, but something else—perhaps just story—constructed "on the well-established foundations of anti-Puritan satire" (135). I believe, however, that the most important moments of *A Tale* are *not* playful and agree with Clark that "one might well question an examination of the *Tale*'s serious artistry that is resolved by implying that playfulness in itself is the work's end or purpose" (67). Swift's vehicles seem to be deliberately sabotaged—as opposed to accidentally in the odes—so as not to go very far before breaking down, as Clark shows in regard to the opening "parable" of the tub. The Grand Committee itself cannot arrive at a suitable tenor: *A Tale* is supposed to divert schemers, but in the analogy "whales, tubs, and even the Grand Committee itself are all so many schemers, dangerous to government; and the reader finds himself in perilous and confusing waters" (58). Clark finds a similar metaphorical confusion in the definition of wisdom. He finally suggests that wisdom, "that something of value beneath the rind, after all the pains of the journey, is in reality valueless, offensive" (59). Such an unpleasant nothingness, I would add, lurks behind all the significant analogical vehicles of *A Tale*, including, of course, the "Carcass of *Human Nature*" as it is read (dissected) by the Hack. This *nothing* is paradoxically *something* in the context of so many panegyrical schemes and topics—a surprising fulfillment of the nebulous addressees of the "Odes."

The Range of Analogy in *A Tale*

The analogies of *A Tale* range from the extended allegory of the three brothers and their coats to the concentrated analogizing in the emphasis on names and naming. These include analogies that work through inversion or reversal, through inappropriateness of the vehicle (usually due to a disturbing difference in kind or quality), and through a gradual development that seems to cause the tenor to change or reverse itself from a good thing to a bad. Such kinds are by no means distinct, and nearly all of the analogies of *A Tale* work through the identification of a vehicle with a tenor on the basis of a partial, irrelevant, or even mistaken similarity, which is after all a type of reversal.

The clothes analogy seems to have infiltrated the "Apology" of *A Tale* and even established colonies. Swift accuses the "*weightiest* Men in the *weightiest* Stations" of conniving in their humorlessness at "pulling up those very Foundations wherein all Christians have agreed." This "pulling up" is identical to Jack's ripping and tearing, and perhaps motivated more by hatred

5 / From Cheated Sight to False Light

for other brothers (Catholics) than love for the Father. While not exactly Jack, they are certainly his abettors:

> The Abuses in Religion he proposed to set forth in the Allegory of the Coats and the three Brothers, which was to make up the Body of the discourse. Those in Learning he chose to introduce by way of Digressions. ("Apology," 4)

It is curious that after speaking of the brothers' bodily garb he refers to their story as a body. The book or "discourse" clothes their story just as their coats clothe their bodies, and as their church "clothes" their lives. *A Tale* is itself implicitly a coat, a "vehicle." This early emphasis on surfaces helps prepare us for the "findings" of the sect of "tailor-worshippers" of "Section III," which all stem from an abuse of analogical relationships. In the preference for the surfaces of things, for vehicles over tenors, all they appreciate is the superficial aspect of things. Thus their "findings" disturb, not always because they are false but because they are incomplete. Their failure to arrive at knowledge, or worse, to arrive at *true* knowledge, stems from a greater failure to understand the inherent nature of analogical knowledge. Partial knowledge mistaken for complete knowledge makes for a tremendous falsehood probably worse than plain ignorance. Thus the wrongness of their assertion that the universe is "a large *Suit of Cloaths*" derives from taking as complete the incomplete knowledge provided by an analogy between the way "the Earth is invested by the Air; the Air is invested by the Stars" and the way the body is covered by layers of clothing. Thus like the Hack himself they consistently identify the vehicle with the tenor. These postulates being admitted, as the Hack says, or allowing a whole series of identifications to be made on the basis of slight similarities, it is possible to remake man as a kind of sartorial Frankenstein, patched together out of a whole series of stolen parts; but the result is considerably less viable than even that monster.

Still, the reader's sense of the impropriety of the Hack's procedure is probably complicated and maybe even blunted by having encountered just such monsters in positions of authority and respect. It is hard for the reader not to implicate himself in the Hack's obviously very foolish mental processes, especially given the element of truth that they *seem* to discover. But this occurs on a height fathoms above the Hack himself, who remarks with an air of cheerful, uncritical discovery that "so, an apt Conjunction of Lawn and black Sattin we intitle a *Bishop*" (sec. 2, 79). The hack can no more *feel* the truth of this than the falsehood. He himself resembles the tailor-worshippers—could even be one with his own obvious preoccupation with the surfaces of things. Some of the uneasiness one feels reading the Hack's description of the sect stems from the impression created by his presentation there and elsewhere that he is in some ways himself a member of this sect; one readily perceives through his dark mystifying prose that the "idol" is in fact just a tailor.

The description of the tailor-worshippers' analogical abuses is itself a vehicle, of course, for the similar abuses perpetrated by the brothers on their coats. They proceed the same way, identifying vehicle with tenor on the basis of slight and arbitrarily chosen similarity. Their procedure is complicated somewhat by the existence of the father's will, but this proves no major obstacle once they begin. Just as the tailor-worshippers eventually assemble a man from the pieces, namely the vehicles of violated analogies, they assemble a word (S.H.O.U.L.D.E.R.) from the letters of other words. Like the tailor-worshippers' soulless "man," this "word," in terms of the father's will at least (which comprises after all, all the terms that matter), has no tenor. Eventually they obtain desired vehicles from other less legitimate sources, or get rid of undesirable vehicles by giving them false tenors, as when they ignore the injunction against "fringe" by deciding that "fringe" means broomsticks—another false identification based on partial and indeed rather selective similarities.

The Hack's procedure with *critic* is not unlike the brothers' with *fringe*. He too dispenses with the obvious tenor ("such Persons as invented or drew up Rules for themselves and the World, by observing which, a careful Reader might be able to pronounce upon the Productions of the *Learned*" [sec. 3, 92]), but substitutes for it one derived from the spurious identifications of other analogies by virtue of which the critic, in some ways like a collector of faults, becomes indeed "*a Discoverer and Collector of Writers Faults*" (sec. 3, 95). By a typical reversal of tenor and vehicle, the "true critic" actually becomes the faults, or "an *Abstract* of the *Criticisms* themselves have made" (sec. 3, 96). The Hack can now read history exactly as the brothers read the will, by ignoring obvious meanings and substituting others derived from faulty procedures. The brothers and the Hack treat all texts as their own. Their selfishly motivated substitution of obvious tenors by abstruse ones derived from the vehicles-become-tenors of other analogies mentally prepares us for the reversals of the ancients versus moderns controversy (as when, in "Section V," he criticizes Homer for not having read the moderns, effectively making *them* the ancient and Homer the modern). It also prepares us for all the other "great revolutions" (sec. 4, 50) of *A Tale*, which include such diverse events as the hack's despotic placement of a preface (sec. 5) in the middle of the book to Peter's overthrow of Constantine and Jack's overthrow of Peter and, finally, "great" men's overthrow of their reason.

The brothers' sartorialism seems to be reflected in the Hack's obsession with outwardness (always disguised as a desire for inwardness and profundity), as when he remarks,

> I have some Time since, with a World of Pains and Art, dissected the Carcass of *Humane Nature*, and read many useful Lectures upon the several Parts, both *Containing* and *Contained*; till at last it *smelt* so strong, I could preserve it no longer. Upon which, I have been at a great Expence to fit up all the Bones with exact Contexture, and in due Symmetry, so that I am ready to show a compleat Anatomy thereof to all curious *Gentlemen and others*. (Section 5, 123).

The Hack's vehicle of a dissecting session for his analysis of human nature suggests that human nature, at least for him, is a rotting corpse. For us the analogy suggests, among other things, the offensiveness of the Hack's version of humanity and the offensiveness of his treatment, his technique. The vehicle is surprising in that, as *dissection*, it suggests inwardness and meaningfulness, which I identify with the tenor, at the same time it is consistent with all the other analogies of the hack in its overemphasis on exuberant and even runaway presentation. The vehicle is also, I think, highly paradoxical in that it employs a vehicle for depth (of sorts) in what is after all a most materialistic and hence (I think it is fair to say) superficial presentation of human nature.

Of course, the Hack has probably confused things by mixing metaphors or mixing analogies. A vehicle for a movement from inside to outside has been used for a movement from physical to spiritual; consequently, what ought to suggest spirituality or spiritual things (the essence of human nature) suggests instead just more internal physical things.[8] Similarly, the skeleton that he reassembles after his analysis suggests not the essence that he supposedly was after but instead something reductive and even grotesque. What he offers as the final result of this dissection, the old cliché about instruction and diversion, is neither. And he forces this into the same inside-outside vehicle as the spiritual and the physical, a kind of Horatian sandwich: "with a *Layer* of *Utile* and a layer of *Dulce*" (sec. 5, 124).

The tailor-worshippers' use or abuse of analogy anticipates the wind-worshippers or Aeolists of "Section VIII"—indeed, provides an intertextual vehicle for them. The spirit of the world may in some ways be like wind, but it is not wind. The Aeolists' wind is the madmen's vapors in "Section IX"— though I admit this is itself an identification based on similarity. The madmen's zeal of "Section IX" should be compared to Jack's in "Section VI." It is their zeal that leads the madmen to innovate and form schools and philosophies, just as Jack's leads him to found the Aeolists. And their zeal is for "things impossible to be known" (sec. 9, 166) or "Things Invisible" (sec. 9, 169), like Jack's for a pristine coat, a tenor he can never arrive at, or like those things (such as goodness) that are traditionally the object of analogy. Like the sartorialists, like the Aeolists, like the Hack himself in his analyses, the madmen seem to have constructed whole systems out of partial and indeed slight similarities.

Swift demonstrates considerable skill at analogizing, through a character singularly inept at it even though it is something he consciously endeavors to excel at:

> [T]he *Grubaean* Sages have always chosen to convey their Precepts and their Arts, shut up within the Vehicles of Types and Fables, which having been perhaps more careful and curious in adorning than was altogether necessary, it has fared with these Vehicles after the usual Fate of Coaches over-finely painted and gilt; that the transitory Gazers have so dazzled their Eyes, and fill'd their Imaginations with the outward Lustre, as neither to regard nor consider, the Person or the Parts of the Owner within." (Introduction to *A Tale*, 66).

The Hack complains about the overemphasis on presentation, on the vehicular side of things, with a vehicle that has clearly got away from him (though not, of course, from Swift). He is clearly not the one for the task he has undertaken, of "untwisting and unwinding" Grub Street works. His confession that he is "somewhat liberal in the Business of Titles" refers not just to paratextual matters like the "Treatises written by the Author" at the start of *A Tale* but also more generally, I think, to his preference for names, indeed for all aspects of signification over things signified.

The arbitrariness of these analogical procedures is not unlike simple naming, a theme the *Tale* anticipates as early as the "Apology." There Swift complains that, while out of respect he forbears to name his hoped-for protectors and actual detractors, they "fix a Name upon the Author of this Discourse" (6) and to works that he never wrote. This concern with names, part of the larger concern with arbitrary signification and imbalanced presentation pertinent to analogy, is carried over into the Bookseller's arbitrary use and abuse of titles both literary and aristocratic: he cares no more for Lord Somers, the dedicatee of *A Tale*, than for the book itself, of which he admits "I am altogether a Stranger to the Matter" (23). Similarly the Hack's list of subscribers' names tends to become just a series of "tenorless vehicles" as the poets' works and the poets themselves are forgotten by time: "I am preparing a Petition to *Your Highness*, to be subscribed with the Names of one hundred thirty six of the first Rate, but whose immortal Productions are never likely to reach your Eyes" (33). His manipulation of names and titles is as arbitrary as the Bookseller's, only less successful, and certainly less *profitable*. His one solution for modern obscurity—of validating their titles by limiting them to the immediate present—is clearly no solution at all. He says in a piece addressed to posterity: "[W]hat I am going to say is literally true this Minute I am writing" (Posterity, 36).

This foundation of truthfulness on the sheer *assertion* of its signification should be counted among the "common Privileges of a Writer" claimed by the Hack. The devices may be as uncommon and extravagant as those attributed by Marvell to Parker, such as the "understanding" that "whatever word or Sentence is Printed in a different Character shall be judged to contain something extraordinary either of *Wit* or *Sublime*" (Preface, 47). In other words, meaning may be affected (even *effected*) by typeface. *That* the text means is all it indicates, never *what*. The latter is arguably the writer's jurisdiction, the former the reader's. He abnegates one to usurp the other. Meaning's reduction to a matter of the writer's assertion establishes the validity of self-praise as merely a form of *self*-assertion. The absence or presence of any quality can be asserted just as the absence or presence of meaning itself: "[W]hen an Author makes his own Elogy, he uses a certain Form to declaire and insist upon his Title, which is commonly in these or the like Words, '*I speak without vanity*'" (Preface, 47). The Hack's vehicle for the modern right to self-praise is a lump sum received by those who formerly received just the interest from it. Such beneficiaries acquire complete control at the expense of not having anything to control. The analogy brings us back to the Hack's initial and indeed fundamental dilemma, of making meaning entirely a matter of assertion, or arbitrary signification.

The vehicle of the "Fee Simple" illustrates both modern self-praise and the "common Privileges of the Writer." A more general discussion of praise and blame follows in Swift's text.. Satirists are to their public what pedants are to their naughty students. They "first expostulate the Case, then plead the Necessity of the Rod from great Provocations, and conclude every Period with a Lash" (Preface, 48). Like the boys' bottoms, the "World's Posteriors" become callous. One might well ask, Just what are the "World's Posteriors"? The Hack wishes that satire may at least be as oblivious to the world as the world is to it. Consistently with other things in *A Tale*, satire "triumphs" at the cost of anything to triumph over. Curiously, his analogy of the razor ("it is with *Wits* as with *Razors*, which are never so apt to *cut* those they are employ'd on, as when they have *lost their Edge*" [Preface, 49]) seems almost to reverse its tenor as it develops. Dull razors cut the face by cutting hair awkwardly, and so cannot stand for dull wits, which presumably would not cut at all; but perhaps Swift is making a distinction between good satire and bad along the lines of Dryden's. Without further elaboration the analogy seems to begin as a vehicle for bad satire and end as a vehicle for good. Analogies in *A Tale* have both specific and complementary general application, mainly because one of the main tenors of *A Tale* is analogy itself.

It is important that all this analogical abuse occurs in the context of much discussion of panegyric and satire. Indeed, the confusion over good and bad indicated by blame delivered as praise and vice versa has much to do with the inversions of tenors and vehicles described above. For one, the analogical abuses create an atmosphere of topsy-turviness in which one *expects* other reversals. Moreover, Swift seems to imply that where such analogical reversals occur others *ought* to be expected. Indeed, when identification is based on spurious similarities it is extremely easy to make the bad the good or vice versa. One simply bases the identification on a spurious similarity to the appropriate vice or virtue—the Aeolists' wind, the madmen's vapors. No doubt the sheer epistemological uncertainty created by Swift's manipulation of analogy also creates an uncertainty about the possibility of knowing good and bad, but such uncertainty lies entirely with the reader. The point may be that one *ought* to be uncertain, whereas the Hack is not only certain about good and bad but convinced that what he is writing contains not "one grain of Satyr intermixt" (Preface, 48). At its most abstract level, Swift's satire seems to be of the epistemological certainty of good and evil on which satire is based.

5 / FROM CHEATED SIGHT TO FALSE LIGHT 123

Whereas "cheated sight" seems to have rendered old virtues less accessible, false light and delusion discover new virtues—really just new kinds of "unpleasant nothingness"—by means of analogy. The Aeolists' elevation of wind to a virtue in "Section VII," like the tailor-worshippers' elevation of clothes or the philosophers' elevation of trinity, prepares us for the treatment of princes. As "unpleasant nothings" are elevated into virtues, so men deemed great in past ages are seen to be great for . . . well, nothing—indicating that something more sinister than a simple inversion has taken place. The tenor of virtue itself has changed, causing the tenor of "princes" to change with it. Thus the princes of panegyric are exposed as madmen; they are "Persons, whose natural Reason hath admitted great Revolutions" (162), and who should not be surprised at revolution in their states. The assassination topos, so negative in panegyric, here becomes at least a necessary remedy, a cure for the "nothing" in princes that drives them to bother their subjects:

> In the midst of all these Projects and Preparations; a certain *State-Surgeon*, gathering the Nature of the Disease by these Symptoms, attempted the Cure, at one Blow performed the Operation, broke the Bag, and out flew the *Vapour*; nor did anything want to render it a complete Remedy, only, that the Prince unfortunately happened to Die in the Performance. (164)

The reconciliation kings were expected to achieve is replaced by madmen, each with "Parties after his particular Notions" (171). They are as exclusive and chauvinistic as the other system makers of *A Tale* or as "Learning" seems to be in the "Ode to the Athenians":

> Learning's little household did embark
> With her world's fruitful system in her sacred Ark,
>
> (lines 12–13)

Finally, the ceremonial, public aspect of panegyric, the feeling of spaciousness, of poet addressing a head of state before some vast national gathering, seems to be deliberately frustrated in the microcosmic Bedlam, with its representative "officers in a state, ecclesiastical, civil, and military." It is no longer strictly an analogy at all, but an identification.

6
The Preface as Vehicle in *A Tale of a Tub:*
The Panegyrical Paratext (2)

I.

NOUS sommes au seuil d'une époque paratextuelle, au seuil d'un seuil, stationnés à la frontière d'un moment exégétique, 'dispositionnel,' qui privilégie les marges, s'y institue, s'en fait partie," declares Richard L. Barnett, rather grandly, in his *avant-propos* to a recent issue of *L'Ésprit Créateur* devoted entirely to aspects of "paratextuality."[1] For the following discussion of prefaces in Swift and Marvell, I have used terminology developed by Gérard Genette in his aptly titled *Seuils* (1987)[2] as a part of his "paratextual" emphasis. Genette defines "le paratexte" as "ce par quoi un texte se fait livre et se propose comme tel à ses lecteurs, et plus généralement au public" (7). The paratext is a "seuil," a threshold between the inside ("le texte") and the outside ("le discours du monde sur le texte" [8]), comprised of "épitexte" and "péritexte." The "épitexte" is "tous les messages qui se situent, au moins à l'origine, à l'extérieur du livre" (10–11); the "péritexte" is all messages "autour du texte" (10). Here I will deal mainly with one aspect of the "péritexte," the preface, as it is described by Genette in *Seuils* and as it appears in Marvell's *Rehearsal Transpros'd*[3] and Swift's *Tale of a Tub*.[4]

Genette defines the preface (succinctly) as "toute espèce de texte liminaire (préliminaire ou postliminaire)" (150). It is, both by virtue of its function and its (usual) placement before the text of a book, a threshold (Genette treats it as only one of many "thresholds," like titles, footnotes, endnotes, glosses, etc.). While not itself a boundary, or at least not a "water-tight" (7) one, as Genette remarks, it is frequently concerned with establishing interpretive boundaries and guidelines out of which the reader, like modern wit in *A Tale*, is warned not to "stray the breadth of a Hair, upon peril of being lost" (43). Even if we choose to ignore such boundaries, in a sense, by the very "choosing," we admit that we cannot utterly ignore them. This is the reason that prefacers often seem to attach such importance to what they say, as if they felt they had to say something and on that something depended interpretive order, if not the future of Western civilization, too. In a sense, in their small but sometimes not-so-modest way, prefacers *are* staving off interpretive chaos; they are really registering the fact that if not very much more than some prefaced text is at stake, very much more is at play.

Genette's use of a term like "seuils" for such things as prefaces indicates, I think, the modern realization that such things are *not* distinct from their texts but may, in fact, *be* the text. The attempt on the part of critics like Genette to systematize such things follows naturally from the exploitation of them by significant modern (or postmodern) writers, who attempt to expand *outward* from the text and, as Luiz Fernando Valente says in an article on Guimaraes Rosa's prefaces to *Tutameia*, "open a dialogue with other texts by the author."[5] For Borges the preface in particular represents a kind of ideal:

> To compose vast texts is a laborious and diminishing extravagance; that of expounding in five hundred pages an idea whose perfect oral exposition takes a few minutes. A better device is to pretend that those books already exist and to offer a summary, a commentary.[6]

In several collections of prefaces from Henry B. Wheatley's *Dedication of Books to Patron and Friend* (1887)[7]—which he describes in his own preface as "the first instance of a book being entirely devoted to the history of this topic" (v)—to Guy R. Lyle's *Praise from Famous Men: An Anthology of Introductions* (1977),[8] a common hallmark of the preface is precisely this interpretive anxiety. Wheatley's examples illustrate well how the dedicatee in a prefatory dedication could be used to dispel anxiety in the reader, if not altogether in the writer; clearly the dedicatee was also intended to influence the reading from the start, if only by giving the writer—and his book—a preliminary recommendation (Genette would say "valorization"). One Dr. Turner, dedicating his *Herbal* to Queen Elizabeth, mentions just this function, something—typically, considering the eventual prominence of booksellers in these things—his printer suggested:

> The Printer had geven me warninge there wanted nothinge to the settinge oute of my hole Herbal saving only a Preface, wherein I might require some both mighty and learned Patron to defend my labours against

> spitefull and envious enemies to all mennis doyinges saving their owne, and declare my good minde to him that I am bound unto by dedicating and geving these my poore labours unto him. (52)

Herbert Grierson, in *The Personal Note* (1946),[9] a collection of prefaces and postfaces intended to illustrate "personal feelings, which have been kept in check in the effort to be objective or conciliatory" (2), reprints Jonson's dedication of *Volpone*, in which, sounding a very Swiftian note (or does Swift rather sound a Jonsonian note?), he protests

> I know, that nothing can be so innocently writ or carried, but may be made obnoxious to construction; marry, whilst I bear mine innocence about me, I fear it not. (39)

and complains

> Application is now grown a trade with many; and there are that profess to have a key for the deciphering of everything: but let wise and noble persons take heed how they be too credulous, or give leave to these invading interpreters to be overfamiliar with their fames, who cunningly and often utter their own virulent malice under other men's simplest meanings. (39–40)

These are, in fact, instances of what Genette describes for us as directions "how to read" (194). There are many other instances of it, such as Donne's preface to *Biathanatos* (where not judging harshly can be seen in terms of the subject [suicide], the treatment [*Biathanatos*], and Christian charity), and Johnson's famous preface to *A Dictionary of the English Language* (where he, too, wants charity in the reader, but also—in the reading—some fraction of the diligence that went into the writing):

> [A] few wild blunders, and risible absurdities, from which no work of such multiplicity was ever free, may for a time furnish folly with laughter, and harden ignorance into contempt; but useful diligence will at last prevail, and there never can be wanting some who distinguish desert; who will consider that no dictionary of a living tongue ever can be perfect. (91)

The idea of the preface occurs often enough (and usually in vivid, metaphorical language) in *The Rehearsal Transpros'd* to be thematic, if not ubiquitous, and in *A Tale of a Tub* prefatory pieces comprise the first five parts (six, if one counts "The Introduction"), "Section V: A Digression in the Modern Kind," which performs functions "proper in a preface," and "Section X: A Further Digression," which acts like a postface although it is only the penultimate section.

Perhaps the "learned reader," already impatient with loitering on the threshold, would be appalled to know that even before Marvell's day it was possible to make a career out of reading just prefaces, as Archbishop Laud is said to have done. His job was "to look over Epistles Dedicatory and Prefaces to the Reader" and (anticipating Swift's "true critic") "see what fault may be found" (127). In our day it is still possible for critics like Gérard Genette to do almost the same thing and sound rather like Swift's Hack, "just come from perusing some hundreds of Prefaces" (45): "Parmi les nombreuses préfaces que j'ai eu l'occasion de lire en vue de cette étude...." (184).

The Rehearsal Transpros'd and *A Tale of a Tub* sometimes present themselves as books only in the bookseller's sense of so many bound paper objects to be sold.[10] In the deeper sense of book as metaphor for wisdom and knowledge, like the Bible or Homer's epics, they do not appear to be books at all but self-conscious accretions of the conventions of which books are made but which do not make books—not, at least, in the highest sense. The most salient of these conventions, and the one that finally comes to stand—I think—as a metaphor for all the others, is the preface. As Genette remarks in the conclusion to his discussion of prefaces in *Seuils*, "[L]a préface est peut-être, de toutes les pratiques littéraires, la plus typiquement littéraire, parfois au meilleur, parfois au pire sens" (270).

Marvell's "animadversions" on Parker's preface, virtually a reading of it with and through Marvell's eyes,[11] really comprise a satirical preface to Parker's entire *oeuvre*, devalorizing where Parker valorized, and worse, devalorizing Parker himself. The various "lies" that Parker is faulted for in his preface discredit him in the main body of his other works. In Genette's terms, his paratext is made—retroactively—to corrupt his text, or, in Marvell's language: "I am sure our Author had died no other death but of this his own *Preface*... if the swelling of Truth could have choak'd him" (13).

The preface is also, both in Marvell and in much earlier polemicists, closely connected to the issue of religious ceremonies in particular, and religious ridicule in general. The preface can quite naturally be seen as a formal abuse in literature, on the part of those wanting to impose formal abuses in religious matters; moreover, as a kind of dressing of the text it prefaces, it nicely connects with the sartorial nature of some of these abuses. As discussed in chapter 4, Parker's prefaces encrust other men's works the way the ceremonies they are written in defense of encrust Christianity.

In *A Tale of a Tub* the preface comes to represent that awful condition in which literariness and talk about literature have actually cankered literature itself. The abuse of the surface has become profound, in a way that can best be understood in terms of a confusion of vehicle and tenor. The distance between who is talking and what he is talking about ultimately collapses. From the egotistical Parker prefacing the vindication of a dead bishop (who comes increasingly to resemble the egotistical Parker himself), to the self-sufficient Hack writing about nothing because all he can write about is what is in himself—and *he* is empty—is a short but telling distance.

The preface itself expresses what is arguably the central theme of *A Tale*, the relationship (or want of relationship) between container and contained (to use Korkowski's terms)[12] or between vehicle and tenor (to use Richards's).[13] The same theme is expressed in what Wyrick[14] (and others) have identified as the main metaphor, the clothes analogy, effectively introduced by the prefaces of *A Tale*, with their inherent sartorialism. Clearly the numerous prefatory pieces of *A Tale* emphasize the "vehicular side" of things—what means over what is meant. Clearly this too can be seen as a development of the contentious literature of the seventeenth century and, certainly in Parker's case, of the anxiety of partisans to show not just the meaning of the work but rather to determine how that meaning can be reapplied or enlisted to their cause, mainly by redirecting it in a preface. The risk of such procedure, is that with every additional "redirection" or "remeaning" a bit of the original gets lost—a "piece of the main." This precipitates a crisis for panegyric, at least for the paratextual kind that occurs in dedications and prefaces, since its tripartite structure requires clear distinctions between the parts, between who means (the poet) and who is meant (the prince).

Genette, in *Seuils*, describes the emergence of the preface, its gradual separation from the text, as a print-related phenomenon (152). It is, moreover, linked to the translation and dissemination of classical texts in the modern era (243), and is therefore an important means of cultural appropriation and assimilation.[15] Genette remarks that this appropriation could be opportunistic, a chance to "déborder quelque peu l'objet prétendu de son discours au profit d'une cause plus vaste, ou éventuellement toute différente" (250).

Opportunism is precisely what Marvell accuses Parker of in his *Preface Shewing what grounds there are of Fears and Jealousies of Popery* (1672) prefixed to Bishop Bramhall's *Vindication of himself and the Episcopal Clergy from the Presbyterian Charge of Popery*. The immediate target of Marvell's satire is naturally the preface, for the above reasons and because the book he is attacking *is* one. Marvell wonders "whether the Author made his Preface for Bishop *Bramhal's dear sake*, or whether he published the Bishop's Treatise for sake of his *own dear Preface*" (9). From Buckingham's play, *The Rehearsal*, Marvell borrows the point that Bayes's prologue could equally be an epilogue: "I do not see but the Preface might have past as wel for a Postscript, or the Headstal for a Crooper" (9). He compares it to a horse whose motion may be directed by the head or the tail. Marvell imagines a game of leap-frog as, in subsequent editions, the preface and the "Vindication" proper trade places, now Parker first, now the bishop. The disjunction of the preface and the work is further seen in the remark that it is merely "the Tap-droppings of his *Defence*" (38). In other words, the preface is not merely unrelated to Bramhall's work, but unrelated to Bramhall's precisely because it is related to Parker's own. Parker's preface to Bramhall is really a thinly disguised postface to his latest book..

Marvell calls Parker "Bayes" after Dryden's caricature in *The Rehearsal*. It is unlucky for Parker, but quite lucky for Marvell, that Bramhall in his "Vindication" had identified a "*cursed Bay-tree*" (a metaphor for insistence on transforming indifferent opinions into necessary articles of faith) as the "*cause of all our brawling and contention*" (99). Thus Marvell establishes the basis for the relationship between Parker's preface and its text, and instead of allowing the "Vindication" to support the policy advanced in the preface, he has it actually subvert it—and by means of the prefacer's very name!

That Marvell is conscious that this kind of opportunism has been facilitated by print is made clear by the metaphorical treatment of printing on nearby pages:

O *Printing!* how hast thou disturb'd the Peace of Mankind! that Lead, when moulded into Bullets, is not so mortal as when founded into Letters! There was sure a mistake in the story of *Cadmus*; and the Serpents Teeth which he sowed, were nothing else but the Letters which he invented. (5)

Before the printed text the function of the preface ("préface intégrée") was assumed by the first few lines if it was poetry (as in the classical invocation) or the first few paragraphs if it was prose (as in Herodotus's *History* or Lucian's *True History*). The prologue of tragedy (which preceded the chorus) is not a preface in Genette's sense of "avertissement au public" [154], but the prologue to a comedy like Plautus's *Amphitryon* is ("commentaire bonimenteur" [154] was evidently inappropriate to tragic dignity). Genette and Swift would have concurred then, in attributing the "Invention, or at least the Refinement of *Prologues*" (*Tale*, 101) to the theater. That Marvell should have been inspired to his parody of Parker's *Preface* partly by Buckingham's play, *The Rehearsal*, is no mere coincidence, given that the comic use of prefaces (or prologues, nearly the same thing) was part of a dramatic tradition:

> Bayes: Now, gentlemen, I would fain ask your opinion of one thing. I have made a prologue and an epilogue which may serve for either (that is, the prologue for the epilogue, or the epilogue for the prologue—do you mark? Nay, they may both serve too, I gad, for any other play as well as this . . . I come out in a long black veil, and a great, huge hangman behind me, with a furred cap and his sword drawn; and there tell 'em plainly that if, out of good nature, they will not like my play, I gad, I'll e'en kneel down, and he shall cut my head off.
>
> (act 1, scene 1)[16]

I cannot resist reproducing here Bouilhet's remark from the preface (Flaubert's) to *Dernières Chansons*: "Il se serait pendu plutôt que d'écrire une préface" (245).

This transposition of prologue and epilogue is but one of many transpositions in *The Rehearsal*, the first being of prose and verse:

> Bayes: I take a book in my hand . . . if there be any wit in't . . . I transverse it: that is, if it be prose, put it into verse (but that takes up some time), and if it be verse, put it into prose.
>
> Johnson: Methinks, Mr. Bayes, that putting verse into prose should be called transprosing.
>
> (act 1, scene 1)

Transposing, with its punning connection through transversing to transprosing, is fundamental to Marvell's technique in applying the mock-heroics of a play (itself a burlesque of heroic drama) to a burlesque of Parker's "Preface" and a satire of his theology. This transposition of preface and epilogue, back and front, becomes the motive metaphor in Marvell's *Rehearsal Transpros'd*, generating most of the other mock-heroic ones:

> Here you might see one put on his Helmet the wrong way: there one buckle on a Back in place of a Breast. Some by mistake catched up a Socinian or Arminian Argument, and some a Popish to fight a Papist. (120)

The most common, and important, transposition Parker is seen to make in his preface is that of praise into blame and blame into praise. This amounts to a failure of what Genette sees as the principal function of this type of preface ("préface allographe"), "recommandation" (246). Parker himself seems to be aware that this is his task. That the following has already been quoted in the context of a different dispute (religious ceremony) suggests the economy of Marvell's technique:

> *The ensuing Treatise of Bishop* Bramhall's *being somewhat superannuated, the* Bookseller *was solicitous to have it set off with some Preface that might recommend it to the Genius of the Age and reconcile it to the present juncture of affairs.* (4)

Besides sartorialism, in this kind of recommendation Marvell sees mainly a mistaken and self-serving condescension:

> A pretty task indeed: That is as much to say, To trick up the good old Bishop in a yellow Coif and a Bulls-head, that he might be fit for the Publick and appear in Fashion. (4)

Worse, Parker fails to heed Aristotle's implicit warning, in his discussion of praise and blame in his *Rhetoric*,[17] that the difference between vice and virtue, for the hearer or the reader at least, can be entirely a matter of shading or emphasis ("the choleric and passionate man may be spoken of as frank and open, the arrogant as magnificent and dignified") (97). Parker says of Bramhall,

> *Tis true, the Church of* Ireland *was the largest scene of his Actions; but yet there, in a little time, he wrought out such wondrous Alterations, and so exceeding all belief, as may convince us that he had a mind large and active enough to have managed the Roman Empire at its greatest extent.* (12)

Praising is intended to promote a course of action, and this praise (or panegyric) ends as unintentional satire. "Mr *Bayes* [Parker] at any time, will make the same thing serve for a Panegyrick or a Philippick" (24), Marvell remarks, recalling again the transposition of epilogue and prologue. Such praise fails at something else very important to its kind of epideictic rhetoric: the ethical kind of proof, the creation of a good impression of the speaker's (or the writer's) character. We know that Bramhall really was none of the things Parker describes (which is just as well), so we suspect that what the description represents is Parker's own ego-maniacal self.

Marvell's subsequent exploitation of Parker's failure at praise enables him to depict Parker as a madman whose "head runs upon nothing but Romane Empire and Ecclesiastical Policy" (29) and to devastate the panegyric he elsewhere addresses to the king. Marvell himself, of course, uses praise moderately and skilfully to further his cause, writing the kind of deliberative panegyric that Aristotle suggests in the *Rhetoric* ("if you desire to praise, look what you would suggest; if you desire to suggest, look what you would praise" [103]):

> And you Mr. *Bayes* [Parker], had you lived in the days of *Augustus Caesar* ... would not you have made, think you, an excellent Privy Counsellour? His Father too was murdered ... And His Majesty ... will in all probability not be so forward to hearken to your advice as to follow their Example ... Kings have, I doubt, a shrewd understanding with them. (108)

Finally, Marvell transposes Parker's *Preface* in a much more important way than suggesting it "might have past as wel for a Postscript, or the Headstal for a Crooper" (9). He transposes its ideas, which are already topsy-turvy, and so restores order:

> Our Author translates Joy to *Chearfulness*, Peace to *Peaceableness*, and Faith to *Faithfulness*: What ignorance, or rather, what Forgery is this of Scripture and Religion? ... Joy is not Chearfulness, but that *Spiritual Joy which is unspeakable* ... Peace is not Peaceableness in his Sense, but *that Peace of God which through Jesus Christ is wrought in the heart of Believers by the Holy Ghost* ... Faith in God is there intended not faithfulness in our Duties, Trusts or Offices. (87)

The above is arguably less transposition than translation, but remembering the myth of Cadmus above, it is apparent that the two are related. Transposing a few letters may result in a significant translation, the letters of the alphabet being relatively few (especially compared to the number of letters in print):

the transposition only of a letter a, another time in the name of a goat, by some called *Crabe,* and by others *Cabre,* was the loss of more men's lives than the distinguishing but by an Aspiration in *Shiboleth* upon the like occasion. (103)

One gets from the above and similar passages in *The Rehearsal Transpros'd* the sense of a relatively small number of limitations and conventions capable of infinite and infinitely dangerous permutation. In a work intended to explode a particular preface, the preface itself becomes the central metaphor for a synchrony of conventions that extend from the alphabet to God. Of course, if such transpositions are both easier to create and more dangerous in a post-Gutenberg world, they are also easier to correct (provided that the press is free).

I think it is the sense of access to convention facilitated by print that accounts for Marvell's notable neutrality regarding convention itself. Much of Marvell's argument consists of exposing the establishment archdeacon as an intensely unconventional man ("Why he gives us a new Translation of the Bible, and a new Commentary" [93]). Convention is generally a good thing, and the conventional world of print is no exception. Marvell mocks Parker's complaint against the press ("such is the mischief, that a Man cannot write a Book but presently he is answered" [5]) and defends linguistic convention ("even *Augustus Caesar,* though he was so great an Emperour, and so valiant a man in his own person, was used to fly from a new word" [103]). Finally, the extreme literariness of *The Rehearsal Transpros'd,* in its quotations from classical authors as well as church fathers, from plays, etc., seems to belie if not preclude any real contempt for that most literary of conventions, the preface.

II.

The hypocrisy of the print-oriented man who declaims in a preface against other print-oriented men is exploited by Swift in the preface to *A Tale of a Tub,* in the story of the fat man in Leicester Fields. Those who complain about the press of writers should consider that if they would "bring [their] own Guts to a reasonable Compas" there would be "room enough for us all" (46). One difference, of course, is that the fat man complaining about the "press" (the word becomes something of a pun in the context) doesn't stand for an individual like Parker, but for a typical patron. The difference, though small in itself, is typical of Swift's far greater cynicism about convention. The preface continues to provide a focus and a major (if not *the* major) metaphor for the discussion, but the treatment of convention is both more exhaustive and more nihilistic than it is in *The Rehearsal Transpros'd*.

Some of the best examples of the exploitation of the preface in Swift's own time are found in Robert Boyle's *Works* (1772).[18] *The Works* bristle with prefaces, advices, advertisements, and postscripts, as well as occasional digressions and animadversions, just as one imagines Boyle's desk must have bristled with scientific apparatuses (like that displayed on the title page, perhaps). The paratextual "apparatus," in particular the liminary texts, is as haphazard and ongoing as the enquiries it attempts to surround. Indeed, such enquiries seem to require an elaborate apparatus, both scientific and literary, as if no less is needed to make the book than to conduct the experiment. Swift is indebted to Boyle in the same sense that he is to John Dunton—almost as much as to Marvell. Boyle in turn is also clearly indebted to Marvell and other polemicists. Indeed, his very nervousness in his prefaces about *avoiding* polemics betrays the polemical nature of his writing, as well as a preoccupation with religion.[19]

I have no space here to undertake a detailed description of Boyle's paratexts, but a few examples should suffice to indicate the connections between Boyle and *A Tale*. Boyle's *Excellency of Theology Compared with Natural Philosophy* begins, like *A Tale*, with "The Publisher's Advertisement to the Reader." This piece functions like an apology: the bookseller undertakes to excuse the lack of what we call today "acknowledgment of sources," because the work was written some time before (1665), when there was a plague going on (not to mention the Second Dutch War), and the author had "frequently to pass from place to place, unaccompanied with most of his books" (1). (The idea of Boyle writing a defense of theology while dodging *bacilli* strikes me as a trifle mad.) The "Publisher's Advertisement" is followed by "The Author's Preface," in which Boyle uses some of that condescending "prefatory" language that Marvell hated so much in Parker and that Swift satirizes in *A Tale*: "I am not so little acquainted with the temper of this age, and of the persons, that are likeliest to be perusers of the following tract," he begins. He continues by apologizing for his subject, and the fact that he wrote it, but ends by establishing the importance of his subject, and that no one could be more qualified for it than himself. He yields to his fans—"there are divers persons, for whom I have a great esteem and kindness, who think they have as much right to solicit me for composures of the nature of this, that they will now have to go abroad, as the virtuosi have to exact of my physiological pieces" (2)—with the same gawky grace with which Parker yielded to his bookseller.

He also sees that his preface performs the functions appropriate to it. Thus, we encounter *thème du comment* in "equitable readers will consider, not only what is said, but on what occasion, and with what design it is delivered" (3); *génèse* in "the just indignation I conceived, to see even inquisitive men depreciate that kind of knowledge, which does the most elevate" (4); and *choix d'un public* in "I despair not, that what is here represented, may serve to fortify in a high esteem of divine truths those, that have already a just veneration for them" (4).

One other writer is especially appropriate to illustrate the prefatory conventions that Swift satirizes in *A Tale*—the notorious John Dunton (for whom Swift wrote "Ode to the Athenian Society"). Robert Adams Day describes him as Dr. Bentley's equal at writing *scaz*, which he defines, after the Russian formalists, as "naïve, unadorned, idiomatic speech, an idiolect in fact, transferred to paper."[20] Day connects the rise of *scaz* to the rise of print culture and what he calls—with reference both to the visual orientation of print and to the element of egotism it allows—"Eyethink" (135). According to Day, Swift hated Dunton (and satirized him in *A Tale*) for more than Dunton's having hoodwinked him over the *Athenian Society;* he would have seen in him the shift from discourse with a strong rhetorical sense to discourse more visually oriented, personal and (in a classical sense at least) disordered.[21]

While still pursuing Day's lead, I would like to qualify his ideas a little, and bring them into line with my discussion of prefaces, by considering them in the light of Dunton's prefaces to his own *Life and Errors of John Dunton*.[22] The title alone seems to confirm Dunton's boast that "his own personality was his sole and darling theme" (128). What is curious, and even disturbing about Dunton's prefaces, is not just their degree of *scaz*, but the strange effect of *scaz*—which is essentially nonrhetorical—combined with a high degree of rhetorical self-consciousness stemming from the author's awareness of the fact that he is, after all, writing a preface. Day remarks that, with printing, "The author need not woo the collective audience with the devices of the classical exordium, nor yet carefully prepare his transitions; he can present his unmediated self instantly" (127). This, however, is a bit of an overstatement, as well as an oversight. The preface is itself a kind of exordium, but a typographical platform or podium that, while it retains some degree of rhetorical place and occasion, allows for a *scaz*-like degree of intimacy as well. Now Dunton can reach privately, in print, as many as could only be reached publicly before, in speech; his egotism seems animated by the awareness that he is going "one on one" with multitudes.

Of course, this combination of the private and the public in Dunton's prefaces is disturbing because it creates, or at least aggravates, a troublesome uncertainty in the reader about how to take what is written. The reader is never sure what tone it is written in. Day, confronted with Dunton's *Voyage Round the World*, concludes that "a mad facetiousness predominates" (134). Indeed, it may be that Dunton *was* mad; if so, his excesses only illustrate a little more clearly the abuses to which prefaces were prone, and the fact that a *madman* could so aggrandize himself in a preface argues for its accessibility as a print-created private/public podium, a platform that *anyone* could climb up on and avail himself of.

The very title of Dunton's first prefatory piece seems to glance at Genette's *choix d'un public*—"To the Impartial Readers," which rather precludes any modern readers. He then writes, in the first paragraph, of the need to "prepare [his] Reader's mind a little" (xi). Though what follows was written in 1704, it sounds remarkably like the prefatory pieces of *A Tale*. The Hack begins his "Epistle Dedicatory to Prince Posterity" with what sounds like an excuse, if not a complaint:

> I here present *Your Highness* with the Fruits of a very few leisure Hours, stollen from the short Intervals of a World of Business, and of an Employment quite alien from such Amusements as this. . . . (30)

Dunton begins similarly:

> My retreat from the world and business has given me not only the leisure, but the inclination, to become more thoughtful than before. . . . (xi)

As implied by his title, Dunton—like most prefacers—is concerned about judgment, but he himself seems confused about whether the judge is himself, the reader, or God, and whether the judgment is self-criticism, literary criticism, or the Last Day of Judgment. He takes pains to establish his good intentions—he says "design," a word that Swift does arabesques on in his "Apology"—but he is never very clear exactly what they are, and one probably would not believe him if he were, because he sounds so dishonest. He insists, in a preface to a whole book about himself, "I know very well, and am satisfied with, my low obscurity" (xii). Describing the book to follow, he inadvertently suggests a scam—"the burthen of my *New Idea* is no less than the business of the Christian Life"—as if he were really less concerned with the business of life than a life of (constant and rather shady) business. When he allegorizes "Christian Life" in bookseller's terms—"if any have been so unfortunate as to copy after my *real Life*, I here take the opportunity to tell them, that I solemnly disown the original" (xii)—he sounds *worse* than dishonest.

Dunton, conventionally, indicates the originality or novelty of his work, his "*New Idea*" being a kind of autobiography interleaved with repentance, the life he really lived with the life he *wishes* he had lived. In his hand, unfortunately, novelty turns immediately into bathos, and bathos into the grotesque. Though speaking in rather commonplace terms of "old life" and "new life," he still finds it necessary to explain to the reader (whom he must suppose is as stupid as himself) that "according to the best evidence he can get, he was living the tenth of October, 1704" (xii), when he wrote this preface. He is like Swift's Partridge, *after* Swift got through with him. Worse, too delighted with the obvious to leave it alone—Day also remarks "his whims" which Dunton called "maggots"—he worries it to death and putrefaction:

> I confess, six years ago, I printed my *Living Elegy* (or represented John Dunton as dead and buried, in an "Essay upon my own Funeral"), and perhaps some may think it a little *maggoty*, that I should come again from the Dead to write "The History of my own Life"; but, Gentlemen, cease to wonder at this, for I have almost finished "The Funeral of Mankind; or, an Essay proving we are all dead and buried, with a Paradox, shewing what we call Life is Death, and that we all live and discourse in the Grave," & c. (xv)

There is a paradox here, but it is that Dunton has nothing to say, least of all in public, and says it in a preface. He is constantly, like Swift's Hack, addressing himself to readers (and only those "impartial" readers) who have had the very same experiences he has had, while recommending his work as written entirely from experience. He has—indeed, he only can have—nothing to impart.[23]

Swift offers us several kinds of preface.[24] The "Bookseller's Dedication," technically an "épître dédicatoire (fictive) à fonction préfacielle" (181), is a "préface allographe fictive," and the "Dedication to Prince Posterity" is a "préface authoriale fictive." "The Preface" is another "préface authoriale fictive" and the "Apology" is a "préface authoriale authentique" (and "*ultérieure*," because it was attached only to the fifth and subsequent editions). Of course, "A Digression in the Modern Kind" is really a preface dropped into the middle of the book, and "A Further Digression" is a postface (even though the book isn't quite finished yet). What is especially interesting about all these different types of preface is the way each type explodes the conventions that Genette sees as peculiar to it. This suggests both the accuracy of Genette's generalizations and, since Swift must have made his own generalizations two centuries earlier, the rightness of Genette's assertion that the conventions of the preface developed and became fixed very early in the development of the preface itself.

> [L]a plupart des thèmes et des procédés de la préface sont en place dès le milieu du XVIᵉ siècle, et les variations ultérieures ne relèvent pas d'une véritable évolution, mais plutôt d'une série de choix divers dans un répertoire beaucoup plus stable qu'on ne le croirait *a priori*. (152)

The disjunction between prefatory piece and prefaced text can be seen, exaggerated, in the disjunction between the prefatory pieces themselves, in particular between the two dedications. The Bookseller dedicates the book to Somers, over the author's own dedication to Prince Posterity. Wheatley, incidentally, gives us a real-life version of the very thing, when Dryden, at loss of considerable profit, nobly refused to dedicate his translation of the *Aeneid* (1697) to King William, only to have Tonson dedicate it for him. He caused every likeness of Aeneas in the engravings to resemble the monarch, so that the wits could say "old Jacob has placed old Nassau's hook-nos'd head on young Aeneas' shoulders" (137).

The problems of praise that were seen by Marvell in Parker's *Preface* remain in Swift's parodic prefaces, if only because they are endemic. The ostensible objects of the "préface authoriale originale" being to "1. *obtenir une lecture*, et 2. *obtenir que cette lecture soit bonne*" (183), this kind of preface employs a strategy of "*valoriser le texte*" (184) while implicating the author only minimally. In such a preface the author tends to emphasize his subject at the expense of his treatment of it. One way to emphasize the subject is to stress its utility, and we find the Hack doing precisely this in "The Preface"; the Swiftian version of the convention is slightly askew, however, in that this is a utility of uselessness:

6 / The Preface as Vehicle in *A Tale of a Tub*

[I]t was decreed, that in order to prevent these *Leviathans* from tossing and sporting with the *Commonwealth* . . . they should be diverted from that Game by a *Tale of a Tub*. And my Genius being conceived to lye not unhappily that way, I had the Honor done me to be engaged in the Performance. (41)

The same sort of convention is satirized in "Section V," where the "Endeavours" of the moderns are characterized as "highly serviceable to the general Good of Mankind" (123).

Novelty and originality are also conventions of this kind of valorization. It may be the desire to achieve such novelty that led to what, to my mind, is one of the most "original" prefatory pieces every penned, Lacy's dedication of *Dumb Lady* (1672) to Lord Limrick, one of Charles's bastards by the duchess of Cleveland. The passage is quoted in Wheatley:

When I began to write this dedication my hand shook, a fear possessed me, and I trembled; my pen fell from me, and my whole frame grew disordered as if blasted with some sudden upstart comet. Such awe and reverence waits on dignity, that I now find it fit for me to wish I had been refused the honour of my dedication, rather than undertake a task so much too great for me. (148)

Clearly the desire to write *not* another "stale bundle of flattery" has induced a state of dementia—but surprise us he does. Here the emphasis has shifted—typically, in a world of runaway convention—from the novelty of the work being prefaced to the novelty of the preface itself (a distracting effect that Genette calls *l'effet Jupien* (89), a tendency to loiter in the vestibule with a too-distinguished servant):

[M]y more successful Brethren the *Moderns* . . . will by no means let slip a Preface or Dedication without some notable distinguishing Stroke to surprise the Reader at the Entry, and kindle a Wonderful Expectation of what is to ensue. (42)

This stroke is provided in "A Digression in the Modern Kind" by inserting what is essentially a preface in the middle of the book. Originality has also its pragmatic side, to foil the reader who would "twirl over forty or fifty Pages of *Preface* and *Dedication*, (which is the usual *Modern* Stint) as if it were so much Latin" (131).

Perhaps the most interesting convention Swift exploits for his "préface authoriale originale fictive" is what Genette calls "excusatio propter infirmitatem" (193). It is related to the strategy of valorization because by stressing the author's infirmity it, too, emphasizes the subject at the expense of its treatment. It is also a means of anticipating and thereby frustrating the critics (see "préface paratonnerre" [192]). We encounter something of the sort in the Hack's "circumstances and postures of life":

> [T]he shrewdest Pieces of this Treatise were conceived in Bed, in a Garret: At other times . . . I thought fit to sharpen my Invention with Hunger; and in general, the whole Work was begun, continued, and ended, under a long Course of Physic, and a great want of Money. (44)

Of course, the change here is that the infirmity has been made out to be a positive thing; moreover, it is combined with another convention, that of advice on how to read a book ("thème du comment" [194]), which naturally obviates the question of *why*:

> Whatever Reader desires to have a thorow Comprehension of an Author's Thoughts, cannot take a better method, than by putting himself into the Circumstances and Postures of life, that the Writer was in upon every important Passage as it flow'd from his Pen. (44)

We get, incidentally, more of the same business at the start of the "Epistle Dedicatory to Prince Posterity":

> I here present *Your Highness* with the Fruits of a very few leisure Hours, stolen from the short Intervals of a World of Business, and of an Employment quite alien from such Amusements as this: The poor Production of that Refuse of Time which has lain heavy upon my Hands, during a long Prorogation of Parliament, a great Dearth of Forein News, and a tedious Fit of rainy Weather. . . . (30)

The "how to read this book" occurs again as late as the penultimate section of "A Further Digression," where it is so late as to be utterly pointless:

> I do here humbly propose for an Experiment, that every Prince in *Christendom* will take seven of the *deepest Scholars* in his Dominions, and shut them up for *seven* Years, in *seven* Chambers, with a Command to write *seven* ample Commentaries on this comprehensive Discourse. (185)

The conventional discussion of the origins ("génèse" [195]) of the book, the expression of thanks for those who were involved in it, and the acknowledgment of sources, are also aspects of valorization, if only because "un auteur qui a tant d'amis et de compagnes ne peut être absolument mauvais" (197). We find this, changed of course, in the relation of the "important Discovery . . . made by a certain curious and refined Observer" (40) in "The Preface" and in the acknowledgment in "A Further Digression" of all sorts of people who had nothing to do with *A Tale of a Tub*:

> I do here return my humble Thanks to *His Majesty*, and both Houses of *Parliament*; To the *Lords* of the King's most honourable Privy-Council, to the Reverend the *Judges*; To the *Clergy*, and *Gentry*, and *Yeomanry* of this Land. . . . (181)

The most serious implication of "The Preface" regarding praise has to do, oddly enough, with the decline of individual satire and the rise of general satire too sparing in nature. The idea in "The Preface" is that this forbearance has hurt not only blame, but praise too; after all, how can one praise effectively, how can praise mean anything, if the praiser is not equally free—and able—to blame? This situation is shown, in the conclusion of "The Preface," to have done infinite harm to not just prefaces (though they are naturally a good beginning) but to what we have come to call today "the fabric of society."

The "painter-poems" and *The Rehearsal Transpros'd* provide a significant illustration of the importance of individual satire (that is, blame) to individual praise, and the importance of praise to blame. It is surely no coincidence that one of the things that one cannot do in the world of *A Tale* is blame in this specific way. One may not, as Marvell did, describe "How *such a one*, starved half the Fleet, and half-poisoned the rest" (52–53). "The Preface" starts with a self-manifestation of specific and rather narrow rhetorical problems, but quickly moves to the illustration of those same problems at work at large in society. The decline of a literary kind of social writing—the preface—mirrors the decline of social discourse generally.

The "choix d'un public" (197), oddly enough, occurs in the postface, "A Further Digression," where (like the "how to read this book") it is so out of place as to be useless:

> Readers may be divided into three Classes, the *Superficial*, the *Ignorant*, and the *Learned*: And I have with much Felicity fitted my Pen to the Genius and

Advantage of each . . . But the Reader truly *learned*, chiefly for whose Benefit I wake, when others sleep, and sleep when others wake, will here find sufficient Matter to employ his Speculations for the rest of his Life. (185)

Clearly Swift knew what conventions went where, and knowingly transgressed. Moreover, the uselessness of "A Further Digression" corroborates Genette's argument that the postface is among the rarest variations of the preface (219), for the obvious reason that it comes too late to obtain a good reading. Rather than write a postface, the author might as well wait for a second edition and write a "préface ultérieure," good modern examples of which are also relatively scarce, thanks to the decline of the "critique moralisante" (228) that necessitated it in the first place.[25]

This brings us to Swift's own "préface ultérieure": "An Apology (for the Tale of a Tub)." Here, where he seems to assert the positive value of convention, we sense that he has written himself into a corner or (to mix metaphors) pulled the rug out from under his feet in a way that Marvell (narrowly!) avoids doing. For here Swift attempts to use in earnest many of the very same prefatory conventions he has so thoroughly exploded in the body of his work—he becomes, if not the first, the most conspicuous victim of his own nihilism.

For all the sensitivity to conventions that enables Swift to violate and expose them so effectively, in "An Apology" he comes remarkably close to ignoring the first convention of such a preface ("originale" or "ultérieure"), which is never to insist on one's own genius, talent, style, cleverness at composition, etc. (184). He comes too close sometimes to self-praise, to stating the obvious in a way that makes it *less* obvious:

Another Thing to be observed is, that there generally runs an Irony through the Thread of the whole Book, which the Men of Tast will observe and distinguish, and which will render some Objections that have been made, very weak and insignificant. (8)

The principal function of the "préface ultérieure"—the "réponse aux critiques" (223)—"An Apology" performs adequately enough, but not without employing many of the same conventions exploded above. We encounter "choix d'un public" in remarks like "those who approve it, are a great Majority among the Men of Tast" (3) and (reminding us of the "Dedication to Prince Posterity") "This Apology [is] chiefly intended for the Satisfaction of future Readers" (9). Similarly, we get a great deal about "génèse":

> The greatest Part of that Book was finished about thirteen Years since, 1696, which is eight Years before it was published. (4)

> his Discourse is the Product of the Study, the Observation, and the Invention of several Years; that he often blotted out much more than he left.... (10)

And about "how to read this book":

> Had the Author's Intention met with a more candid Interpretation from some whom out of Respect he forbears to name, he might have been encouraged ... (5–6)

> [S]ome have endeavour'd to squeeze out a dangerous Meaning that was never thought on. (8)

We even have the assertion of originality, which the Hack himself couldn't have claimed more vociferously:

> [T]hrough the whole Book he has not borrowed one single Hint from any Writer in the World; and he thought, of all Criticisms, that would never have been one. He conceived it was never disputed to be an Original, whatever Faults it might have. (13)

Finally, Swift's assertion that

> He was then a young Gentleman much in the World ... he gave a Liberty to his Pen, which might not suit with maturer Years, or graver Characters. ... (4)

resembles the "excusatio propter infirmitatem"—*propter iuventum*, perhaps.[26]

Besides being inconsistent with the main body of *A Tale*, "An Apology" is inconsistent with itself. Swift criticizes Dryden's language in his own prefaces, where he tells us "that he *possesses his Soul in Patience*" (7). This is in dangerous proximity to Swift's own rather thin expressions of patience in the "Apology." Also, in dangerous proximity to his own injunction against unfavorable or uncharitable applications, he urges the reader to make uncharitable applications: "I believe the Reader may find more Persons to give that Passage an Application" (7). How is his preface any different? Uncharitable applications are welcome, provided they are to parodied authors and not to the "real" one, the author of the "Apology," even though it is extremely hard to tell them apart.

Swift is finally left without any ground to stand on. He is caught up in the very problems of convention that he diagnosed so well, as Marvell did before him. But Marvell did not deny convention entirely or hamper his own ability to use it effectively, or, when necessary, to appear conventional. Swift's exploitation of conventional forms of valorization and recommendation in *A Tale of a Tub* seems to have destroyed his capacity to assert any positive values, least of all conventional ones, and amounts almost to a cancellation of one branch of epideictic rhetoric by another, namely, of panegyric by satire. The effect of this epideictic breakdown can be detected in Swift's treatment of Lord Somers (once considered positive, but now, at best, ambiguous). Swift's dilemma in "An Apology" is similar to that of his creation, the Bookseller's. Both have to invent new conventions, new virtues, which will ipso facto be spurious, or use the old Aristotelian ones that have become counterfeit in print, and which are only introduced by way of parasepiopesis: "But to ply the World with an old beaten Story of your Wit, and Eloquence, and Learning, and Wisdom, and Justice . . . I confess, I have neither Conscience, nor Countenance to do it" (25–26). The predicament is as bad as the Hack's, who must praise satire because the conventions of panegyric have been exhausted. He must praise blame—constantly contradicting himself—and blame praise. The screw has been turned once too often and the thread has been stripped.

7

Swift and Churchill: Postmodern Panegyric

Peter Schakel remarks that "when he wrote 'Directions for a Birthday Song' (1729), Swift reflected the optimistic assumption of the moment that Walpole was vulnerable" (131).[1] Swift expected at any moment in the 1730s to be returned to power and influence, but the poem is premised on a divorce between political (and every other) reality and signification that leaves Swift nothing to be optimistic about. While it is tempting to regard this spate of panegyrical activity as a kind of "last hurrah," the intensely panegyrical nature of later poems by Swift and others, such as Churchill's *Gotham*, suggests that panegyric and satire continue to implicate one another in a tradition of self-consciously analogical signification.

"Stella Poems"

In the introduction to *A Tale of a Tub* the Hack complains that it is "as hard to get quit of *Number* as of *Hell*" (55), and inadvertently suggests an equation between the two. The problem of escaping them is central to Stella's birthday poems. John Irwin Fischer in "Faith, Hope, and Charity" in *Contemporary Studies of Swift's Poetry*[2] speaks of "the objective world of number, weight, and measure" as a "nightmare from which he [the Christian] has been awakened by faith" (82).

In the first of Stella's birthday poems, "Stella's Birthday: Written in the year 1718,"[3] virtue is treated mathematically, the way it is in the "Odes" and *A Tale of a Tub*. Mathematical, quantitative treatment is violently applied to qualitative things,

> Oh, would it please the gods to *split*
> Thy beauty, size, and years, and wit . . .
>
> (lines 9–10)

in a list of mingled qualities and quantities that seems intended to awaken us to their difference. The second birthday poem, "Stella's Birthday: Written in the Year 1720–21," at first appears to be less concerned with differences in kind among Stella's attributes than with differences between Stella's beauty and Chloe's. But the same jarring distinctions between quantity and quality, qualitative tenor and quantitative vehicle, soon emerge. Stella is compared to an old inn that, despite its battered appearance ("the painting grows decayed" [7]), is preferred to the "new angel two doors from us" (10) by swains who continue to be entertained by Stella's "breeding, humour, wit, and sense" (25). As in the previous birthday poem, part of the humor lies in treating these infinite commodities mathematically and so finitely ("and had her stock been less, no doubt / She must have long ago run out" [31–32]), but there is also much (uneasy?) humor in the treatment in overtly sexual language of Stella as something resorted to by the men for "the liquor and the meat" (4). And how is Stella's "painting" (7) better than Chloe's "daubing" (11), except that the former is decayed and the latter new? The difference is as hard to detect in the diction as it is in the reality. The difference is less in packaging and advertisement than in "trade," as Swift calls it repeatedly in the poem—a word, like other "appearances," capable of a wide range of applications, from sexual to social intercourse. Swift seems to indicate by that very word both the difference in kind between quality and quantity and the problematic similarity of their presentation. Perhaps signification is always quantitative and materialistic. With its split between decaying appearances and (in some "cases") wholesome interiors, the poem presents the obvious problem (compounded by the fact that physically, at least, Stella and her rival "inns" have much in common) of distinguishing appearance from reality and getting at a good "interior" through an unprepossessing "front"—or a prepossessing one, for that matter. The problem with appearance, indeed with the relationship of all signifiers to their signifieds, is arbitrariness.

In the 1723 poem, Swift worries that

> They'll call it all poetic license:
> And when I brag of aid divine
> Think Eusden's right as good as mine.
>
> (lines 28–30)

It becomes obvious that Stella has displaced national figures as Swift's focus here; he praises her much as Eusden the laureate praises Queen Caroline and others (only better). By praising her annually, he vindicates his right to a kind of shadow-laureateship, ironically more genuine than Eusden's. Stella's praise "crowns the year" (80) as praise of George or Caroline should have done.

Stella's unusual importance lends pathos to the last birthday poem, in which Swift confronts her death. Her death has all the significance of the passing of a public figure, with none of the public continuity that helps to make such a passing bearable. Consequently, her death intensifies questions about signification raised in the previous birthday poems, and prompts Swift to rephrase them in larger terms, not as questions of the relationship of virtue to appearance but as questions of the relationship of this life to an afterlife:

> Then, who with reason can pretend
> That all effects of virtue end?
>
> (lines 65–66)

Unfortunately, he offers no indication that the arbitrariness that characterizes signification here below does not characterize it above. His comparison of the effects of good food to the effects of good deeds is similarly ambiguous or even inappropriate. The problem here may be similar to that encountered in the earlier birthday poem comparing Stella to an inn, where we must somehow approach internal qualities through the external quantities of appearances, where "what draws us in" must always be different in kind from what "entertains" us once inside. Evaded is the leap of faith required of the "guest," of the reader, and initially of Swift himself, to enter at all. The dilemma of how the guest gets into the inn is oddly similar to that of Stella getting into heaven. But the leap from eating to virtue is harder. Swift's analogy here, like the use of quantity throughout, seems almost *deliberately* inappropriate. Not only does the vehicle seem unsuited to its virtuous tenor (eating to the afterlife), but the tenor itself seems to be unsatisfactory.

"Directions for a Birthday Song"

The composition of Stella's birthday poems might be regarded as the practical experience that qualified Swift to advise other would-be laureates in "Directions for a Birthday Song" (1729). The real poet laureate, Eusden, died in 1730, and it is not hard to see Swift's "Directions" as advice to

Eusden's successor; it is a parody of the kind of panegyric (like "Threnodia Augustalis") that would be written to his successor on the death of a monarch.

The "Directions" presents some interesting formal problems because, like much of Swift's verse, it pretends to be formless. A. B. England remarks that, as in "The Furniture of a Woman's Mind" (1727), Swift constructs "sequences of details that take on the characteristics of the catalog" and "accumulates a large number of satiric comments into a sequence that is ostentatiously unstructured" (106). As in the earlier poem, in "Directions" he "throws the list open to additions by the reader." The theme of the poem is no less than signification itself, and in developing this theme in the context of a conspicuously absent authority, the displaced addressee of panegyric, Swift places it securely in the tradition of panegyrical satire.

The "Directions" can be divided into four sections: (1) a list of gods, dealing mainly with George II (lines 1–104); (2) a passage on encomium or, more precisely, *mock*-encomium (105–50); (3) lines on Caroline and Frederick, Prince of Wales (151–208); and (4) a passage on names (Hanover, George, Brunswick, Hesse Darmstadt, Guelph, Caroline, Sabrina, Medway, Thames, Albion, Nassau, Kinsley, Walpole, etc.) (209–82). These describe a movement away from George and Caroline, the king and queen, towards G, E, O, R, G, E, C, A, R, O, L, I, N, and E. As in Marvell's depiction of Parker's reduction of meaning to phonemes, in the "Directions" there is a movement from sense towards nonsense, from words as representations of reality to words as representations of the stuff of which, in a reductive sense, reality is made.

The "Directions" begins like a cake recipe:

> To form a just and finished piece
> Take twenty gods of Rome or Greece . . .
>
> (lines 1–2)

The joke is similar to the one we encountered in the Stella poems. Again we have the inappropriateness of quantitative treatment for what is unquantifiable—which here reminds us of the real absence of the qualitative (and unquantifiable) virtues in George II. This absence is, of course, glaring in the kind of poem that traditionally praises virtue. This split between the qualitative and the quantitative, as in "Stella's Birthday" (1719),

> Oh, would it please the gods to split
> Thy beauty, size, and years, and wit. . . .
>
> (lines 9–10)

prepares us for, and is the beginning of, a split between words and what words signify. Eventually it is a charm.

Nothing adequately expresses George's "virtue." The "laws of song" (21) and reality are at odds, and every attempt to reconcile them only confounds them more. Literature, represented by panegyric, becomes a machine, the smooth running of which precludes the presence of the real George.

There are two patterns, an ancient and a modern one, of monarchs eating their sons. The first is that of Saturn (of course), and the second George I (by implication). Here applying the conventions to George results in a kind of tautology, because he is notoriously bad enough to require no "vehicle." He even supplants existing patterns by becoming one himself.

Panegyric traditionally, as a form of epideictic, uses analogy to make us understand "the good" king; here, a surfeit of analogies helps us to understand "the bad" George. The surfeit of them evokes the sense of inexpressibility, but inexpressibility of "the bad." The conclusion of the stanza,

> But this I think will not go down
> For here the father kept his crown.
>
> (lines 13–14)

works on several levels, as a modernization of cannibalism into usurpation (or is it vice versa?), as a rather disgusting pun on "go down" as "swallow" and "believe," and finally as an unsatisfactory evasion. If George and his father are not the pattern but just another application (and an imperfect one at that, though not for want of trying on the father's part), what is the pattern? When the analogy is positive, George is absent; when negative, he is the only man present.

The "broad innuendoes" of lines 69–80 (a sample of how and what the "birthday bard" ought to write) are that George's reign produces monsters. The insult is all the more telling because it is a variation of the "Nile" topic, traditionally used to illustrate the benefits of royal power, the reciprocity of people and prince, and the ideal of *tranquilla potestas*. While, in his earlier use of the topic, Swift suggests that an awareness of the source of good may detract from our enjoyment of it, here he suggests that the source, George, whose "bounty flows" (73) rather like a sewer, has been poisoned and so creates monsters—not crops that grow on the bank but reptiles, the poets, that crawl in the slime on the bottom (at Oxford and Cambridge):

> On Learning how his bounty flows,
> And with what Justice he bestows.
> Fair Isis, and ye banks of Cam,
> Be witness if I tell a flam:
> What prodigies in arts we drain
> From both your stream in George's reign!
> As from the flowery bed of Nile....
>
> (lines 73–79)

George has become a kind of negative Nile (it is tempting to say "Nihil"): instead of generosity, there is meanness; instead of benign power, malignancy; instead of calm, stagnation. The earlier use of the topos argued for the reality of a good that might be, but should not be, confounded with its "vehicle." Here the same topos is used to argue precisely the opposite: the unreality or nothingness that is the "tenor" of evil, that (at least in an ethical sense) *ought* to be identified, so far as possible, with its expressions (though the problem of *adequacy* remains). Whatever the deeper meanings, the shallower one is that George will not get them, since he cannot *read*:

> He'll get it read, and take the hint
> . . . .
> And will be so much more your debtor
> Because he never knows a letter.
>
> (lines 84–88)

In the third section Swift advises the "birthday bard" how to praise Queen Caroline and other members of George's family ("breed"). Goddesses like Venus are said to be six thousand years old, when in fact they are immortal and ageless; however, this gives the poet the chance to remark that Caroline "hardly fifty odd is" (162), as if what were nothing to a goddess were not "middle aged" to a woman. Complementing George's description as Apollo, Caroline's suggests Cynthia at the same time it rejects the identification. By insisting that Caroline is *not* Cynthia (the moon), Swift suggests that somehow she must be, or that while she may not be in some ways, she may be in others—in having "Apollo" for her brother, for instance. Besides hinting at incest, Swift implies that George has been "usurped" by his wife, at least so far as the conventions of panegyric are concerned. Caroline appears to be a star in her own right and George a weak sun whose absence, during which Caroline acts as his regent, far from casting his nation into darkness, is of no consequence. George is physically absent (in Hanover most of the time), but this absence is not noticed because as king he is essentially a *vacuum* anyway. He is treated here as he is treated in Pope's "To Augustus": as a lacuna occupied by others —a tenorless vehicle. Caroline, too (as the poem takes off in a Handelian direction), falls away from her signifier, but into putrefaction:

> May Caroline continue long
> Forever fair and young—in song.
> What though the royal carcass must
> Squeezed in a coffin turn to dust. . . .
> (lines 233–36)

The rest of the stanza, like stanza 8, approximates the very language of Whig panegyric. Its indirectness alone would be enough to make it parodic. Language that could be excused if it were spontaneous becomes inexcusable when prescribed—a hazard of the "painter-poems," for example. Words like "now," "then," and "but now" set off the purple passages like laughing parentheses—orderly and sensible foils for disorderly nonsense. Qualifying expressions in the midst of much fulsomeness have a similar mock-panegyric effect:

> But swear his line shall rule the nation
> For ever—till the conflagration.
> (lines 297–98)

The growing tension between tenors and their vehicles seems finally to snap in the last section; at least there is no longer even a pretense of connecting words to things, but rather a wholehearted embrace of nonsense, names, and noise. The final section reads like a mock-panegyric addressed to Caroline (and other members of George's family), until one remembers that the George and Caroline addressed are not rulers or even people, but merely names, and that this section is therefore a panegyric to certain combinations of letters that will sound—one cannot say good—in the "birthday poet's" poem (or in a musical setting by Master Handel).

This is the ultimate explosion of the "inexpressibility" topos, used by Marvell in his description of the duchess of York in the "Second Advice," and in "Epitaph upon———":

> Enough: and leave the rest to Fame.
> 'Tis to commend her but to Name.
>
> (lines 1–2)

and by Dryden in "Heroic Stanzas":

> How shall I then begin, or where conclude
> To draw a fame so truly circular?
>
> (lines 17–18)

George and family are inexpressible, not because they are nonpareils of virtue who render their poets speechless with admiration, but because they are dreadful people and, worse, because the very sound of their names is inimical to poetry and therefore inexpressible in it:

> A skilful critic justly blames
> Hard, tough, cramp, guttural, harsh, stiff names.
>
> (lines 209–10)

Only part of the problem with these names is their foreignness. To clear Swift from charges of xenophobia, one should note the good old English names with which there is also something wrong: "Albion's cliffs are out at heel" (244); that is, the expression is as worn out as the country. The target is rather words as words, than words as foreign (or anything else). That we deal only with words, in a hermetically sealed "world of words" where embarrassing qualifications and parentheses are *almost* entirely eliminated, is made manifestly clear. The queen's name is analyzed phonetically, then addressed in lieu of Caroline herself:

> May Caroline continue long,
> Forever fair and young—in song.
>
> (233–34)

What qualifications remain ("in song") serve only to remind us that we are now in a world without much reference to things, without much meaning. What words are in Caroline's song is no more than what her body is in decomposition:

> What though the royal carcass must
> Squeezed in a coffin turn to dust;

> These elements her name compose
> Like atoms are exempt from blows.
>
> (lines 235–38)

Caroline "sung" will continue as long as Caroline "dung," because her song itself has been decomposed into phonetic elements as eternal as chemicals and as nugatory. The Caroline that "may fill your gaps" (239) may be equally the name that can fill out a line in a poetic text, the fat woman herself, or the fat woman's carcass stuffed into a hole somewhere ("consult the maps" [240]), or "all of the above."

Likewise the Nassau of line 251 is both William III and the poetic name for him. It is pejorative not just for being William's but for being a poeticism, too. Again the mock-panegyrical and the meretriciously poetical are identical. Nassau the name is a "hanger-on" (233) brought in by "old acquaintance"—that is, a cliché introduced into poetry by bad poets (Whig panegyrists in particular). Nassau the man (William III) might also be described (uncharitably) as a hanger-on (husband of Mary) brought in (invited) to rule England by his friends the Whigs.

The Walpole of line 255 is similarly both name and man; consequently, "lend a line" (255) means both to give a certain amount of space in a line of poetry and to help out. "In decline" (256) would mean, as far as poetry goes, "out of fashion," but as far as politics goes, "out of office." There is a kind of seesaw movement, a cause-and-effect relationship, an "in" with William and an "out" with Walpole, appropriate perhaps for the Whiggish king and the Whig prime minister, and reinforced by the teeter-totter image of line 260: "Whom you once sing up, sing down." Like the treatment of words as phonemes, this treatment is also reductive, making poetry brainlessly mechanical or, at best, spasmodic.

One of the principal ideas of panegyric is mocked ("Reject with scorn that stupid notion / To praise your hero for devotion" [261–62]). As the poem ends, we take a parting glance at a glibly cynical court, and the "birthday poet" has his poem set to music by Handel. It is the final stage in the apotheosis—not of a king into a god, but of a poem into nothing.

"The Delany Poems"

Swift continued to write *oblique* panegyrics throughout the early 1730s. Like the "Directions," they do not address a figure of authority but another poet who does. The panegyric is not heard (as if one were oneself the addressee) but overheard. "An Epistle upon an Epistle" and "A Libel on the Reverend Dr. Delany and His Excellency John, Lord Carteret" respond to Delany's "Epistle to Lord Carteret," itself a panegyric (if not a very good one). The viceroy replaces the king as the addressee of Delany's poem, and Swift in turn addresses Delany, an arrangement that should by now be only too familiar.

In "An Epistle" Delany is depicted as one who seeks preferment by means of flattery, because he cannot live within his means. Delany would use Carteret as the Bookseller of *A Tale* would use Somers, whose name "on the front in capital letters will at any time get off one edition," except Delany is frustrated by Carteret's more upright refusal to cooperate:

> Nor will my Lord so far beguile
> The wise and learned of our isle;
> To make it pass upon the nation,
> By dint of his sole approbation.
>
> (lines 17–20)

Because there appears to be a laureateship for the viceroy just as there is for the king, Delany becomes the successor to Jonathan Smedley (the previous viceroy's "laureate"), whose poem is quoted twice. Smedley is used to state part of Swift's case for him—that Delany should live more simply—only in language that reveals its insincerity. Swift demolishes Smedley's poem by using the insincerity of its poeticisms as a foil for its good ideas; thus set off, the latter are turned against the poet. The quotation of panegyrical poems out of context to the discredit of all poetry is a common trait of Swift's later work, as panegyric becomes a metaphor for arbitrary and empty signification.

"A Libel," also addressed to a panegyrist, is more explicit about the problems of patronage as it elaborates the connection between arbitrary and empty signification and arbitrary power. The arbitrariness of the politicians is reflected in the submission of their poets, writers like Congreve, Steele, Gay, and Addison, to a language divorced from reality, in which signifiers like "true politicians" and "solid work"—or "libel," for that matter—no longer have any meaningful relation to their signifieds. The "true politicians" are not interested in poetry and regard it as "useless," "useful" having lost its meaning too. Typically, the "poetical" passages that Swift quotes (165–70) are inferior to the "unpoetical" (185–92).

Swift's reaction to such arbitrariness is to simply reverse it. If, as in the "Directions," power maintains that blame is praise, in "To Mr. Delany on the Libels Writ Against Him" he suggests the opposite, and moreover offers passages of praise whose blame is only too transparent:

> The Irish senate's praises sing:
> How jealous of the nation's freedom,
> And, for corruptions, how they weed 'em.
> How each the public good pursues
> How far their hearts from private views . . .
>
> (lines 56–60)

If power presents an order in which all literature becomes panegyric, he offers an alternative in which the only literature worthy of the name would be satire. Ultimately, he suggests, the effect of officially sanctioned praise is blame. Essentially he reiterates the old insistence on praise and blame, panegyric and satire, as mutually sustaining kinds of writing.

Carteret himself, an oblique addressee in the "Delany Poems," becomes the principal human metaphor for the problems of signification the poems describe. His office no longer has any but an arbitrary relationship to himself, due to the arbitrariness of the power he represents. The identity of man and office is conventionally emphasized in panegyric; here, this conventional emphasis enables Swift to invoke a positive idea of authority as an absence: "I hate the Viceroy, love the Man" (152). Unlike the negative authority figures of *A Tale*, Carteret has real substance, but one positive signified is inevitably negated in a sea of otherwise arbitrary signification.

Charles Churchill's Revisionary Panegyric: *Gotham*

Roughly thirty years after Swift's panegyrical "Delany Poems," panegyric was renewed by the peculiar circumstances of the start of George III's reign. George was perceived by Churchill as a would-be despot, and this, along with the fact that his principal advisor was a Scot and a Stuart, naturally proved congenial to the revival of a kind of writing closely associated with arbitrary rule and the Stuarts. In reviving this kind of writing Churchill inherited not only its rhetorical topics and formal arrangements, but also its preoccupation with aspects of signification, with analogizing and naming. These continue to have political as well as epistemological implications.

The setting of *The Rosciad*—the selection of a judge to choose the successor to Roscius, king of the actors—provides, as well as an occasion for panegyric (or mock-panegyric) and serious diatribe, an opportunity for the analysis of signification. At the same time, the attitude of the poet to panegyrical adornment and ceremony, as implied in the idea of "naked" merit, is (to say the least) skeptical. The occasion, the day of the coronation, is not like Samuel Daniel's "great day," but a day like any other. The presentation is a consistent, ironic deflation of the expectations of high-blown, panegyrical praise: "Nothing magnificent appear'd, but Art / With decent modesty perform'd her part" (249–50). "Nothing" functions as an epistemological pun, as simply nothing and also as "Magnificent Nothing," like the significant *nothings* of *A Tale*.

As in his description of the tribunal (251–58), Churchill constructs elaborate vehicles for the bad that begin as vehicles for the good. More generally, Churchill's unreal thespian society works both as tenor and as vehicle, imparting its own unreality to the world of kings and politicians, but also having imparted to it a considerable degree of unreality already a part of that "real" world. Sometimes the thespian world is a vehicle for the political world, and sometimes vice versa.

When Common Sense regards Fitzpatrick, the instigator of the Fizzgiggo Riots that plagued Garrick's theater, as "usurping" the actors' throne, "It" is revealed for what it is—nothing, but a nothing disturbingly decked out in the trappings of public poetry:

> Plain Common Sense appear'd, by Nature there
> Appointed, with Plain Truth, to guard the chair;
> The pageant saw, and, blasted with her frown,
> To Its first state of nothing melted down.
>
> (lines 167–70)

The insistence on *plain* sense and *plain* truth has to make one suspect a joke, as must their anything-but-plain appearance as quasi-allegorical figures. It is typical of Churchill's transitional character that, while mocking panegyrical excess, he fails to endorse an "honest" alternative. It is a good illustration of what Lockwood sees as a problem in late-eighteenth-century satire, and especially in Churchill, "the propriety of calling one abstraction an empty name without calling all abstractions empty names" (90). As abstractions, "Plain Truth," etc., are obviously as empty as the expressions they are meant to replace. One has to think of how Jack, trying to get at the tenor, comes to resemble Peter (trying to get away from it by adding on more vehicles).

I think one also has to suspect that any genuine sense and truth would not have stopped at melting just Fitzpatrick down. As happens occasionally in "Directions for a Birthday Song," the introduction of some more solid element only underscores the unreality of the whole. This type of satire, invoking political poetry, panegyrical topics, and epistemological arrangements, is prone to such uncontrollable moments, which are like eddies that can potentially draw the whole poem under.[4] Churchill's use of sartorial imagery, his invocation of Swiftian pairs like "knaves and fools," his insistence on reason—all suggest that, consciously or not, he is working within and perpetuating what amounts to a body of almost "folk" lore on surprisingly abstract questions involving the application to social questions of the relationship of form to substance, vehicle to tenor. The loosely panegyrical setting and the obviousness of the theatrical analogy suggest the broader application without actually stating it.

Significantly, one of the faults the actors "ape" is the pride of kings (504). In satirizing these player-kings the poet is satirizing the real king. But their obsession with Opinion—

> What! shall Opinion then, of Nature free,
> And liberal as the vagrant air, agree
> To rust in chains like these, imposed by things
> Which, less than nothing, ape the pride of kings?
>
> (lines 501–4)

—suggests that the focus of Churchill's society (and of Churchill's attack on it) is not kings, but something much more middle class. Churchill refuses to let custom be imposed by player-kings, although by implication real kings are imposed by it.

A long section of female praise is a strikingly Swiftian attack on the overemphasis on appearance, and a restatement of the idea that virtue is qualitative, not quantitative:

> Are foibles then, and graces of the mind,
> In real life, to size or age confined?

> Do spirits flow, and is good-breeding placed
> In any set circumference of waist?
>
> (lines 825–28)

The split between appearance and reality is less the principal target, I would argue against critics like Raymond J. Smith, than a symptom.

But it is not that Churchill has anything against appearance, some sort of antipathy for the "vehicular" side of things, as the lines in praise of female beauty are meant to show. He desires only that it be whole and, in this way, natural. Thus he faults an actor whose enunciation overemphasizes the particles, "In monosyllables his thunders roll, / He, she, it, and, we, ye, they, fright the soul" (889–90)—or another who emphasizes one virtue over all others (931–34). He desires appearances that do not distract from substance, vehicles that do not draw so much attention to themselves that they become their own tenors. Sincerity is the way to achieve this kind of balance: "Those who would make us feel, must feel themselves" (962). This is, after all, the point of the epigraph, which emphasizes the sincerity of *both* praise and blame:

> Unknowing and unknown, the hardy muse
> Boldly defies all mean and partial views;
> With honest freedom plays the critic's part,
> And praises, as she censures, from the heart.

But for this, panegyric, with its positive emphasis on the external and ceremonial, can only act as a kind of foil. Arguably, I hope, it is a most (perhaps *the* most) effective one, but no more than that, since the virtue (sincerity) for which it is a foil is actually profoundly inimical to it.

The first few lines of *Gotham* are about *naming*, and the arbitrary—and proprietary—effect of it. Imperialists' claim to the New World is no less shaky than Churchill's claim to England for naming it Gotham. The name is significant in other ways, of course, since (a footnote tells us) "Gotham is a parish six miles south of Nottingham, proverbial for the simplicity of its inhabitants, a simplicity which is said to have been simulated in order to avert the anger of a king" (note 308).[5] In the preoccupation with naming and in the concern with the arbitrariness of the relationship between signifiers and their signifieds, there is then an *epistemological* focus to Churchill's panegyric that, I believe, is characteristic of latter-day epideictic writing. This typically leads to a rather bewildering confusion of tenors and vehicles, revolving around the idea of kingship. It soon becomes unclear whether Churchill's king is a vehicle for the abstract goodness of kingship (the *optimus* of *princeps*), for George III, for the native chiefs who sell their people's country "for a bit of glass" (44), or for Churchill himself.[6]

Perhaps the ultimate in what is perceived (pre-poststructurally?) as arbitrary signification (with all the appropriate political connotations) is the colonizer's planting of Christ's cross, "his royal master's name thereon engraved" (19), upon an island he wishes to enslave. There is nothing Christian about the process of colonization, and there is nothing of the royal colonizer about Christ. As a flattering vehicle or an insulted tenor, the cross stands for both the arbitrariness that imposes and the arbitrariness that is imposed on—that is, *both* vehicle and tenor. Obviously, in some ways it too is just another vehicle for George III, who was the last constitutional monarch to really reign and himself something of an imposed-on imposition. On him would be superimposed the names of financiers, stockbrokers, merchants, and politicians, conspicuous among whom would be (of course) the earl of Bute. That there would be nothing kingly about capitalist exploitation or capitalistic about George only made him more instrumental for capitalism. One must ultimately ask of this kind of poetry two questions that suggest connections between cognition, epistemology, and politics: (1) Who is the king? (2) What is the tenor of the analogy?[7]

Along with a counterfeit cross and crown go pastors who cannot read or write; the Gospel itself has lost its proper tenor and become just another vehicle of oppression:

> Pastors she [Europe] sends to help them in their need,
> Some who can't write, with others who can't read;
> And on sure grounds the Gospel pile to rear,
> Sends missionary felons every year . . .
>
> (lines 69–72)

The gulf between signifiers and signifieds will eventually be bridged by revolutionary violence, as the system of signification is turned against its initiators, the only way for the oppressed to return the tenors to the vehicles. Thus the virtues will, from the standpoint of the oppressor, return as the daemonic inversions or vices of the "ten times more the sons of Hell" (88), because directed against themselves. Prudence, wisdom, and faith will return, but as cunning, resentment, and stoic resolve—all directed against those who banished them initially, who created and subsequently rather comfortably exploited the gulf between their appearance and the reality. Churchill is the poet of epistemological breakdown but also the prophet of revelation: the two go together. Churchill insists throughout the poem that no mere act of signification or symbolic exchange, however sanctioned its appearance, may override what he considers a more natural system of signification, in which vehicles stand for the real qualities of their tenors.

One can argue that Churchill discredits European claims to the New World by likening them to his own arbitrariness in calling England — or some never-never land —Gotham in order to make himself king of it.[8]

> Europe discover'd India first; I found
> My right to Gotham on the self-same ground;
> I first discovered it. . . .
> With Europe's rights my kindred rights I twine;
> Hers be the Western world, be Gotham mine.
>
> (lines 103–10)

But one can, consistently with the epistemological uncertainty of the poem, also argue the other way: that Churchill substantiates his personal arbitrariness by seeing it as established on the same footing as no less than half the globe. Churchill seems to confirm his private willfulness at least as much as he denies *their* public arbitrariness. Epistemological acts of violence seem to be as good for individuals as they are bad for states. Thus, after discrediting Europe, he proceeds to credit himself, and for nearly the same things:

> All instruments, self-acted, at my name
> Shall pour forth harmony, and loud proclaim,
> Loud but yet sweet, to the according globe,
> My praises, whilst gay nature, in a robe,
> A coxcomb doctor's robe, to the full sound
> Keeps time, like Boyce, and the world dances round.
>
> (lines 153–58)

This occurs in an amphionic passage that seems to allude not entirely satirically to similar passages in Waller's and Marvell's panegyrics to Charles I and Cromwell. Rather than a mock-panegyric, it is a redirection of panegyric to something kinglike yet not precisely a king.

The refrain merely insists on the point. The subsequent passage, a kind of temporal procession poem uniting praise from different age groups, continues to develop this theme of positive naming and even delightful arbitrariness. On one level the poem praises Churchill for naming himself king of Gotham, and on another it celebrates the human arbitrariness or human freedom (as one wishes) that such naming expresses.

The second part of *Gotham* develops the theme of signification by considering problems of poetic composition and craft:

> when to use the powers
> Of Ornament, and how to place the flowers,
> So that they neither give a tawdry glare,
> 'Nor waste their sweetness in the desert air';
> . . . .
> To make proud Sense against her nature bend,
> And wear the chains of Rhyme, yet call her friend.
> (lines 17–28)

He divides poets into those who stress vehicles at the expense of tenors, or what he calls "sense,"

> Who make it all their business to describe
> No matter whether in or out of place;
> Studious of finery, and fond of lace
> (lines 30–32)

and those who stress tenors, who "depend / On sense to bring them to their journey's end" (55–56). The first he likens, again with characteristic reference to a panegyrical topic, the union of ceremony and power, to "idle monarch boys":

> Neglecting things of weight, they sigh for toys;
> Give them the crown, the sceptre, and the robe,
> Who will may take the power, and rule the globe.
> (lines 49–52)

The second he compares to monarchs who, though they may have power, lack popularity (so may not have power long):

> Sense, mere dull, formal Sense, in this gay town,
> Must have some vehicle to pass her down;

> Nor can she for an hour insure her reign,
> Unless she brings fair Pleasure in her train.
>
> (lines 73–76)

Though it is often confused with the austerity of its presentation, virtue itself, which ought ultimately to be the poet's subject, is neither austere nor otherwise but "acts from love" and finally is simply invisible: "In her own full and perfect blaze of light / Virtue breaks forth too strong for human sight" (107–8). Thus, in his epideictic verse Churchill seems painfully conscious of the fact that he is dealing with moral absolutes (for I think the same could implicitly be said for vice) that can only be approximated by analogy. The ideal for what epideictic might do is Christ or at least *Christlike*, a kind of ultimate in terms of word made flesh: "Like God made man, she lays her glory by, / And beams mild comfort on the ravish'd eye" (113–14). The more practicable model is that of the greatest English writers who "held the golden mean" (144) between sense and grace, tenor and vehicle. Churchill finds himself, not surprisingly, among those who fail conspicuously at such a compromise, whose thoughts fail to get adequate expression. The thoughts are likened, significantly, to children who may not live long enough to be baptized, or in other words to get a name. This returns us to what I see as the central preoccupation of the poem: the arbitrariness of naming as epistemological act with various linguistic, political, and economic implications. Moreover, this arbitrary epistemological act is *seen* variously as a form of public tyranny, as an expression of private freedom and positive self-sufficiency, and as a necessary compromise and accommodation, as a prerequisite for life.

Increasingly, though, in the second book of *Gotham* Churchill appears to side with the tenor over the vehicle, with the things named against the act of naming itself. Rather than be bound up with the words themselves, his meaning seems to transcend them as freedom and wildness bound up with "loose Digression" (205) and "gay Description" (211). Of course, it is arguable that this apparent siding with the tenor over the vehicle is really no such thing, but rather just a siding with different tenors of different vehicles. Clearly, however, there is at least an important change in the nature of the vehicle from the word to something else, larger and harder to pin down. And clearly whatever side Churchill is really on, he wishes to come out strongest for meaning over whatever means; it is this that, whatever his better sense, arouses his best feeling and some of his best lines, as when he describes the lines (with rather precise naming, one must note): "Materials rich, though rude, inflamed with thought, / Though more by fancy than by judgment wrought" (227–28). This poem is really itself the vehicleless tenor of the poem that you, the craftsperson, might want to write. *Name* it then, and "Swear it surpasses Rome, and rivals Greece" (236).

Not surprisingly, since Churchill prefers meaning over means, he opposes the very panegyrical tradition and all its emphasis on means and ceremony, which he exploits by writing *Gotham*. This preference of tenor over vehicle is identified with detestation of George III's minister, the earl of Bute, since Bute and detestation of Bute—he tells us finally—is really his meaning (and it excuses all).[9] The whole second half of the book is a kind of reprise of Stuart history and a revision of the kind of poetry associated with it, as Churchill "pays back" the Stuarts for all the lies said about them in panegyrics. He does so in another panegyric addressed (ostensibly) to himself. Of course, this is also a screen for getting at George III. Churchill himself, as king of Gotham, becomes a vehicle for the king of England, and Churchill's detestation of Bute becomes an example for George to follow: "Cursed be the cause whence Gotham's evils spring, / Though that cursed cause be found in Gotham's king" (275–76).

The arbitrariness of naming is given its strongest political corollary in Churchill's seemingly double vision of Charles I. On one hand, Charles is king and so "could do no wrong" (536); on the other, he is clearly a liar and a wrongdoer of the first order. The arbitrariness of this act of naming is best understood historically, and indeed the violent discontinuity of the king's name or vehicle with the king's tenor or real self seems a direct consequence of that other violent discontinuity that separated his head from his body:

> ... hadst thou laid down in death
> As in a sleep, thy name by Justice borne
> On the four winds, had been in pieces torn.
>
> (lines 542–44)

Not inappropriately, arbitrary naming here defends arbitrary rule, and even moves that other arbitrary namer, Charles Churchill, who regarded Charles I as a martyr even though he knew better. Charles II, though described as better than his father at seeing through things to their tenors, is still too lazy to do anything about them. Finally, James II is neither duped by appearances nor too lazy to address reality, but rather too much an aberration to be himself other than an appearance or a bad dream without reality. He is a tenorless vehicle, so much closer to fiction than to history that "the relation would mere fiction seem, / The mock creation of a poet's dream" (645–46).

After finding a savior in Nassau, Churchill begins Book Three with rather cloying scenes of domestic bliss. These establish him as feeling father of his people, as "Patriot King." At this point, then, he permanently usurps George III as Gothamite king, though now the naming seems especially presumptuous:

> Will I, or can I, on a fair review,
> As I assume that name, deserve it too?
>
> (lines 51–52)

> A patriot king—why, 'tis a name which bears
> The immediate stamp of Heaven; which wears
> The nearest, best resemblance we can show
> Of God above, through all his works below.
>
> (lines 63–66)

These lines replace the tenor of kingship with something more mundane, describing the crown itself as a deceptive vehicle that "glistens" (106) but is "lined with thorns" (112), and the king worthy of the name as Christlike in more ways than one:

> Be it my task to seek, nor seek in vain,
> Not only how to live, but how to reign,
> And to those virtues which from reason spring,
> And grace the man, join those which grace the king.
>
> (lines 219–22)

He must avoid being a tenorless vehicle, a "royal cipher" (260), a disgrace of "All that is royal in his name" (316). The effect of this is to make other names equally arbitrary and unsuited, especially "Rebellion" (303), which then becomes a bad name for a good thing, for an act that is not rebellion at all but rather national conservation. Apparently one way to avoid this is to read this poem, since he writes us (561–65) that as Patriot King history will become his special study. While he must not forget that "monarchs are for action made" (474), he must also demonstrate an ability to deal successfully with the very epistemological problems posed here; he must do generally what he says he must do specifically with religion: "find out there / What's form, what's essence" (581–82).

If these are the things the Patriot King must do, then Churchill, by his own admission possessed of a marked preference for tenor over vehicle, for meaning over means, would be too radical and, in a sense, too arbitrary for the job. Careful sifting of the wheat from the chaff is clearly not for Churchill; of the three brother's of *A Tale*, he is closer to Jack than to Peter or even Martin. Less significantly, the impartial reading of history would have been similarly inimical to him, as he might have expected us to notice. Finally, his naming himself Patriot King, always vaguely conditional and hortatory, is itself suspect of the same ambivalence that generally surrounds naming in *Gotham*. Naming is as attractive privately as it is publicly ugly. It *might* be splendid to name oneself Patriot King, provided one *were*. But how can one know? Yet, as Bertelsen indicates, knowledge is offered as the panacea for the ills of monarchy.[10] How many Patriot Kings would there be? How many could we stand? These are just some of the nagging questions Churchill tries to answer in his poem. Churchill provides a significantly more offhand (and even positive) version of Swift's Hack's "promise" to the "truly learned" reader everywhere that *here* he will "find sufficient Matter to employ his Speculations for the Rest of his Life": "Something I do myself, and something too, / If they can do it, leave for them to do" (187–90).

Afterword

I have made at least two discoveries that have enlarged my sense of panegyric's longevity and even cast some doubt on the "fact" of its decline. First, Swift's mock-panegyrics of the 1730s ought to be distinguished from mere mock-encomia, because what they mock is much more than fulsome or exaggerated praise. They mock abusive relationships, not just of patrons and clients, but also of tenors and vehicles. The simultaneous presence of both targets is no coincidence, but an indication of the subtle connections between the way we address authority and the way we address the rest of the world.

Second, this deeper than anticipated sense of panegyric is not restricted to the first half of the eighteenth century, but survives virtually intact into the 1760s. In fact, the connection between panegyric's innately political relationships (poet, prince, and people) and the innately epistemological relationships of language itself (meaner, meaning, "meanee") is as strong in Churchill as it ever was in Swift.

Clearly, from panegyrists and mock-panegyrists alike Churchill inherits a theme, a tradition of self-conscious and arbitrary signification, principally analogical, to which he himself is extremely ambivalent. The arbitrariness comes to be seen as probably unavoidable, and certainly not all bad. Thus what is a negative in Swift's satire begins to be positive again in Churchill's, but with at least one major difference. While Churchill indicates some of the Hack's capacity for arbitrariness, he indicates nothing of his capacity for certainty. Churchill's epistemology is almost a contradiction in terms, since it lacks the confidence, the "knowledge," of knowledge.

Critics like Wedgwood and Doody have already indicated how significant, sophisticated literary techniques may reveal an unsophisticated or even naïve origin in response to extraliterary events. Panegyric seems to have started as a somewhat *recherché* kind of writing (though necessarily a response to extraliterary events), and then to have lent itself to more popular, polemical treatment in works like the "painter-poems" and *The Rehearsal Transpros'd;* they in turn provided some of the principal motifs (like the preface and clothing) for the epistemological (and political) satire of *A Tale of a Tub.*

What develops in the panegyric tradition, I believe, is a sophisticated understanding of the problems of signification that is widespread and popular; it is not restricted to any particular class, level of education, or political persuasion. Thus Churchill, in his panegyrical poems, seems to understand as well as Swift the need of virtue for *some* kind of qualitative representation, some kind of "vehicle," at the same time he seems even more sensitive than Swift to the problems of such representation in a world of increasingly *quantitative* criteria. It makes little difference, for this, that Swift was a Tory churchman and Churchill a libertine and a supporter of Wilkes. Marvell's earlier anticipation of this new, quantitative world, where religious principles are secondary to problems of supply and taxation, helps to make him what Legouis calls "modern." Ironically, of all the writers discussed here, Waller is both the most indicative of such changes and the least indicative; he who praised them most *quantitatively,* understood them least *qualitatively.*

That panegyric was affected by capitalism and democratization is less surprising than the degree to which these changes may be traced in literature. In inferior writers like Waller this manifests itself in an awkward betrayal of quality to increasingly paramount quantity, a betrayal often achieved by analogical techniques that seem to have gone out of control, lost their reference, created a new one, or even created an entirely new version at odds with the poet's original intention. After all, if the focus of "the good" has in fact shifted to "the many," all analogy can argue is that "the many" may be more or less. At best, analogy reverts, as it does in the "Instructions," to its initial, strictly mathematical, and morally neutral significance. Swift satirizes this very point; he makes this neutrality negative by showing how horrible, even nightmarish, it is, not in itself, but when it is offered by some mistaken "birthday bard" as a vision of the Good, in particular the good ruler.

In Marvell, Swift, and Churchill the analogies tend to describe analogy itself, in particular some analogical vehicle, whether a painting of a painted woman, or a "painting" of a poem, or (in Churchill's *Rosciad*) a representation of an actor representing another actor representing some bad actor of a king, etc. All are conspicuously caught up in quantitative processes in which our judgment is also implicated. The fact that these vehicles usually stand for or have displaced either a king or some other figure of authority, suggests a tantalizing nexus between social and literary developments.

In his study, *The Origins of the English Novel*, Michael McKeon shows how the novel became an instrument for the investigation of what he calls questions of truth and virtue, and ultimately a gauge for the calculation of their divergence. Clearly another important gauge is epideictic writing, whose conventional subject is similar, if not identical, to the unconventional subject matter of the novel. McKeon describes the rise of a new, quantitative virtue similar to what one can discern in panegyrics like Waller's "Instructions" or in the personified "Opinion" and "Prudence" of Churchill's later poetry. As forms of epideictic, panegyric and satire make their own contribution to epistemological probing, a probing that contributes, like everything else, it seems, to the more thorough investigation of the novel.

The integrity of the panegyric tradition, at least until the time of Churchill, is surprising. No doubt, it is partly due to its intimate connection to the Stuarts, for whom it was practically a family business. The Stuarts were still on Churchill's mind in the 1760s (his great enemy, the earl of Bute, was a Stuart), and they doubtless helped keep panegyric there, too. The integrity of this tradition suggests that it may have collapsed under its own weight.

The virtual monopoly of a genre by one family or dynasty must be unique in literature. That the afterglow of this era also coincided with the great age of English satire tends to confirm that satire and panegyric are profoundly linked by their techniques, topics, and formal arrangements, and also by their topicality; the conditions that give rise to one are bound to give rise to the other. It is hardly surprising that satire and panegyric both exploit analogical techniques quite self-consciously for the sake of their respective transcendentals; nor is it surprising that together they facilitate a certain "consciousness raising" about the cognitive process itself, given the significant role of analogy in cognition and the sheer difficulty of *knowing* that such topical, "competing" versions tend to alert one to.

The frequent occurrence of panegyric in paratexts, its tendency to develop in self-consciously "literary" directions, and its association with a (for want of a better word) "sartorial" attitude to language cannot be mere coincidence. Lockwood argues that the growing sense, in the eighteenth century, of the opacity of language, noticeable in Churchill's difficulty with abstractions, contributed to a subversion of sense, standards, and consequently, of satire. The development must be, if anything, more harmful for panegyric, since its tripartite structure, its stress on mediation, and all their epistemological implications are based on a sense of the transparency of words. Typically, a change in thinking that affected panegyric must have eventually affected satire, and in the same way.

In an essay in *Literary Meaning and Augustan Values* dating from the mid-seventies Irvin Ehrenpreis argues that eighteenth-century writing is characterized by what amounts to an ease and confidence of analogizing, a "conception of style as the frame of meaning or even worse as ornament applied to meaning" (5). This is truer of earlier eighteenth-century satire than later, when ease and confidence appear to have degenerated into their opposites. On its abstract level Swift's satire seems to be of the very epistemological certainties on which satire is premised. I think of Martin who, in his acceptance of the corruptions of his "coat," becomes the least convincing brother of *A Tale*. The self-conscious analogizing of Swift and Churchill exhibits both an impatience with its own epistemology and a failure to discover a better alternative. Satire, according to Leon Guilhamet and many others, typically expresses dissatisfaction with the very arrangements it is nostalgic for. Eighteenth-century satire ridicules the conventions of a discredited genre, panegyric, while exploiting them to expose current abuses. The object of its ridicule and the object of its nostalgia are briefly and curiously one, and its expression as part of the same kind of writing is only sharper for this awareness: a self-reflective art-form, written in obvious awareness of the full implications of its subject matter and of the strengths and limitations of its characteristic means of representation.

Notes

Chapter 1. "Panegyrike Congratulatorie"

1. Aristotle, *The "Art" of Rhetoric*, trans. John Henry Freese (London: William Heinemann, 1921), 13

2. See Charles Allen Beaumont, *Swift's Classical Rhetoric* (Athens: University of Georgia Press, 1961). He defines it as "using the better word or implying the better motive to name or evaluate an act or person" (55).

3. Quintilian, *De institutione oratoria*, trans. H. E. Butler (London: William Heinemann, 1980), 465.

4. James D. Garrison, *Dryden and the Tradition of Panegyric* (Berkeley: University of California Press, 1975).

5. Brian Vickers, ed., *Rhetoric Revalued* (New York: Medieval and Renaissance Texts and Studies, 1982), 18.

6. See Henry Knight Miller, "The Paradoxical Encomium: With Special Attention to its Vogue in England, 1660–1800," *Modern Philology* 53: 145–78. Miller discusses some of the ironic panegyrics of *A Tale*, but without the deeper understanding of the genre that is mainly due to Garrison's study.

7. Warren L. Chernaik, *The Poetry of Limitation* (New Haven: Yale University Press, 1968).

8. Phillip Harth, ed., *New Approaches to Eighteenth-Century Literature* (New York: Columbia University Press, 1974).

9. Ralph Cohen, "On the Interrelations of Eighteenth-Century Literary Forms," in Harth, *New Approaches*, 42.

10. Ralph W. Rader, "The Concept of Genre and Eighteenth-Century Literary Forms," in Harth, *New Approaches*, 83–84.

11. Leon Guilhamet, *Satire and the Transformation of Genres* (Philadelphia: University of Pennsylvania Press, 1987).

12. Isabel Rivers, *The Poetry of Conservatism, 1600–1745: A Study of Poets and Public Affairs from Johnson to Pope* (Cambridge: Rivers Press, 1973).

13. Rachel Trickett, *The Honest Muse: A Study in Augustan Verse* (Oxford: Clarendon Press, 1967).

14. Nilli Diengott, "Analogy as a Critical Term: A Survey and Some Comments," *Style* 19 (1985): 227–41.

15. For example, Charles O. Hartman, "Cognitive Metaphor," *New Literary History: A Journal of Theory and Interpretation* 13 (1982): 327–39.

16. Aristotle, *The "Art" of Rhetoric*, 397. Freese's translation reads: "the simile . . . is a metaphor differing only by the addition of a word" (the term of comparison), but a note explains that the original might mean "manner of setting forth."

17. I. A. Richards, *The Philosophy of Rhetoric* (Oxford: Oxford University Press, 1936).

18. Cecil C. Seronsy, "The Doctrine of Cyclical Recurrence and Some Related Ideas in the Works of Samuel Daniel," *Studies in Philology* 54 (1957): 393.

19. Joan Rees, *Samuel Daniel: A Critical and Biographical Study* (Liverpool: Liverpool University Press, 1964).

20. Charles Howard McIlwain, *The Political Works of James I* (New York: Russell & Russell, 1965), 30.

21. Seronsy, "Doctrine of Cyclical Recurrence," 388. Seronsy states, "The doctrine of recurrence is a familiar classical theme," and traces its influence in Plato *(The Statesman)*, Virgil *(Fourth Eclogue)*, and Seneca.

22. Graham Parry, *The Seventeenth Century: The Intellectual and Cultural Context of English Literature, 1603–1700* (New York: Longman, 1989), 25.

23. Howard Erskine-Hill, *The Augustan Idea in English Literature* (London: Edward Arnold, 1983).

24. Chernaik, *The Poetry of Limitation*, 150–51.

25. See, for example, Howard D. Weinbrot, *Augustus Caesar in "Augustan" England* (Princeton: Princeton University Press, 1978).

26. George Parfitt, ed., *Ben Jonson: The Complete Poems* (London: Penguin Books, 1988), 335.

27. Maurice Platnauer, trans., *Claudian* (Cambridge: Harvard University Press, 1963), 1:308–9.

28. L. E. Kastner, ed. *The Poetical Works of William Drummond of Hawthornden*, 2 vols. (1913; New York: Haskell House, 1968).

Chapter 2. Andrew Marvell's Political Poetry and the Panegyric Tradition

1. Garrison, *Dryden and the Tradition of Panegyric*, 131.

2. Franklin G. Burroughs, Jr., "Marvell's Cromwell and Mays's Caesar: 'An Horatian Ode' and the *Continuation of the Pharsalia*," *English Language Notes* 13 (1975): 118.

3. G. D. Monsarrat, "Marvell's Use of 'Nor Yet,' with Special Reference to the 'Horatian Ode'," *English Language Notes* 18 (1980): 107–8.

4. Nicholas Guild, "The Context of Marvell's Allusion to Lucan in 'An Horatian Ode'," *PLL* 14 (1978): 412.

5. Patterson, *Marvell and the Civic Crown*, 62.

6. Blair Worden, "The Politics of Marvell's Horatian Ode," *Historical Journal* 27 (1984): 539.

7. J. M. Newton, "What Do We Know about Andrew Marvell?" *Cambridge Quarterly* 4 (1973): 129.

8. Michael Wilding, "Marvell's 'An Horatian Ode Upon Cromwell's Return from Ireland', The Levellers, and the Junta," *Modern Language Review* 82 (1987): 5.

9. John Wallace, *Destiny his Choice: The Loyalism of Andrew Marvell* (Cambridge: Cambridge University Press, 1968), 75.

10. Ibid., 100.

11. A. J. N. Wilson, "Andrew Marvell's 'The First Anniversary of the Government Under Oliver Cromwell: The Poem and Its Frame of Reference," *Modern Language Review* 69 (1974): 268.

12. Nicholas Guild, "Marvell's 'The First Anniversary of the Government Under O.C.'," *PLL* 11 (1974): 1.

13. Stephen N. Zwicker, "Modes of Government in Marvell's 'The First Anniversary," *Criticism* 16 (1974): 1.

Chapter 3. "Competing Versions"

1. Sir George Clark, *The Later Stuarts, 1660–1714* (Oxford: Clarendon Press, 1955), 63.

2. Warren L. Chernaik, *The Poetry of Limitation* (New Haven: Yale University Press, 1968), 188–89.

3. Annabel M. Patterson, *Marvell and the Civic Crown* (Princeton: Princeton University Press, 1978), 142.

4. Edward Niles Hooker and H. T. Swedenberg, Jr., eds., *The Works of John Dryden*, vol. 1. (Berkeley and Los Angeles: University of California Press, 1956). All quotations of *Annus Mirabilis* are from this edition.

5. See George deF. Lord, ed., *Poems on Affairs of State: Augustan Satirical Verse, 1660–1714*, vol. 1 (New Haven: Yale University Press, 1963). All quotations of the "painter-poems" are from this edition.

6. Quoted in Chernaik, *Poetry of Limitation*, 68.

7. Pat Rogers, ed., *Jonathan Swift: The Complete Poems* (New Haven: Yale University Press, 1983). All quotations of Swift poems are from this edition.

8. Isabel Rivers, *The Poetry of Conservatism* (Cambridge: Rivers Press, 1973), 119.

9. Nicholas Jose, *Ideas of the Restoration in English Literature* (Cambridge: Harvard University Press, 1984), 102.

10. Paul Seaward, *The Cavalier Parliament and the Reconstruction of the Old Regime, 1661–1667* (Cambridge: Cambridge University Press, 1989), 252–53.

Chapter 5. From Cheated Sight to False Light

1. E. W. Rosenheim, "Swift's Ode to Sancroft: Another Look," *Modern Philology* 73 (1976): 33.

2. Fischer, *On Swift's Poetry*, 17.

3. Brian Vickers, "Analogy Versus Identity: The Rejection of Occult Symbolism, 1580–1680," in *Occult and Scientific Mentalities in the Renaissance*, ed. Brian Vickers (Cambridge: Cambridge University Press, 1984), 95–163.

4. Ibid., 102.

5. Deborah Baker Wyrick, *Jonathan Swift and the Vested Word* (Chapel Hill: University of North Carolina Press, 1988).

6. John R. Clark, *Form and Frenzy in Swift's "Tale of a Tub"* (Ithaca: Cornell University Press, 1970), 69.

7. Rosenheim, *Swift and the Satirist's Art*, 133.

8. See Michael McKeon, *The Origins of the English Novel, 1600–1740* (London: Century Hutchinson, 1987), 61. McKeon remarks that the Hack's "dismay at superficial and deep reading alike is one version of the central problem of the *Tale*, the untenable choice between being a fool and a knave." I think it should be noted that such distinctions are misleading, since the Hack is *always* a superficial reader. For him "deep" reading is the identification of the tenor with a vehicle to which it is only superficially similar. He pretends to offer two alternatives, but practices only one.

Chapter 6. The Preface as Vehicle in *A Tale of a Tub*

1. Richard L. Barnett, "En guise d'avant-propos," *L'Ésprit Créateur* 27 (1987): 5–6.
2. Gérard Genette, *Seuils* (Paris: Éditions du Seuil, 1987).
3. Andrew Marvell, *The Rehearsal Transpros'd and The Rehearsal Transpros'd The Second Part*, ed. D. I. B. Smith (Oxford: Clarendon Press, 1971).
4. Jonathan Swift, *A Tale of a Tub*, ed. A. C. Guthkelch and D. Nichol Smith, 2d ed. (Oxford: Clarendon Press, 1958).
5. Luiz Fernando Valente, "Fiction and the Reader: The Prefaces of *Tutameia*," *Hispanic Review* 56 (1988): 350.
6. Jorge Luis Borges, *Obras completas, 1923–1972* (Buenos Aires: Emecé, 1975), 429. Quoted as translated by Oviedo, "Borges: The Poet According to His Prologues," in *Borges the Poet*, ed. Carlos Cortinez (Fayetteville: University of Arkansas Press, 1986): 121–33.
7. Henry B. Wheatley, *The Dedication of Books to Patron and Friend* (London: Elliot Stock, 1887).
8. Guy R. Lyle, ed. *Praise from Famous Men: An Anthology of Introductions* (Metuchen, N.J: Scarecrow Press, 1977).
9. Herbert J. C. Grierson and Sandys Watson, *The Personal Note or First and Last Words from Prefaces, Introductions, Dedications, Epilogues* (London: Chatto & Windus, 1946).
10. See William Kinsley's "Le Mock-Book," *Études Françaises* 18 (1982): 43–60, for a discussion of *A Tale of a Tub* as "mock-book." Kinsley's article deserves to be less unknown than it is.
11. Just as we (reading Marvell reading Parker, to use modern jargon) seem to be on a walk accompanying Marvell through Parker's text (Marvell uses the walk as a metaphor for animadverting), we seem to be right with Marvell when he breaks off his reading for the night and resumes the next morning. One paragraph ends, "And so, Mr. *Bayes*, Good night," and the next begins, "And now Good-morrow" (117). Reading and commentary are signs of authorial presence.
12. Eugene Korkowski, "With an Eye to the Bunghole: Figures of Containment in *A Tale of a Tub*," *Studies in English Literature* 15 (1975): 391–408.
13. I. A. Richards, *The Philosophy of Rhetoric* (Oxford: Oxford University Press, 1936).
14. Deborah Baker Wyrick, *Jonathan Swift and the Vested Word* (Chapel Hill: University of North Carolina Press, 1988). See especially 132–35.
15. Wheatley noted the same thing in 1887, with particular reference to dedications: "At the revival of learning in Europe, when the grand works of the classic authors were rescued from their long slumber, few of them were published without a dedication" (4).
16. George Villiers, duke of Buckingham, et al., *The Rehearsal*, in *Restoration Plays* (New York: Modern Library, 1953), 3–57.

17. Aristotle, *The "Art" of Rhetoric,"* trans. John Henry Freese (Cambridge: Harvard University Press; London: William Heinemann, 1939).

18. Robert Boyle, *The Works of the Honourable Robert Boyle in Six Volumes* (1772; Hildesheim: George Olms Verlagsbuchhandlung, 1966).

19. See the preface to "Animadversions upon Mr. Hobbes's Problemata de Vacuo," *Works,* 4:104. He refers to "resolutions" he "had taken against writing books of controversy," but proceeds nevertheless to quarrel with Hobbes's "gross conception of a corporeal God" (105).

20. Robert Adams Day, "Richard Bentley and John Dunton: Brothers under the Skin," *Studies in Eighteenth-Century Culture* 16 (1986):125–38.

21. Dunton has his revenge, of sorts, in the preface to his *Life and Errors,* where he endeavors to turn Swift's satire into compliment: "to use the words of the *scoffing Tub-man,* the History of my *Life and Errors* is 'a faithful and painful Collection, wholly gathered from my own breast'" (xvi).

22. John Dunton, *The Life and Errors of John Dunton, Citizen of London; with the Lives and Characters of More than a Thousand Contemporary Divines, and Other Persons of Literary Eminence, etc.* 2 vols. (London: J. Nichols, Son, and Bentley, 1818).

23. As a last backward glance at Dunton, I wonder who it was who wrote to the *Athenian Oracle* asking, "Which in your Opinion is the best Preface that ever was written?" Dunton, or some other "Athenian," answers, in rather garbled and *scazzy* fashion, "It's impossible for any Person to determine, since no one has seen all, or could that be supposed, perhaps as no one has Judgment exact enough to criticize on all Subjects, some would have these Three to be the best, Monsieur *Thou's* Preface to his History, *Causabon's* to his Edition of *Polybius,* and *Calvin's* to his *Institutions.* That of *Plutarch* to his *Lives,* and of *Hooker* to his *Ecclesiastick Polity,* are very Curious, perhaps not inferior to the first Three. *Sanderson, Jewel, Taylor,* and several others have done something too fine for our Arbitration." See, if you are lucky enough to find a copy, *The Athenian Oracle: Being an Entire Collection of all the Valuable Questions and Answers in the Old Athenian Mercuries, etc.,* 3d ed. (London, 1728), 4:336.

24. This is a good place to reproduce Genette's charts in *Seuils,* p. 169. The preface may be described according to "régime" (its order of truth) and "role" (the relationship of the prefacer to the prefaced text).

	ROLE		
RÉGIME	auctorial	allographe	actorial
authentique	Hugo pour *Cromwell*	Sartre pour *Portrait d'un invonnu*	Valéry pour *Commentaire de Charmes*
fictif	"Laurence Templeton" pour *Ivanhoe*	"Richard Simpson" pour *Gulliver*	"Gil Blas" pour *Gil Blas*
apocryphe	"Rimbaud" pour *la Chasse Spirituelle*	"Verlaine" pour *la Chasse Spirituelle*	"Valéry" pour *Commentaire de Charmes*

25. Genette remarks that Nabokov was one of the moral critics' "dernière victimes" (228); hence, the "postface ultérieure" to *Lolita*.

26. This autobiographical, even retrospective aspect of the "Apology" resembles what Genette calls the "preface tardive" (228), good modern examples of which would be Borges's prologue to his *Obras Completas* of 1974, in which he sometimes expresses a sense of alienation from the prefacer as well as the work prefaced: "I have changed this book very little. It is no longer mine" *(Obras Completas,* 55). Borges's preference for "prologue" over "preface" no doubt reflects his appreciation of the theatrical, role-playing potential of the form. Some of Borges's prologues would be closer to the "preface ultérieure" (like the prologue to *El hacedor*, 1960), but clearly the distinctions between such "seuils" are no more watertight than the "seuils" themselves.

Chapter 7. Swift and Churchill

1. This judgment may have to be revised, in light of my own discoveries in Churchill's poetry of the 1760s.

2. John Irwin Fischer and Donald C. Mell, eds., *Contemporary Studies of Swift's Poetry* (Newark: University of Delaware Press, 1981).

3. Pat Rogers, ed., *Jonathan Swift: The Complete Poems* (New Haven: Yale University Press, 1983).

4. This may sound extreme, but it is consistent with the way Churchill's predicament is described by others. See, for example, Peter M. Briggs, "'The brain, too finely wrought': Mind unminded in Churchill's Satires," *Modern Language Studies* 14 (1984): 39–53 at 52. "He had followed his satiric intelligence where it led him, and it had carried him away from all the traditional sources of validation for satire—common experience, a common language, shared ideals and aspirations, a framework of cultural values which served to differentiate heroism from chaos."

5. See Bertelsen, *The Nonsense Club,* 224 for a version of the story of how, by feigning madness, the Gothamites averted King John's anger at them for having denied him passage through their fields. Bertelsen connects this story to the carnivalesque function of "lords of misrule" like the mayors of Garret and even John Wilkes himself.

6. See Briggs, "The brain," 40 for a discussion of what he terms Churchill's "wavering epistemology, a faltering ability to grasp his satiric objects *and* his own values firmly." While Briggs sees the problem of Churchill's epistemology as one of mental penetration impossible to sustain without it becoming solipsistic, I see it in terms of I. A. Richards's nomenclature of tenor and vehicle.

7. See James D. Garrison's *Dryden and the Tradition of Panegyric* (Berkeley and Los Angeles: University of California Press, 1975). Garrison defines panegyric as "an oration addressed to a monarch, or other figure of 'conspicuous power,' on a public, ceremonial occasion" (37). While properly a branch of epideictic rhetoric, panegyric became deliberative as its praise became advice. Many of its topics can be found in *Gotham*, particularly in Book III. In panegyric the king must raise the humble and lower the proud, as in the Virgilian ideal of *parcere subiectis:*

> To be a common father, to secure
> The weak from violence, from pride the poor
>
> (lines 79–80)

He must "exile the vices,"

> Vice and her sons to vanish in disgrace . . .
>
> (line 81)

"restore,"

> To bid afflicted Virtue take new state
> And be, at last, acquainted with the great;
>
> (lines 83–84)

be a "patron,"

> To love the arts, nor let the artists starve;
>
> (line 88)

"rule by example,"

> How can a king (yet on record we find
> Such kings have been, such curses of mankind)
> Enforce that law 'gainst some poor subject elf
> Which Conscience tells him he hath broke himself?
>
> (lines 195–98)

and combine power with piety (or power with virtue):

> When kings,—and none but fools can then rebel,—
> Not less in virtue, than in power, excel,
>
> (lines 215–16)

Churchill's poem offers strong evidence for the longevity of the rhetorical sense of what panegyric was all about. More generally, and more significantly, panegyric is about the proper relationship between prince and people. According to Lance Bertelsen in *The Nonsense Club*, "a discussion of the proper relationship of the monarch, his ministers, and the people" is the subject of at least two books of *Gotham*. In his treatment of what he terms "middling culture," in which "the centripetal processes of assimilation, mimicry, mystification, and education by which the myriad elements constituting 'hegemony'—the stabilizing rules, values, and symbols of the social order—were continually renegotiated" (4), Bertelsen should give more acknowledgment to the specific rhetorical contribution, as many of the topics and formal arrangements of the panegyric get translated into popular culture by writers like Churchill.

8. As does Ronald Hatch in his "Charles Churchill and the Poetry of 'Chartered Freedom'," *English Studies in Canada* 15 (1989): 277–87.

9. Bertelsen calls this "a rather unimpressive transition" (*Nonsense Club*, 228), but I imagine it would have worked with the contemporary audience for whom the earl of Bute was a real concern.

10. See ibid., 230.

Bibliography

Primary Sources

Churchill, Charles. *The Poetical Works of Charles Churchill.* Edited by Douglas Grant. Oxford: Clarendon Press, 1956.

Daniel, Samuel. *The Complete Works in Verse and Prose of Samuel Daniel.* Edited by Rev. Alexander Grosart. 5 vols. 1885. Reprint, New York: Russell & Russell, 1963.

Drummond, William. *The Poetical Works of William Drummond of Hawthornden.* Edited by L. E. Kastner. 2 vols. 1913. Reprint, New York: Haskell House, 1968.

Jonson, Ben. *The Complete Poems.* Edited by George Parfitt. Harmondsworth: Penguin Books, 1988.

Marvell, Andrew. *The Poems and Letters of Andrew Marvell.* Edited by H. M. Margoliouth. 2 vols. Oxford: Clarendon Press, 1971

———. *The Rehearsal Transpros'd and The Rehearsal Transpros'd The Second Part.* Edited by D. I. B. Smith. Oxford: Clarendon Press, 1971.

Swift, Jonathan. *A Tale of a Tub.* Edited by A. C. Guthkelch and D. Nichol Smith. 2d. ed. Oxford: Clarendon Press, 1958.

———. *The Complete Poems.* Edited by Pat Rogers. New Haven: Yale University Press, 1983.

Secondary Sources

Adams, Robert M. "In Search of Baron Somers." In *Culture and Politics*, edited by Perez Zagorin. Berkeley: University of California Press, 1980.

———. "The Mood of the Church and *A Tale of a Tub.*" In *England in the Restoration and Early Eighteenth Century: Essays on Culture and Society*, edited by H. T. Swedenberg, Jr., 71–99. Berkeley: University of California Press, 1972.

Alexander, W. Andrew. "'As Is in That Stile Usual': Debate and Context in Marvell's *The Rehearsal Transpros'd.*" *DAI* 49 (1988): 822A–823A.

Anselment, Raymond. *"Betwixt jest and earnest": Marprelate, Milton, Marvell, Swift, and the Decorum of Religious Ridicule.* Toronto: University of Toronto Press, 1979.

———. "The Oxford University Poets and Caroline Panegyric." *John Donne Journal* 3, no. 2 (1984): 181–201.

Aristotle. *The "Art" of Rhetoric*. Translated by John Henry Freese. Loeb Classical Library. London: William Heinemann, 1939.

Attridge, Derek. "'Damn with Faint Praise': Double Offbeat Demotion." *Eidos* 4, no. 1 (1987): 3–6.

Barnett, Louise K. *Swift's Poetic Worlds*. Newark: University of Delaware Press, 1981.

Barnett, Richard L. "En guise d'avant-propos." *L'Esprit Créateur* 27 (1987): 5–6.

Beaumont, Charles Allen. *Swift's Classical Rhetoric*. Athens: University of Georgia Press, 1961.

Belanger, Terry. "Publishers and Writers in Eighteenth-Century England." In *Books and their Readers in Eighteenth-Century England*, edited by Isabel Rivers, 5–25. New York: St. Martin's Press, 1982.

Billington, Sandra. "An Horatian Ode—Charles I and The Army as Actors." *Notes and Queries* 25 (1978): 512–13.

Bloom, E., and L. Bloom. *Satire's Persuasive Voice*. Ithaca: Cornell University Press, 1979.

Borges, Jorge Luis. *Obras completas 1923–1972*. Buenos Aires: Emecé, 1975.

Boyle, Robert. *The Works of the Honourable Robert Boyle in Six Volumes*. 1772. Reprint, Hildesheim: Georg Olms Verlagsbuchhandlung, 1966.

Bradbrook, Muriel. *Andrew Marvell*. Cambridge: Cambridge University Press, 1961.

Brady, Jennifer. "Jonson's 'To King James': Plain Speaking in the *Epigrammes* and the *Conversations*." *Studies in Philology* 82 (1985): 380–98.

Briggs, Peter M. "'The brain, too finely wrought': Mind Unminded in Churchill's Satires." *Modern Language Studies* 14 (1984): 39–53.

Broadus, Edmund Kemper. *The Laureateship: A Study of the Office of Poet Laureate in England with Some Account of the Poets*. Oxford: Clarendon Press, 1921.

Brown, Laura. *Alexander Pope*. Oxford: Basil Blackwell, 1985.

Browning, J. D., ed. *Satire in the Eighteenth Century*. New York: Garland, 1983.

Burell, David. *Analogy and Philosophical Language*. New Haven: Yale University Press, 1973.

Burnett, Archie. "Sylvester's DuBartas, Marvell and Pope." *Notes and Queries* 29 (1982): 418–19.

Burroughs, Franklin G., Jr. "Marvell's Cromwell and May's Caesar: 'An Horatian Ode' and the *Continuation of the Pharsalia*." *English Language Notes* 13 (1975): 115–22.

Bywaters, David. "*Gulliver's Travels* and the Mode of Political Parallel during Walpole's Administration." *ELH* 54 (1987): 717–40.

Carretta, Vincent. *George III and the Satirists from Hogarth to Byron*. Athens: University of Georgia Press, 1990.

Chernaik, Warren L. *The Poetry of Limitation: A Study of Edmund Waller*. New Haven: Yale University Press, 1968.

———. *The Poet's Time: Politics and Religion in the Work of Andrew Marvell*. Cambridge: Cambridge University Press, 1983.

Chibnall, Jennifer. "Something to the Purpose: Marvell's Rhetorical Strategy in *The Rehearsal Transpros'd* (1672)." *Prose Studies* 9 (1986): 80–104.

Clark, John R. *Form and Frenzy in Swift's "Tale of a Tub."* Ithaca: Cornell University Press, 1970.

Cohen, Ralph. "On the Interrelations of Eighteenth-Century Literary Forms." In *New Approaches to Eighteenth-Century Literary Criticism*, edited by Phillip Harth, 33–78. New York: Columbia University Press, 1974.

Cooper, Marilyn M. "Context as Vehicle: Implicatures in Writing." In *What Writers Know: The Language, Process, and Structure of Written Discourses*, edited by Martin Nystrand. New York: Academic Press, 1982.

Cornelius, David K. "Marvell's Horatian Ode." *Explicator* 35 (1977): 18–19.

Corns, Thomas N. "The Literature of Controversy: Polemical Strategy from Milton to Junius." *Prose Studies* 9, no. 2 (1986): 80–104.

———. "Marvell's Horatian Ode." *Explicator* 35 (1976): 11–12.

Cousins, A. D. "Heroic Satire: Dryden and the Defence of the Later Stuart Kingship." *Southern Review* 13, no. 3 (1980): 170–87.

———. "The Idea of a 'Restoration' and the Verse Satires of Butler and Marvell." *Southern Review* 14 (1981): 131–42.

Crane, David. "Marvell and Milton on Cromwell." *Notes and Queries* 33 (1986): 464.

Creigh, Geoffrey. "Samuel Daniel's Masque *The Vision of the Twelve Goddesses*." *Essays and Studies*, n.s. 24 (1974): 22–35.

Cummings, Robert. "Drummond's Forth Feasting: A Panegyric for King James in Scotland." *The Seventeenth Century* 2, no. 1: (1987): 1–18.

Daniel, Samuel. *The Worthy Tract of Paulus Iouius*, etc. London, 1585.

Day, Robert Adams. "Richard Bentley and John Dunton: Brothers under the Skin." *Studies in Eighteenth-Century Culture* 16 (1986): 125–38.

Diengott, Nilli. "Analogy as a Critical Term: A Survey and Some Comments." *Style* 19 (1985): 227–41.

Donnelly, M. L. "Caroline Royalist Panegyric and the Disintegration of a Symbolic Mode." In *Poetry and Politics in the Seventeenth Century*, edited by Claude J. Summers and Ted-Larry Pebworth. Columbia: University of Missouri Press, 1988.

Duffy, Bernard K. "The Platonic Functions of Epideictic Rhetoric." *Philosophy and Rhetoric* 16 (1983): 79–83.

Dunton, John. *The Life and Errors of John Dunton, Citizen of London; With The Lives and Characters of More than a Thousand Contemporary Divines, And Other Persons of Literary Eminence, etc.* 2 vols. London: J. Nichols, Son, and Bentley, 1818.

Ehrenpreis, Irvin. *Swift: The Man, His Works, and the Age.* 3 vols. Cambridge: Harvard University Press, 1962–83.

Eilon, Daniel. "Did Swift Write *A Discourse on Hereditary Right*?" *Modern Philology* 82 (1985): 374–92.

———. "Swift Burning the Library of Babel." *Modern Language Review* 80 (1985): 269–82.

Elkin, Peter. *The Augustan Defence of Satire.* Oxford: Clarendon Press, 1973.

Elliott, Kenneth. "Andrew Marvell and Oliver Cromwell." *Renaissance and Modern Studies* 26 (1982): 75–89.

England, A. B. *Energy and Order in the Poetry of Swift.* London and Toronto: Associated University Presses, 1980.

———. "Subversions of Logic in Some Poems by Swift." *Studies in English Literature* 15 (1975): 409–18.

Erskine-Hill, Howard. *The Augustan Idea in English Literature.* London: Edward Arnold, 1983.

Farrell, William J. "The Role of Mandeville's Bee Analogy in 'The Grumbling Hive.'" *SEL: Studies in English Literature 1500–1900* 25 (1985): 511–27.

Fisher, Alan S. "An End to the Renaissance: Erasmus, Hobbes, and *A Tale of a Tub.*" *Huntington Library Quarterly* 38 (1974): 1–20.

Fischer, John Irwin. *On Swift's Poetry.* Gainesville: University Press of Florida, 1978.

Fischer, John Irwin, and Donald C. Mell, Jr., eds. *Contemporary Studies of Swift's Poetry.* Newark: University of Delaware Press, 1981.

Fitzgerald, Robert P. "Science and Politics in Swift's Voyage to Laputa." *Journal of English and Germanic Philology* 87 (1988): 213–29.

Fitzgerald, William. *Agonistic Poetry: The Pindaric Mode in Pindar, Horace, Hölderlin, and the English Ode.* Berkeley: University of California Press, 1987.

Flynn, Carol Houlihan. *The Body in Swift and Defoe.* Cambridge: Cambridge University Press, 1990.

Folkenflik, Robert, ed. *The English Hero 1660–1800.* Newark: University of Delaware Press, 1982.

Fussell, Paul. *The Rhetorical World of Augustan Humanism.* Oxford: Clarendon Press, 1965.

Garrison, James D. *Dryden and the Tradition of Panegyric.* Berkeley and Los Angeles: University of California Press, 1975.

Gearin-Tosh, Michael. "The Structure of Marvell's 'Last Instructions to a Painter.'" *Essays in Criticism* 22 (1972): 48–57.

Genette, Gérard. *Seuils.* Paris: Editions du Seuil, 1987.

Gilbert, Jack. *Edmund Waller.* Twayne's English Authors Series. Boston: Twayne Publishers, 1979.

Goldberg, Jonathan. "Fatherly Authority: The Politics of Stuart Family Images." In *Rewriting the Renaissance: The Discourse of Sexual Difference in Early Modern Europe*, edited by Margaret W. Ferguson, Maureen Quilligan, and Nancy J. Vickers, 3–32. Chicago: University of Chicago Press, 1986.

Gray, W. Forbes. *The Poets Laureate of England: Their History and their Odes.* London: Sir Isaac Pitman & Sons, 1914.

Griffin, Dustin. "Augustan Collaboration." *Essays in Criticism* 37 (1987): 1–10.

Grierson, Herbert J. C., and Sandys Wason, eds. *The Personal Note or First and Last Lines from Prefaces, Introductions, Dedications, Epilogues.* London: Chatto & Windus, 1946.

Guild, Nicholas. "The Context of Marvell's Allusion to Lucan in 'An Horatian Ode.'" *Papers on Language and Literature* 14 (1978): 406–13.

———. "The First Anniversary of the Government under O. C." *PLL* 11 (1975): 242–53.

Guilhamet, Leon. *Satire and the Transformation of Genres.* Philadelphia: University of Pennsylvania Press, 1987.

———. *The Sincere Ideal: Studies on Sincerity in Eighteenth-Century English Literature.* Montreal: McGill-Queen's University Press, 1974.

Hammond, Paul. "Dryden's Use of Marvell's *Horatian Ode* in *Absalom and Achitophel.*" *Notes & Queries* 35 (1988): 173–4.

Harris, K. M. "Occasions So Few: Satire as a Strategy of Praise in Swift's Early Odes." *Modern Language Quarterly* 31 (1970): 22–37.

Harth, Phillip, ed. *New Approaches to Eighteenth-Century Literature*. New York: Columbia University Press, 1974.

Hartmann, Charles O. "Cognitive Metaphor." *New Literary History: A Journal of Theory and Interpretation* 13 (1982): 327–39.

Harwood, John T., ed. *The Rhetorics of Thomas Hobbes and Bernard Lamy*. Carbondale and Edwardsville: Southern Illinois University Press, 1986.

Hatch, Ronald B. "Charles Churchill and the Poetry of 'Chartered Freedom.'" *English Studies in Canada* 15 (1989): 277–87.

Helgerson, Richard. *Self-Crowned Laureates: Spenser, Jonson, Milton, and the Literary System*. Berkeley: University of California Press, 1983.

Hill, Christopher. *The Experience of Defeat: Milton and Some Contemporaries*. London: Faber and Faber, 1984.

Hollingshead, Gregory. "Pope, Berkeley, and the True Key to the Dunciad in Four Books." *English Studies in Canada* 10 (1984): 141–55.

Holyoak, Keith J. "An Analogical Framework for Literary Interpretation." *Poetics: International Review for the Theory of Literature* 11 (1982): 105–26.

Hopkins, Robert H. "The Personation of Hobbism in Swift's *Tale of a Tub* and *Mechanical Operation of the Spirit*." *Philological Quarterly* 45 (1966): 372–78.

Howell, W. S. *Eighteenth-Century British Logic and Rhetoric*. Princeton: Princeton University Press, 1971.

———. *Logic and Rhetoric in England 1500–1700*. 1956. Reprint, New York: Russell and Russell, 1961.

Ingram, Allan. *Intricate Laughter in the Satire of Swift and Pope*. London: Macmillan, 1986.

Jaffe, Nora Crow. *The Poet Swift*. Hanover, N.H.: University Press of New England, 1977.

Jose, Nicholas. *Ideas of the Restoration in English Literature, 1660–1671*. Cambridge: Harvard University Press, 1984.

Kenner, Hugh. *Dublin's Joyce*. Bloomington: Indiana University Press, 1956.

Kernan, Alvin B. *The Cankered Muse: Satire of the English Renaissance*. New Haven: Yale University Press, 1959.

Kernan, Alvin B. *The Plot of Satire*. New Haven: Yale University Press, 1965.

Kinsley, William. "Le Mock-Book." *Etudes Françaises* 18 (1982): 43–60.

Klinkenborg, Verlyn. "Johnson and the Analogy of Judicial Authority." *The Eighteenth Century: Theory and Interpretation* 28 (1987): 47–61.

Knafla, Louis A. "The Country Chancellor: The Patronage of Sir Thomas Egerton, Baron Ellesmere." In *Patronage in Late Renaissance England*. Los Angeles: William Andrews Clark Memorial Library, University of California, 1983.

Knights, L. C. *Public Voices: Literature and Politics with Special Reference to the Seventeenth Century*. London: Chatto & Windus, 1971.

Korkowski, Eugene. "With an Eye to the Bunghole: Figures of Containment in *A Tale of a Tub*." *Studies in English Literature* 15 (1975): 391–408.

Korshin, Paul J. *From Concord to Dissent: Major Themes in English Poetic Theory 1640–1700.* Menston, Yorkshire: Scolar Press, 1973.

Kuhns, Richard. "Metaphor as Plausible Inference in Poetry and Philosophy." *Philosophy and Literature* 3 (1979): 225–38.

Lanham, Richard A. *A Handlist of Rhetorical Terms.* Berkeley: University of California Press, 1969.

Larson, Charles. "Marvell's Richard Cromwell: 'He Vertue Dead, Revives.'" *Mosaic* 19 (1986): 57–67.

Leranbaum, Miriam. *Alexander Pope's "Opus Magnum," 1729–1744.* Oxford: Clarendon Press, 1977.

Lock, F. P. *The Politics of "Gulliver's Travels."* Oxford: Clarendon Press, 1980.

Lockwood, Thomas. *Post-Augustan Satire: Charles Churchill amd Satirical Poetry, 1750–1800.* Seattle: University of Washington Press, 1979.

Lyle, Guy R., ed. *Praise from Famous Men: An Anthology of Introductions.* Metuchen, N.J.: Scarecrow Press, 1977.

MacKinnon, Patricia L. "The Analogy of the Body Politic in St. Augustine, Dante, Petrarch, and Ariosto." *DAI* 50 (1989): 438A.

Mason, Sarah. "King John and Marvell's *Horatian Ode.*" *Notes & Queries* 34 (1987): 327.

McIlwain, Charles Howard, ed. *The Political Works of James I.* 1918. Reprint, New York: Russell & Russell, 1965.

Miller, Henry Knight. "The Paradoxical Encomium." *Modern Philology* 53 (1956): 145–78.

Monsarrat, G. D. "Marvell's Use of 'Nor Yet,' with Special Reference to the 'Horatian Ode'." *English Language Notes* 18 (1980): 104–8.

Moritz, Philip A. "Joseph Butler and his Ideas on Ultimate Reality and Meaning." *Ultimate Reality & Meaning* 4 (1984): 213–24.

Mullenbrock, Heinz-Joachim. "Cicero and Quintilian as Mentors of British Journalism: Rhetorical Structure of Swift's 'The Conduct of the Allies.'" *Swift Studies: The Annual of the Ehrenpreis Center* 2 (1987): 57–66.

Murphy, James J. *Rhetoric in the Middle Ages: A History of Rhetorical Theory from Saint Augustine to the Renaissance.* Berkeley and Los Angeles: University of California Press, 1974.

Nelson, Carry. "Reading Criticism." *PMLA* 91 (1976): 801–15.

Nevo, Ruth. *The Dial of Virtue: A Study of Poems on Affairs of State in the Seventeenth Century.* Princeton: Princeton University Press, 1963.

Newton, J. M. "What Do We Know about Andrew Marvell?" *Cambridge Quarterly* 4 (1973): 125–35.

Norlin, George, trans. *Isocrates.* Loeb Classical Library. London: William Heinemann, 1928.

Oviedo, Jose Miguel. "Borges: The Poet According to His Prologues." In *Borges the Poet*, edited by Carlos Cortinez. Fayetteville: University of Arkansas Press, 1986.

Owen, William. "In War as in Love: The Significance of Analogous Plots in Cooper's *The Pathfinder.*" *English Studies in Canada* 10 (1984): 289–98.

Parry, Graham. *The Seventeenth Century: The Intellectual and Cultural Context of English Literature, 1603–1700.* New York: Longman, 1989.

Patterson, Annabel M. *Marvell and the Civic Crown.* Princeton: Princeton University Press, 1978.

Paulson, Ronald. *Theme and Structure in Swift's "Tale of a Tub."* New Haven: Yale University Press, 1960.

Pocock, J. G. A. *Politics, Language and Time.* New York: Atheneum, 1971.

Poulakos, Takis. "Isocrates's Use of Narrative in the *Evagoras*: Epideictic Rhetoric and Moral Action." *Quarterly Journal of Speech* 3 (1987): 317–28.

Preston, Thomas R. *Not in Timon's Manner: Feeling, Misanthropy, and Satire in Eighteenth-Century England.* Tuscaloosa: University of Alabama Press, 1975.

Quintilian. *Institutio Oratoria.* Translated by H. E. Butler. Loeb Classical Library. 4 vols. London: William Heinemann, 1980.

Rader, Ralph W. "The Concept of Genre and Eighteenth-Century Studies." In *New Approaches to Eighteenth-Century Literature*, edited by Phillip Harth, 79–115. New York: Columbia University Press, 1974.

Rawson, Claude, ed. *The Character of Swift's Satire.* Newark: University of Delaware Press, 1983.

Rawson, Claude, ed. *English Satire and the Satiric Tradition.* Oxford: Basil Blackwell, 1984.

Redwood, John. *Reason, Ridicule and Religion: The Age of Enlightenment in England.* Cambridge: Harvard University Press, 1976.

Reedy, Gerard, S. J. "'An Horatian Ode' amd 'Tom May's Death.'" *Studies in English Literature* 20 (1980): 137–51.

Rees, Joan. *Samuel Daniel: A Critical and Biographical Study.* Liverpool: Liverpool University Press, 1964.

Rembert, James Aldritch Wyman. *Swift and the Dialectic Tradition.* New York: St. Martin's Press, 1988.

Richards, I. A. *The Philosophy of Rhetoric.* Oxford: Oxford University Press, 1936.

Richards, Judith. "Literary Meaning and the Historian: Towards Reconstructing Marvell's Meaning in 'An Horatian Ode.'" *Literature and History* 7 (1981): 25–47.

Rivers, Isabel. *The Poetry of Conservatism, 1600–1745: A Study of Poets and Public Affairs from Jonson to Pope.* Cambridge: Rivers Press, 1973.

Rix, Herbert David. *Rhetoric in Spenser's Poetry.* Pennsylvania State College Studies 7. State College: Pennsylvania State College, 1940.

Rodino, Richard H. "'Worse than Swift': 'The Beasts' Confession,' Tradition and Rhetoric." *Swift Studies: The Annual of the Ehrenpreis Center* 3 (1988): 79–90.

Rogers, Pat, ed. *Jonathan Swift: The Complete Poems.* New Haven: Yale University Press, 1983.

Rogers, William. *The Three Genres and the Interpretation of Lyric.* Princeton: Princeton University Press, 1983.

Rosenberg, Betty. *Genreflecting: A Guide to Reading Interests in Genre Fiction.* Littleton, Colo.: Librairies Unlimited, 1986.

Rosenheim, Edward W., Jr. *Swift and the Satirist's Art.* Chicago: University of Chicago Press, 1963.

———. "Swift's Ode to Sancroft: Another Look." *Modern Philology* 73 (1976): S24–S39.

Rowe, George E., Jr. "Ben Jonson's Quarrel with Audience and its Renaissance Context." *Studies in Philology* 81 (1984): 438–60.

Rudd, Niall. "Pope and Horace's 'Epistles', *II*. 2." In *English Satire and the Satiric Tradition*, edited by Claude Rawson, 167–82. Oxford: Basil Blackwell, 1984.

Saccamano, Neil. "Authority and Publication: The Works of Swift." *The Eighteenth Century: Theory and Interpretation* 25 (1984): 241–62.

Schakel, Peter J. *The Poetry of Jonathan Swift: Allusion and the Development of a Poetic Style*. Madison: University of Wisconsin Press, 1978.

Schilling, Bernard N. *Dryden and the Conservative Myth*. New Haven: Yale University Press, 1961.

Scholes, Robert. "An Approach Through Genre." In *Towards a Poetics of Fiction*, edited by Mark Spilka, 41–51. Bloomington: Indiana University Press.

Seidel, Michael. "Crisis Rhetoric and Satiric Power." *New Literary History: A Journal of Theory and Interpretation* 20 (1988): 165–86.

Seronsy, Cecil C. "The Doctrine of Cyclical Recurrence and Some Related Ideas in the Works of Samuel Daniel." *Studies in Philology* 44 (1957): 387–407.

Sharpe, Kevin. *Criticism and Compliment: The Politics of Literature in the England of Charles I*. Cambridge: Cambridge University Press, 1987.

Shuster, George. *The English Ode from Milton to Keats*. 1940. Gloucester, Mass.: Peter Smith, 1964.

Sinnot, Aidan John Barr. *Stuart Politics and the Court Masque*. Ann Arbor, Mich.: University Microfilms, 1974.

Smith, Raymond J. *Charles Churchill*. Twayne's English Authors Series. 197. Boston: Twayne Publishers, 1977.

Speck, Paul Surgi. "Bricolage, Analogies and Hinges: Order in the Recombinant Universe of Tristram Shandy." *South Central Review: The Journal of the South Central Modern Language Association* 2 (1985): 64–82.

Stevens, Wallace. "Effects of Analogy." *The Yale Review* 75 (1986): 255–70.

Sullivan, Alvin. "Donne's Sophistry and Certain Renaissance Books of Logic and Rhetoric." *Studies in English Literature 1500–1900* 22 (1982): 107–20.

Summers, Claude J., and Ted-Larry Pebworth, eds. *The Muses' Commonweale: Poetry and Politics in the Seventeenth Century*. Columbia: University of Missouri Press, 1988.

Tedder, Arthur W. *The Navy of the Restoration: From the Death of Cromwell to the Treaty of Breda: Its Work, Growth and Influence*. 1916. Reprint, London: Cornmarket Press, 1970.

Trickett, Rachel. *The Honest Muse: A Study in Augustan Verse*. Oxford: Clarendon Press, 1967.

Tyne, J. L. "Swift's Mock-Panegyrics in 'On Poetry: A Rhapsody.'" *Papers on Language & Literature* 10 (1974): 279–86.

Uphaus, Robert W. "From Panegyric to Satire: Swift's Early Odes and *A Tale of a Tub*." *Texas Studies in Language and Literature* 13 (1971–72): 55–70.

Valente, Luiz Fernando. "Fiction and the Reader: The Prefaces of *Tutameia*." *Hispanic Review* 56 (1988): 349–62.

Vickers, Brian, ed. "Analogy Versus Identity: The Rejection of Occult Symbolism, 1580–1680." In *Occult and Scientific Mentalities in the Renaissance*, edited by Brian Vickers. Cambridge: Cambridge University Press, 1984.

———. *Rhetoric Revalued*. New York: Medieval and Renaissance Texts & Studies, 1982.

———. "Swift and the Baconian Idol." In *The World of Jonathan Swift*, edited by Brian Vickers. Cambridge: Cambridge University Press, 1968.

Vieth, David, and Dustin Griffin. *Rochester and Court Poetry*. Los Angeles: University of California Press, 1988.

Villiers, George, duke of Buckingham, et al. *The Rehearsal*. In *Restoration Plays*, 3–57. New York: Modern Library, 1953.

Wade, Stephen. "Infinite Mirrors of Analogy: Some Speculations on the Seamless Web." *Agenda* 21–22 (1983–84): 71–77.

Waldrop, Rosemarie. "Shall We Escape Analogy?" *Studies in Twentieth-Century Literature* 13 (1989): 113–28.

Walker, Julia M. "Donne's Words Taught in Numbers." *Studies in Philology* 84 (1987): 44–60.

Wallace, John M., ed. *Destiny His Choice: The Loyalism of Andrew Marvell*. Cambridge: Cambridge University Press, 1968.

———. *The Golden & the Brazen World: Papers in Literature and History, 1650–1800*. Berkeley: University of California Press, 1985.

Wedgwood, C. V. *Poetry and Politics under the Stuarts*. Cambridge: Cambridge University Press, 1960.

Weinbrot, Howard. *Augustus Caesar in "Augustan" England*. Princeton: Princeton University Press, 1978.

———. *The Formal Strain: Studies in Augustan Imitation and Satire*. Chicago: University of Chicago Press, 1969.

Wells, Robin Headlam. "William Cowper as Mock Epideictic Elegist." *Thalia: Studies in Literary Humor* 9 (1986): 3–9.

Wheatley, Henry B. *The Dedication of Books to Patron and Friend*. London: Elliot Stock, 1887.

Wilding, Michael. "Marvell's 'An Horatian Ode Upon Cromwell's Return From Ireland', The Levellers, and The Junta." *Modern Language Review* 82 (1987): 1–14.

Williams, Arthur S. "Panegyric Decorum in the Reigns of William III and Anne." *Journal of British Studies* 21 (1981): 56–67.

Wilson, A. J. N. "Andrew Marvell's 'The First Anniversary of the Government Under Olilver Cromwell': The Poem and its Frame of Reference." *Modern Language Review* 69 (1974): 254–73.

Wooden, Warren W. "Sir Thomas Bodley's *Life of Himself* (1609) and the Epideictic Strategies of Encomia." *Studies in Philology* 83 (1986): 62–75.

Worden, Blair. "The Politics of Marvell's Horatian Ode." *Historical Journal* 27 (1984): 525–47.

Wyrick, Deborah Baker. *Jonathan Swift and the Vested Word*. Chapel Hill: University of North Carolina Press, 1988.

Zimmerman, Everett. *Swift's Narrative Satires*. Ithaca: Cornell University Press, 1983.

Zwicker, Steven N. *Dryden's Political Poetry*. Providence, R.I.: Brown University Press, 1972.

———. "Models of Government in Marvell's 'The First Anniversary.'" *Criticism* 16 (1974): 1–12.

Index

Analogy, 11, 21; and clothing in *A Tale of a Tub*, 114–17; in Daniel's "Panegyrike Congratulatorie," 23–26; deliberate inappropriateness of in "Stella Poems," 147; disorder of and loss of authority, 115; and George II, 149; and identification, 114; and parallels, 78; in Marvell's political poetry; and patronage, 95–100; and problem of transcendence, 108; in satire, 107; in *A Tale of a Tub*, 113–23; and versions of kings, 100–106
Aristotle, 11–13, 52, 112; on analogy, 21; on presentation, 72

Beaumont, Charles Allen: on ethos, 13
Boyle, Robert: prefaces in, 134–35
Brown, Laura, 62

Caesar, 38, 71
Charles I, 74, 106, 160, 163
Charles II, 86; versions of 100–106
Chernaik, Warren L., 18, 29, 61, 85
Churchill, Charles, 166–69; inability to discover satisfactory alternatives to panegyrical excess, 156. Works: *Gotham*, 158–65; *The Rosciad*, 156–58.
Clark, John, 114
Claudian: "Panegyric on the Fourth Consulship of the Emperor Honorius," 34
Cleopatra: as topic, 65
Cohen, Ralph, 19, 53
Cromwell, Oliver, 36–51, 160; as Amphion, 45; as Caesar, 38; as Gideon, 48

Daniel, Samuel, 22. Works: *The Civil Wars*, 24; "Panegyrike Congratulatorie," 22–35, 44
Day, Robert Adams: on *scaz*, 135
Diengott, Nilli, 21
Doody, Margaret Anne, 166
Dryden, John: as Bayes, 129; like narrator of *A Tale*, 71; refuses to dedicate *Aeneas* to William III, 138; satirized in *The Rehearsal*, 132; Works: *Annus Mirabilis*, 68–72; "Astraea Redux," 35; *MacFlecknoe*, 68
Drummond, William: "Forth Feasting: A Panegyricke to the King's Most Excellent Majestie," 34
Dunton, John: and "Athenian Society," 110; prefaces in, 135–37; and *scaz*, 135

Ehrenpreis, Irvin, 169
Elizabeth I, 28
Erskine-Hill, Howard, 26–27
Ethos: abuse by Waller, 13; in *The Rehearsal Transpros'd*, 132

Fischer, John Irwin, 108, 109, 145

Garrison, James D.: definitions of panegyric, 15–16; Dryden and panegyric, 16; on Marvell and Waller, 44; on Marvell's "Horatian Ode," 36; on Marvell's "First Anniversary," 42; Shaftesbury, 18
Genette, Gérard: definition of paratext, 124; on prefaces, 125, 128
George II, 147–53

George III, 155–56, 158–65
Guilhamet, Leon, 19, 83, 169

Hardison, O. B.: on Aristotle's *Poetics* and Averroës's translation, 16
Henry VII, 24–25
Horace: "Fall of Cleopatra," 39

James I: and *Basilikon Doron*, 24, 27, 30, 31–33, 34, 106
James II, 60, 163
Jonson, Ben: dedication to *Volpone*, 126; "A Panegyre, on the Happy Entrance of James, Our Sovereign, to His First High Session of Parliament in This Kingdom," 34
Johnson, Samuel: preface to *A Dictionary of the English Language*, 126
Jose, Nicholas, 73, 84

Legouis, Pierre, 167
Lockwood, Thomas: on Churchill's abstractions, 156, 168
Lucan, 37

Marvell, Andrew, 167. Works: "First Anniversary," 42–51; "An Horatian Ode upon Cromwell's Return from Ireland," 36–42; "painter-poems," 13; *The Rehearsal Transpros'd*, 18, 24, 42; "The Second Advice to a Painter," 60–67; "The Third Advice to the Painter," 72–77; "The Last Instructions to a Painter," 77–83; *The Rehearsal Transpros'd*, 85–106
McKeon, Michael, 168
Michelangelo, 65

Naming: as arbitrariness, 121, 158, 160; and arbitrary rule, 163; in Churchill's *Gotham*, 158–59; in "Directions for a Birthday Song," 148; of Parker "Bayes," 129; and Queen Caroline, 152–53; royal in name, 164; and signification, 156; and Walpole, 153

Panegyric: addressees of, 17; definitions of, 15–16; first in English, 22; displaced addressee of, 148, 154; displacement of public by private people in, 147; and epic, 16; and epistemological focus, 158; in the Greek tradition, 15; as metaphor for all kinds of writing, 155; in "painter-poems" and *Annus Mirabilis*, 54–56; in praise and blame, 91–95; and patronage, 95–100; and the patron, 100–106; and rhetoric, 11–21; and satire, 52, 83–84, 145; and self-praise, 121; and signification, 51; subversion of by Daniel, 35; subversion of by Marvell, 50; tripartite relationships of and political and epistemological implications, 17, 166, 169; tripartite relationships of reproduced throughout *A Tale of a Tub*, 112–13; and variations on tripartite relationships of in *A Tale of a Tub*, 115
Parker, Samuel: conventional expressions of, 89; ethos of, 92; as panegyrist, 95; his preferment, 96; and religious absolutism, 85; and use of analogy, 87; versions of, 90, 98, 100–106
Paratext: as defined by Genette, 124; headings and titles, 88–89; occurrence of panegyric in, 168; prefaces, 89–91, 124–44
Patterson, Annabel: on advice in Waller's "Instructions to a Painter," 54; disagreement with Wallace over meaning of Duchess of Albemarle, 75–76; on Marvell's "An Horatian Ode," 37, 40; on Noah, 66; on *paragone*, 65; on *The Rehearsal Transpros'd*, 85–86
Phaeton, 66
Prefaces: Boyle's, 134–35; and conventions, 133–34, 138, 144; defined by Genette, 124; Dunton's, 135–37; examples of, 125–26; in Marvell, 127–33; Parker a monger of, 90; and print, 136; in Swift, 137–44; as typographical platforms, 135; and valorization, 138–40
Printing: and Cadmus story, 129; and conventions, 133; and Dunton's *scaz*-like intimacy in prefaces, 135; in "Panegyrike Congratulatorie," 31–33; Parker's opposition to, 95; and

prefaces, 128; and print-oriented people in Swift, 133; in *The Rehearsal Transpros'd*, 86–87; and signification, 121; and transposition, 132–33

Quintilian, 14

Rader, Ralph, 19, 53
Rees, Joan, 22–23, 29
Rhetoric: and panegyric, 11–21; a synchrony, 11–12
Richards, I. A.: tenor and vehicle, 21, 53
Rivers, Isabel, 19
Rosenheim, Edward, 107

Schakel, Peter, 145
Second Anglo-Dutch War, 52
Seronsy, Cecil, 22
Signification: arbitrariness of, 121, 146–47, 154; in "Directions for a Birthday Song," 145, 148; in *Gotham*, 159, 161; and interpretation, 124; and panegyric tradition, 167; and paratext, 124; in *The Rehearsal Transpros'd*, 87; as represented by panegyric, 51, 154; in "Stella Poems," 146–47
Somers, Lord, 121, 138, 144

Swift, Jonathan, works: "The Delany Poems," 153–55; "Directions for a Birthday Song," 17, 25, 33, 54, 64, 147–53, 157; "Ode to Dr. William Sancroft," 108–9; "Ode to the Athenian Society," 109–11; "Ode to the King," 107–8; "Stella Poems," 145–47; *A Tale of a Tub*, 18, 20, 24, 29, 42, 44, 107–44, 156

Temple, Sir William: on eloquence 20
Topics, 17
Transposition: of epilogue and prologue, 132; of letters of the alphabet, 132; of praise and blame, 131; and print, 132–33
Trickett, Rachel, 20

Vehicle and tenor: Churchill's ambivalence towards, 157–58, 161–62; as cause and effect, 110–11; as client and patron, 95; as crown of thorns, 164; and danger of vertigo, 115; in Daniel's "Panegyrike Congratulatorie," 35; in deliberate inappropriateness of quantities for qualities, 145–46, 148, 157, 167; as distorted coats of the brothers in *A Tale of a Tub*, 115; failure to find an adequate vehicle for George II's tenor, 149; failure to find an adequate vehicle for George III, 159; in Hack's procedure, 118–20; as inside and outside, 147; as letter and spirit in *A Tale of a Tub*, 114; literary vehicles for political tenors, 99; in "Ode to the Athenian Society," 110; as preface and text, 128; referring to one another rather than to any clear tenor of authority, 105; reversal of polarity in, 156; tenorless vehicles, 121; tenorless vehicle a "royal cipher" and Churchill's fear of becoming same, 164; tension between in "Directions for a Birthday Song," 151–52; vehicleless tenor, 163; as versions of events become versions of versions, 53
Versions: of Archbishop Sancroft, 109; of Samuel Parker, 100–106; of William III, 108;
Vickers, Brian, 16; on analogy in Bacon, 113–14
Villiers, George, 2d Duke of Buckingham: *The Rehearsal*, 69, 130
Virgil, 27, 55, 69
Virtue: of Cromwell, 41; new virtues created by means of analogy, 123; new virtues to replace ones exhausted through print, 144; perversions of prudence, wisdom, etc., 159–60; in "Stella Poems," 58

Wallace, John M., 42; on Duchess of Albemarle, 75–76; on Marvell's "Horatian Ode," 41; on Marvell's "First Anniversary, 42, 45; on *The Rehearsal Transpros'd*, 85
Waller, Edmund, 167; hyperbole in, 53. Works: "Instructions to a Painter,"

Waller, Edmund *(continued):*
    13, 56–60; "Upon His Majesty's
    Repairing of St. Paul's," 44
Wedgewood, C. V., 166
William III, 107

Wilson, A. J. N., 43, 46
Wyrick, Deborah Baker: on metaphor in *A Tale of a Tub*, 114–15

Zwicker, Stephen, 48